HEALING TRAUMA

AT THE CELLULAR LEVEL

The role of the cell danger response
in trauma and PTSD recovery

GREG DONEY

Paperback ISBN: 978-0-646-70904-8
Hardcover ISBN: 978-0-646-70930-7
Epub ISBN: 978-0-646-70954-3

Medical Disclaimer

This book and its contents are provided for informational purposes only. The author and publisher make no representations or warranties regarding the accuracy, completeness, or applicability of the content. They disclaim all liability for any errors, omissions, or inconsistencies that may be present.

The content in this book is not intended to diagnose, treat, cure, or prevent any condition or disease. It is not a substitute for professional medical advice, diagnosis, or treatment. Always consult a licensed healthcare professional before making any changes to your health regimen or treatment plan. The use of this book implies your understanding and acceptance of this disclaimer.

The author and publisher do not guarantee any specific outcomes or results from following the advice or strategies in this book. Individual results will vary, and the examples or testimonials provided are not intended to guarantee similar experiences.

By reading this book, you accept full responsibility for your health and well-being and agree that the author and publisher are not liable for any decisions or actions you take based on its content.

TABLE OF CONTENTS

FOREWORD

Robert K. Naviaux, MD, PhD
San Diego, California

Books with the power to change the course of an entire field of medicine are rare. Books with the power to connect cutting edge discoveries in the lab with practical solutions in the clinic are even rarer. Greg Doney has given us both. In a *tour de force* of medical writing, *Healing Trauma at the Cellular Level—the role of the cell danger response in PTSD and trauma recovery*, is just such a book. Written with understanding, perspective, and compassion, in language that is accessible to patients, therapists, physicians, and scientists alike, this book is a towering intellectual achievement. It unites the silos of medical research with the specialties of therapy and medical practice. Doney's book is a bridge that connects medicine, pediatrics, mental health care, neuroscience, and even the classification of chronic illnesses and mental health disorders, through the mitochondrial nexus.

Mitochondria are often said to be the "powerhouses of the cell". This is because they are responsible for converting the food we eat and the oxygen we breathe into the energy we need to think, talk, love, move, and play. But mitochondria are also much more than this. Mitochondria are the hub of the wheel of metabolism, and the canaries in the coalmine for our cells. Mitochondria are the sensors and the early alarm system that activate an ancient biology called the cell danger response—the CDR. All living things on Earth use the CDR to sense and defend themselves from danger at the cellular level. Indeed, the CDR must be activated to heal from any trauma, infection, stress, poisoning, or injury. Programmed changes in mitochondria unfold to regulate the orderly movement from the first, to the middle, to the last stage of the CDR. This is quite literally the magic we witness every time a cut is healed, an infection is eliminated, or a person recovers from depression, anxiety, PTSD, or any other trauma. This system usually works well. Most of us heal from the vast majority of infections, cuts, and traumas that we experience over a lifetime. However, the latest science has shown that healing can be arrested when the CDR gets stuck. When this happens, it produces the symptoms of chronic pain, anxiety, fatigue, GI abnormalities, neurodevelopmental and neurodegenerative disorders, mental health struggles, heart disease, diabetes, autoinflammatory disorders, and many other disabilities and complex chronic illnesses that affect hundreds of millions of people around the world.

For over 5,000 years physicians have been trained to treat acute illnesses by eliminating the cause whenever it can be bypassed, killed, burned out, or cut out. In this *First Book of Medicine*, acute illnesses are viewed through the lens of *pathogenesis*—the study of what is damaged and how it is damaged. Yet full recoveries are made possible by another process that works silently in the background. This is the process of healing that occurs naturally once the triggers are removed and reinjury is prevented. In an increasingly complex world, it has become apparent that a growing number of chronic illnesses remain after the acute illness or acute trauma is resolved. Something is going wrong with the very process of healing itself. Healing is getting stuck. To study this at the molecular level, I needed a new word. To describe this new biology and to give the new science a sharp focus, I coined the word *salugenesis* in 2018, taken from the root word *Salus*, the Roman goddess of personal health and well-being. It is different than the word salutogenesis that describes the lifestyle choices and coping skills that foster health despite economic and environmental hardships. Salugenesis is the process of self-healing. It is driven by mitochondria that create the molecular, metabolic, and cellular features of the healing cycle. Salugenesis is a whole-body signaling system that begins with mitochondria and the cell. Salugenesis is not the reverse of pathogenesis. The two work hand in hand. Pathogenesis creates the damage, and salugenesis eliminates the threat, effects the repairs, and builds resilience. The word was first used in a public lecture I gave at a meeting of the MINDD Foundation in Sydney, Australia on 23 March 2019, and described in the scientific literature in 2023[1].

Both the CDR and salugenesis are driven by energy and metabolism. As such, they compete for the same limited resources and cannot coexist for long. Chronic activation of the CDR inhibits the molecular, cellular, and cognitive steps needed to heal. Salugenesis signaling breaks this deadlock by redirecting energy to create a regenerative circuit from mitochondria to the brain and back. Remarkable healing and recoveries are possible with this new approach. This book contains descriptions of many of the tools and methods that have been developed to help people recover from trauma—to reboot the stalled CDR and send the signals the body needs to heal. Additional tools for treating other chronic disorders will soon follow. Only time will tell, but Greg Doney's book may be the first salvo in a revolution in medical care for chronic illness. It is a guidebook like no other.

February 2025

Reference

[1] Naviaux, R.K. Mitochondrial and metabolic features of salugenesis and the healing cycle. *Mitochondrion* **70**, 131-163 (2023).

INTRODUCTION:

Trauma, Healing, and the Cell Danger Response

Trauma is often misunderstood as being solely a mental health issue. The truth is, trauma extends far beyond psychological effects—it profoundly impacts both the body and mind, frequently triggering a cascade of biological responses that can leave individuals in a state of chronic stress, pain, and illness. While psychological therapies play a vital role in trauma recovery, a growing body of evidence supports the idea that trauma is not just a psychological event—but a *biological* one. This is where the concept of the Cell Danger Response (CDR) becomes relevant and important.

The CDR is an ancient, evolutionarily conserved cellular response designed to protect the body from threats—whether physical, microbial, chemical, or psychological. When a threat is perceived, the CDR shifts the body into defensive mode, halting normal cellular functions and activating protective measures. In the short term, this response is essential for survival. However, in the context of trauma—particularly chronic or unresolved trauma—the CDR can remain activated long after the threat has passed. This prolonged activation leads to widespread inflammation, mitochondrial dysfunction, and a host of emotional *and* physical symptoms.

The impact of trauma is felt at the body's cellular level, influencing everything from immune function to hormonal balance, sleep cycles, and digestion. When the CDR remains chronically engaged, it alters the functioning of the brain and body, often leading to conditions like chronic fatigue, fibromyalgia, autoimmune disorders, and persistent mental health challenges such as post-traumatic stress disorder (PTSD). This means that healing from trauma will engage not just the mind, but also the body, right down to the cellular level.

This book looks at evidence-based trauma treatments through a biological lens. It explores the complex ways trauma affects both the body and brain, with a particular focus on the pivotal role of the CDR in this process. It delves into the science behind the CDR, explaining how trauma triggers prolonged cellular stress and how this contributes to long-term emotional and physical symptoms. By gaining a deeper understanding of the CDR, we can develop more *integrative* and *effective* approaches to healing from trauma.

Throughout this book, we cover a wide range of topics related to trauma recovery, including:

- **Attachment theory and trauma:** How early attachment wounds, often formed in childhood, activate the CDR and affect emotional and physiological health throughout life.

- **The gut-brain axis and immune function:** How trauma disrupts gut health and immune responses, contributing to chronic inflammation and illness.

- **Nutrition and the CDR:** How specific nutrients, such as omega-3s and antioxidants, support mitochondrial function and help reset the CDR, promoting healing at a cellular level.

- **Holistic therapies for trauma:** Exploring therapies like Brainspotting, **Clay Field Therapy** (see Chapter 25), Family Constellation Work, and other somatic approaches that help release trauma stored in the body and calm the nervous system.

- **Gender differences in trauma response**: How men and women may experience trauma differently, and how gender-specific approaches can aid in recovery.

- **Intergenerational trauma and epigenetics:** How trauma can be passed down through generations via epigenetic changes, and how healing one generation can positively impact future ones.

- **Psychedelics and the CDR:** Investigating how emerging treatments, like MDMA, psilocybin, and ketamine, may influence the CDR and assist in trauma recovery.

Understanding the CDR is essential if we are to fully grasp the extent of trauma's impact on the body. This book not only explains the underlying science, but also provides practical solutions for healing, focusing on nutrition, movement, somatic therapies, and mindfulness. By integrating mind-body approaches with a deep understanding of the cellular processes involved in trauma, we offer a comprehensive and effective path to recovery.

Trauma is not just a psychological issue—it is a full-body experience that can erode physical health over time. As we learn more about the CDR and its role in trauma, it becomes clear that healing must involve both psychological *and* biological interventions.

This book aims to provide the knowledge and tools necessary to address trauma at its root, empowering individuals to fully recover and *thrive*—to lead healthier, more balanced lives.

1.

UNDERSTANDING TRAUMA

From PTSD to Generational Healing

Introduction: What is Trauma?

Trauma is often seen as a profoundly personal experience, yet its impact extends far beyond the individual, rippling through families, communities, and even across generations. While **Post-Traumatic Stress Disorder (PTSD)** is the most well-known trauma condition, trauma manifests in many different forms, each with unique effects on the body, brain, and emotions. Whether from a single, life-threatening event, or from prolonged exposure to adversity, trauma fundamentally changes how the body functions, leaving long-lasting scars.

In this chapter, we explore the various types of trauma, from PTSD and **Complex PTSD** (CPTSD), to Post-Traumatic Stress Injury (PTSI), as well as the more nuanced traumas such as **Adverse Childhood Experiences (ACEs)**, intergenerational trauma, and gestational trauma. We also dive deeper into types of trauma less commonly discussed, but equally impactful: adoption trauma, medical trauma, relational trauma, and betrayal trauma, among others. By understanding this spectrum of trauma and its widespread impact, we can better appreciate the journey toward healing.

Post-Traumatic Stress Disorder (PTSD)

Post-Traumatic Stress Disorder (PTSD) is a condition that develops after an individual experiences or witnesses a life-threatening event. Whether from combat, domestic abuse, a natural disaster, or another source of intense fear, PTSD alters both the brain and body. Flashbacks, nightmares, anxiety, and hypervigilance are common symptoms that keep individuals reliving their trauma *long after* the event has passed.

The nervous system remains in a constant state of fight-or-flight, leading to chronic stress and physical symptoms like headaches, muscle tension, and digestive issues. PTSD is not just a mental health disorder—it is a full-body experience that impacts how the body responds to future stress.

Complex Post-Traumatic Stress Disorder (CPTSD)

Complex Post-Traumatic Stress Disorder (CPTSD) develops from prolonged exposure to trauma, especially in situations where the individual feels trapped or powerless. Unlike PTSD, which is often linked to a single traumatic event, CPTSD stems from ongoing trauma, such as childhood abuse, neglect, domestic violence, or long-term captivity.

CPTSD is characterized by emotional dysregulation, negative self-image, and difficulty forming healthy relationships. Survivors often struggle with feelings of worthlessness and chronic fear, unable to move beyond the constant state of threat they have lived in for so long. CPTSD frequently leads to more complex psychological wounds than PTSD, affecting the individual's mental health and their ability to navigate the world around them.

Post-Traumatic Stress Injury (PTSI)

Post-Traumatic Stress Injury (PTSI) is a newer term that reframes trauma as an "injury" rather than a disorder. This term is particularly relevant in military and first-responder communities, where trauma is often seen as a result of the demanding and dangerous nature of their work. By viewing trauma as an injury rather than a disorder, PTSI helps reduce stigma and emphasizes that trauma can be healed, just like any other physical wound.

PTSI recognizes that trauma leaves both psychological and physiological imprints on the brain and body, but it also emphasizes that recovery is possible with appropriate care. This redefinition is an important shift for those who have felt burdened by the "disorder" label, promoting hope and healing.

Adverse Childhood Experiences (ACEs)

Adverse Childhood Experiences (ACEs) refer to traumatic events that occur during childhood, such as physical or emotional abuse, neglect, or household dysfunction like substance abuse or mental illness. These early-life traumas significantly shape a child's development and are strongly associated with long-term psychological and physical health challenges. High ACE scores are linked to increased risks of mental health disorders, chronic illnesses, addiction, and difficulty forming healthy relationships later in life.

ACEs also illustrate how trauma during critical developmental periods can have a profound, lasting effect on both brain and body development, leading to patterns of hypervigilance, emotional dysregulation, and even chronic illness.

Intergenerational Trauma

Intergenerational trauma, also known as transgenerational trauma, refers to trauma that is passed down from one generation to the next. Trauma caused by historical events—such as slavery, genocide, or war—leaves scars not only on the direct survivors but also on their descendants. This trauma is carried through family systems, manifesting as anxiety, depression, or even physical symptoms in those who may have never directly experienced the original trauma.

Research has shown that trauma can alter the genetic expression of descendants, changing how stress is managed at a biological level. Intergenerational trauma highlights the importance of healing not only for the individual but for the generations that follow, breaking the cycle of trauma transmission.

Gestational Trauma

Gestational trauma occurs when a mother experiences trauma during pregnancy, which can have direct effects on the developing foetus. The heightened stress and **cortisol** levels of the mother during pregnancy can alter foetal brain development, leading to increased susceptibility to mental health disorders, emotional regulation issues, and developmental delays in the child. These effects can last long into adulthood, showing that the prenatal environment plays a crucial role in shaping future mental and physical health.

Gestational trauma indicates the process of trauma can begin even before birth, influencing the health and well-being of the child from their earliest stages of development.

Expanding the Definition of Trauma

Trauma can arise from many sources, not limited to the well-known categories of PTSD or CPTSD. **Adoption trauma**, for example, can leave deep emotional scars tied to identity and attachment. **Medical trauma** refers to the psychological effects of invasive procedures or medical interventions, while **relational trauma** stems from the rupture of significant relationships—whether through betrayal, emotional neglect, or abandonment.

Betrayal trauma occurs when a person, often someone in a position of trust, violates that trust, which can be devastating. **Death trauma** and **traumatic grief** occur when individuals are confronted with the sudden or violent death of a loved one, leaving them to deal with both the immediate shock and the long-term emotional fallout.

In addition to these, **natural disaster trauma** and **refugee trauma** highlight the devastation caused by displacement, war, or climate-induced crises. With the increasing frequency of climate change-related events, **climate-induced existential traumas** have emerged as people face the anxiety and uncertainty of an unstable physical environment.

Trauma can also result from religious or spiritual experiences. **Religious and cult trauma** affects individuals who have been manipulated or harmed within these contexts, while **spiritual trauma** can develop when one's core beliefs are violated or shattered. Furthermore, **pre- and perinatal traumas** involve experiences during pregnancy or childbirth, which can have lasting impacts on the woman's development.

Cultural trauma refers to the collective trauma that can affect entire communities, often rooted in historical oppression, colonialism, or systemic discrimination. This type of trauma is not just personal, but part of a people's collective identity, as seen in many Indigenous communities or groups affected by historical atrocities.

Expanding the Understanding of Trauma

As you can see, the concept of trauma has expanded beyond PTSD to include a wide range of experiences and conditions. Understanding trauma in its various forms—whether it's CPTSD, PTSI, ACEs, intergenerational trauma, or adoption trauma—allows for a more nuanced and comprehensive approach to treatment. Each type of trauma has its own effects on the mind and body, but all forms of trauma affect the nervous system, leading to prolonged states of stress and survival that hinder recovery.

By recognizing the diverse ways trauma manifests, we can create more individualised and effective healing approaches that address not just the mind, but the body and even the family system.

Key Takeaways

- Trauma is a complex condition that affects both the mind and body, manifesting in different forms.

- PTSD is just one type of trauma; prolonged trauma can result in CPTSD, while PTSI reframes trauma as an injury rather than a disorder.

- ACEs, intergenerational trauma, and gestational trauma illustrate how trauma affects families and generations and can even begin before birth.

- Medical trauma, adoption trauma, relational trauma, and cultural trauma are important categories that reveal trauma's breadth.

- Understanding the full spectrum of trauma allows for better treatment approaches that address both emotional and physical healing.

Next Steps

In the following chapters, we'll dive deeper into how trauma affects the body at the cellular level and explore the various treatment options available to help break the cycle of trauma. From cutting-edge therapies to holistic healing practices, here you'll learn about the most effective ways to recover from trauma and reclaim your life.

References

Anda, R. F., Felitti, V. J., Bremner, J. D., Walker, J. D., Whitfield, C., Perry, B. D., Dube, S. R., & Giles, W. H. (2006). The enduring effects of abuse and related adverse experiences in childhood: A convergence of evidence from neurobiology and epidemiology. *European Archives of Psychiatry and Clinical Neuroscience, 256*(3), 174–186. https://doi.org/10.1007/s00406-005-0624-4

Bremner, J. D. (2006). Traumatic stress: Effects on the brain. *Dialogues in Clinical Neuroscience, 8*(4), 445–461. https://doi.org/10.31887/DCNS.2006.8.4/jbremner

Naviaux, R. K. (2014). Metabolic features of the cell danger response. *Mitochondrion, 16*, 7-17. https://doi.org/10.1016/j.mito.2013.08.006

Porges, S. W. (2011). *The Polyvagal Theory: Neurophysiological foundations of emotions, attachment, communication, and self-regulation.* W. W. Norton & Company.

2.

THE FIVE TRAUMA RESPONSES

Introduction: How the Body Reacts to Trauma

When faced with danger or a traumatic event, the body instinctively reacts to protect itself. These responses are deeply rooted in our biology and are designed to ensure our survival in life-threatening situations. However, for individuals with post-traumatic stress disorder (PTSD), these responses often remain "stuck", even when the danger has passed, leading to chronic emotional and physical difficulties. The five primary trauma responses—**Fight**, **Flight**, **Freeze**, **Fawn**, and **Flop**—are survival mechanisms, but when these responses persist after the danger has passed, they can cause distress in daily life.

Fight Response

The **fight response** is activated when a person perceives a threat and feels the need to defend themselves. This reaction involves a surge of adrenaline and heightened alertness, preparing the individual to confront the danger. In a fight response, the body tenses up, and the individual may feel irritable, angry, or even aggressive.

While this response can be helpful in the face of short-term, real-life threats, it becomes problematic when it manifests as chronic anger or irritability in situations where no real danger exists. Individuals stuck in the fight response may have relationships that suffer frequently with conflict, struggle with impulse control, and often feel as if they're on the verge of losing their temper.

Flight Response

The flight response is triggered when the body's primary goal is to escape danger. In a flight state, a person's body floods with adrenaline, creating a strong urge to flee or avoid the perceived threat. People in this response may experience restlessness, anxiety, or a constant need to be on the move.

For individuals with PTSD, this response can turn into **avoidance behaviours**, where they try to escape or avoid anything that reminds them of the trauma. Over time, this can lead to **social isolation**, avoiding public places, certain people, or even personal thoughts and memories related to the trauma.

Freeze Response

When fighting or fleeing seems impossible, the **freeze response** kicks in. This response is a form of **immobilization**, where the person becomes "frozen" in place, unable to react or move. It is often accompanied by feelings of numbness, detachment, or dissociation.

In people with PTSD, the freeze response can manifest as emotional numbness or feeling disconnected from reality. Individuals in this state often describe feeling like they are "stuck" or "frozen" in place, unable to make decisions or act. This response may also lead to **dissociative episodes**, where the person feels like they are outside of their body or disconnected from the world around them.

Fawn Response

The **fawn response** involves people-pleasing behaviours, typically in an effort to avoid further harm or conflict. This response is common in individuals who have experienced relational trauma—such as abuse or neglect—where pleasing others was the only way to maintain safety.

People stuck in the fawn response may develop **co-dependency** or constantly prioritize the needs of others over their own. They may find it challenging to set boundaries, express their own needs, or stand up for themselves, fearing that doing so will provoke conflict or harm.

Flop Response

The **flop response** occurs when an individual surrenders completely. In this state, they feel powerless to act, fight, or even freeze. The body's energy levels drop, and there is a sense of helplessness or defeat. People who experience the flop response may feel exhausted, passive, or apathetic.

This response is commonly seen in individuals who have experienced chronic, long-term trauma—where resistance seemed futile, and survival depended on total surrender. Over time, this can result in extreme fatigue, low motivation, and a lack of engagement with life.

Understanding the Nervous System and Trauma

All five trauma responses are tied to the **autonomic nervous system (ANS)**, which regulates the body's fight, flight or freeze responses through two branches: the **sympathetic** and **parasympathetic nervous systems**. When trauma occurs, the **sympathetic nervous system** is activated, triggering either fight-or-flight. In the absence of escape, the parasympathetic nervous system may engage, leading to freeze or flop.

For many individuals with PTSD, these responses become chronically activated, even in the absence of actual danger. The **polyvagal theory**, developed by Dr. Stephen Porges, provides insight into how the brain's **vagus nerve** controls these responses. The theory highlights the importance of **nervous system regulation** in trauma recovery and emphasizes the need to move from a state of survival to a state of safety.

How Trauma Responses Impact Daily Life

While these trauma responses are adaptive in moments of actual danger, they can create challenges in daily life when they persist. For example, individuals stuck in the fight response may struggle with anger management, while those in flight may experience chronic anxiety. People who freeze may have difficulty making decisions or expressing themselves, while those who fawn might struggle with setting boundaries or maintaining healthy relationships.

By understanding how these responses operate, individuals can begin to recognize patterns in their behaviour and seek appropriate treatment to regulate the nervous system and reduce the intensity of these reactions.

Key Takeaways

- The five trauma responses—Fight, Flight, Freeze, Fawn, and Flop—are instinctive survival mechanisms that can become dysfunctional in individuals with unresolved trauma.

- Each response serves a specific role in helping the body survive perceived threats, but when these responses are chronically activated, they can lead to emotional, physical, and relational difficulties.

- Trauma is deeply tied to the nervous system, and treatment often involves learning to regulate these responses and restore a sense of safety.

Next Steps

In the next chapter, we will explore the **Cell Danger Response (CDR)**, a groundbreaking concept that explains how trauma affects the body on a cellular level. Understanding the CDR sheds light on why PTSD can cause chronic physical symptoms alongside emotional distress.

References

Levine, P. A. (1997). *Waking the Tiger: Healing trauma*. North Atlantic Books.

Ogden, P., Minton, K., & Pain, C. (2006). *Trauma and the Body: A sensorimotor approach to psychotherapy*. W. W. Norton & Company.

Rothschild, B. (2000). *The Body Remembers: The psychophysiology of trauma and trauma treatment*. W. W. Norton & Company.

3.

TRAUMA AND CHRONIC ACTIVATION OF THE CELL DANGER RESPONSE

Introduction: The Long-Term Impact of Trauma

When a traumatic experience strikes, the body's immediate response is to survive the danger. But for many people, the effects of trauma don't end when the event is over. Instead, trauma leaves a lasting imprint on the body's cellular functions. One of the most critical examples of this is the chronic activation of the Cell Danger Response (CDR), a cellular mechanism designed to protect the body from perceived threats.

In this chapter, we will explore how the prolonged activation of the CDR leads to persistent physical, emotional, and cognitive symptoms. By understanding how trauma affects the body at a cellular level, we can begin to grasp why trauma is such a pervasive condition and how it contributes to chronic illnesses.

Understanding the Cell Danger Response (CDR)

The Cell Danger Response (CDR) is a universal defence mechanism that activates whenever the body detects a threat—whether it be physical injury, infection, toxins, or psychological trauma. When this happens, the cells enter "defence mode", halting their usual functions, such as growth, repair, and metabolism, in order to focus on survival. The mitochondria, which are responsible for energy production in cells, shift from producing energy to conserving it, which leads to significant physiological changes.

This temporary shift is designed to protect the body from immediate harm. In a healthy system, once the threat is neutralized, cells return to their normal state, resuming regular functions. However, in people with trauma, the CDR can become *chronically* activated, meaning the cells remain in defence mode *long after* the original danger has passed. This ongoing state of cellular distress contributes to many of the physical symptoms associated with PTSD, such as chronic fatigue, inflammation, and cognitive dysfunction.

Simplifying the CDR

To expand further on this topic: think of the CDR as the body's emergency mode. When a threat like trauma, injury, or even a toxin, appears, your cells temporarily stop what they usually do—like producing energy or repairing tissue—and they focus instead entirely on survival. This change is meant to protect you in the short term, but if the emergency mode stays on for too long, it can lead to long-term problems like chronic fatigue or inflammation. Imagine a superhero constantly staying in battle mode, even when the threat is gone—that's what happens when the CDR is stuck in "on" mode. This can contribute to many of the physical and emotional symptoms seen in trauma survivors.

History of the Cell Danger Response (CDR)

Dr. Robert K. Naviaux, a physician-scientist specializing in mitochondrial medicine and metabolic psychiatry, developed the Cell Danger Response (CDR) theory. Dr. Naviaux first introduced the concept in his 2014 paper, *"Metabolic features of the Cell Danger Response"*, which highlighted how the CDR is an evolutionary mechanism designed to protect the body from threats such as trauma, infection, and toxins. His work has been pivotal in demonstrating how the chronic activation of the CDR can contribute to a wide range of chronic illnesses, including **chronic fatigue syndrome (CFS)**, autoimmune disorders, and neurodegenerative diseases. Naviaux's research has transformed the way we understand the role of mitochondria, (organelles within our cells) not just in energy production but as central players in the body's defence and healing processes.

How Trauma Disrupts Cellular Function

When trauma activates the CDR, it interrupts the normal functioning of the body's cells, particularly their ability to produce and use energy. This is because the mitochondria—the "powerhouse" of the cell—switch from energy production to a protective state, conserving resources to deal with the perceived threat.

While the Cell Danger Response (CDR) is a critical mechanism that places the body in a state of defence during trauma, it must eventually be resolved for healing to occur. This resolution is achieved through **salugenesis** *signalling*, promoting cellular healing and restoring normal function. In later chapters, we will explore how various therapies can stimulate salugenesis to support the body's natural healing pathways.

This survival response can be beneficial in the short term. However, prolonged activation of the CDR results in metabolic imbalance, which manifests as chronic physical and cognitive symptoms.

Here's how the CDR affects critical processes in the body:

- **Energy production:** Mitochondria slow down energy production to conserve resources, leading to chronic fatigue and low energy levels in individuals with trauma.

- **Inflammation:** Trauma triggers an inflammatory response in the body, which is helpful for healing in the short term. However, when inflammation becomes chronic, it leads to various health issues, such as autoimmune disorders, digestive problems, and pain.

- **Cell communication:** In CDR mode, cells cease their normal communication functions, which affects the functioning of tissues and organs. This disruption in cell signalling can lead to cognitive difficulties, brain fog, and memory problems—all common symptoms of trauma.

CDR and the Brain: A Neurobiological Perspective

The effects of the CDR extend beyond physical health—they impact brain function as well. Trauma significantly alters the brain's structure and connectivity, affecting how an individual processes information, responds to stress and regulates emotions.

Key brain areas affected by trauma include:

- **Amygdala:** Known as the brain's "fear centre", the amygdala becomes overactive in response to trauma, causing individuals to remain in a hypervigilant state. This hyperactivity keeps the body and mind in a state of high alert, which is central to maintaining chronic CDR activation.

- **Hippocampus:** The hippocampus, responsible for processing memories, often shrinks in individuals with trauma. This makes it harder to distinguish between past trauma and present safety, leading to flashbacks and intrusive thoughts. The hippocampus is susceptible to cellular stress, making trauma survivors prone to memory difficulties.

- **Prefrontal cortex:** The prefrontal cortex helps regulate emotions and make rational decisions. Trauma reduces activity in this part of the brain, contributing to emotional dysregulation, impulsive behaviour, and trouble concentrating.

How the CDR Becomes Chronically Activated

The CDR is meant to be a temporary response. However, in individuals with trauma, several factors can cause it to remain chronically activated:

- **Unresolved trauma:** When trauma is not fully processed—whether through therapy or other means—the body continues to perceive it as an ongoing threat. This keeps the CDR active, trapping the individual in a prolonged state of defence.

- **Repeated exposure to stress:** Individuals who experience repeated trauma or live in stressful environments are more likely to experience chronic CDR activation. Constant exposure to stressors keeps the body from ever fully returning to a state of rest-and-repair.

- **Implicit trauma memories:** Trauma is often stored in implicit memories, which reside deep in the brain and body and can be triggered without conscious awareness. These implicit memories reactivate the CDR even when there is no immediate danger.

Chronic CDR Activation and Its Physical Symptoms

The chronic activation of the CDR has widespread consequences for the body and brain, contributing to the long-term physical symptoms commonly seen in PTSD:

- **Chronic fatigue:** The body's inability to produce sufficient energy leads to persistent exhaustion, even with adequate rest.

- **Inflammation:** Chronic inflammation caused by prolonged cellular stress can result in physical pain, autoimmune disorders, and gastrointestinal issues.

- **Cognitive dysfunction:** The brain's normal functioning is disrupted by the CDR, leading to issues such as brain fog, memory loss, and concentration difficulties.

The Role of the Vagus Nerve and Polyvagal Theory

The vagus nerve plays a critical role in regulating the body's response to stress, mainly through the polyvagal theory, developed by Dr. Stephen Porges. The vagus nerve is the longest cranial nerve, connecting the brain to the heart, lungs, and digestive system. It helps regulate the parasympathetic nervous system, which is responsible for rest and relaxation.

In individuals with trauma, the vagal tone is often reduced, meaning the body struggles to switch from the fight-or-flight response back to a state of calm. This keeps the CDR active and contributes to the chronic symptoms of trauma. Strengthening the vagus nerve through therapeutic techniques such as breathwork, mindfulness, and somatic therapy can help reduce chronic CDR activation and restore nervous system balance.

The Connection Between Trauma and Chronic Illness

Research shows that individuals who have experienced trauma are more likely to develop long-term health conditions, many of which are linked to chronic inflammation, immune dysfunction, and metabolic imbalances caused by the CDR.

Some common chronic conditions associated with trauma include:

- **Chronic fatigue syndrome (CFS):** CFS, which shares many characteristics with the chronic activation of the CDR, is frequently diagnosed in trauma survivors who experience profound, unexplained fatigue.

- **Fibromyalgia:** A chronic pain condition characterized by widespread pain and tenderness, fibromyalgia is thought to result from dysregulated pain processing, which can occur when the CDR remains activated.

- **Autoimmune disorders:** Conditions like lupus and rheumatoid arthritis are more common in individuals with PTSD, as the immune system can become overactive and attack healthy tissues when the CDR is chronically engaged.

- **Gastrointestinal issues:** The gut-brain connection is disrupted in trauma survivors, leading to conditions like irritable bowel syndrome (IBS) and other digestive disorders.

Key Takeaways

- **Chronic CDR activation:** The chronic activation of the CDR is a significant contributor to the long-term physical and emotional symptoms of trauma.

- **Salugenesis signalling:** Resolving the CDR and shifting the body from defence to repair is achieved through salugenesis signalling, which restores normal cellular functions and supports healing. Holistic therapies such as somatic work, breathwork, and vagus nerve activation are essential for stimulating salugenesis and facilitating cellular recovery.

- **Impact on physical health:** A chronically activated CDR leads to energy deficits, inflammation, immune dysfunction, and cognitive impairment, contributing to conditions such as chronic fatigue syndrome and fibromyalgia.

- **Brain involvement:** The amygdala, hippocampus, and prefrontal cortex are affected by the CDR, leading to emotional dysregulation, memory problems, and hypervigilance.

- **Role of the vagus nerve:** Strengthening vagal tone through somatic therapies can help reduce chronic CDR activation and promote healing.

Next Steps

If you are dealing with trauma-related symptoms that could be linked to chronic CDR activation, here are some steps to begin the healing process:

- **Focus on restoring mitochondrial function:** Mitochondria play a critical role in the CDR. Look for therapies that promote mitochondrial health, such as **Frequency Specific Microcurrent (FSM)**, **Photobiomodulation**, or supplements that target cellular energy production.

- **Explore therapies that reduce inflammation:** Chronic inflammation is a hallmark of prolonged CDR activation. Consider therapies such as **Hyperbaric Oxygen Therapy (HBOT)**, **herbal anti-inflammatories**, and **anti-inflammatory diets** to reduce inflammation and support cellular repair.

- **Incorporate mind-body practices:** Therapies like **Somatic Experiencing, Eye Movement Desensitization and Reprocessing (EMDR)**, or **mindfulness-based stress reduction (MBSR)** help to resolve trauma by calming the nervous system and supporting the body's transition from defence to healing.

- **Monitor progress with tools like HRV: Heart Rate Variability (HRV)** monitoring can provide insights into your autonomic nervous system's balance, showing how well your body is recovering from chronic stress and trauma.

- **Work with a trauma-informed therapist:** Partner with a therapist experienced in addressing the physical and emotional effects of trauma, who can help guide you through therapies that target your mind *and* body for complete healing.

References

Afari, N., & Buchwald, D. (2003). Chronic fatigue syndrome: A review. *American Journal of Psychiatry, 160*(2), 221-236. https://doi.org/10.1176/appi.ajp.160.2.221

Clauw, D. J. (2014). Fibromyalgia: A clinical review. *JAMA, 311*(15), 1547-1555. https://doi.org/10.1001/jama.2014.3266

Naviaux, R. K. (2014). Metabolic features of the cell danger response. *Mitochondrion, 16*, 7-17. https://doi.org/10.1016/j.mito.2013.08.006

Porges, S. W. (2011). *The Polyvagal Theory: Neurophysiological foundations of emotions, attachment, communication, and self-regulation.* W. W. Norton & Company.

Siegel, D. J. (2012). *The Developing Mind: How relationships and the brain interact to shape who we are.* Guilford Press.

van der Kolk, B. A. (2015). *The Body Keeps the Score: Brain, mind, and body in the healing of trauma.* Penguin Books.

4.

NUTRITION AND THE CELL DANGER RESPONSE

Introduction: Nutrition as a Tool for Healing the CDR

When the CDR is chronically activated—often due to trauma or prolonged stress—it leads to mitochondrial dysfunction, inflammation, and various health problems. One of the most potent ways to help deactivate the CDR and support healing is through targeted nutrition. Specific nutrients and diets can promote mitochondrial health, reduce inflammation, and restore balance in the body, making nutrition *a vital tool* in trauma recovery.

Mitochondrial Health and the CDR

When the Cell Danger Response (CDR) is triggered, mitochondria—the cell's energy producers—shift from their usual role of generating ATP (the cell's energy currency) to a defensive mode. In this state, they reduce ATP production and increase oxidative stress, which causes cellular damage. This prolonged shift can lead to fatigue, cognitive issues, and inflammation—all common in trauma survivors.

Supporting mitochondrial health is critical for deactivating the CDR and restoring normal cellular function. Several vital nutrients and dietary strategies play a significant role in supporting mitochondrial function and promoting recovery from trauma.

Key Nutrients for Mitochondrial Support

Omega-3 Fatty Acids:

- **Source:** Found in fatty fish, like salmon, sardines, and mackerel, as well as plant-based sources like flaxseeds and chia seeds.

- **Function:** Omega-3s are essential for brain health and have potent anti-inflammatory properties. These fatty acids help stabilize mitochondrial membranes and promote efficient energy production, reducing oxidative stress. Omega-3s are vital in mitigating the effects of prolonged CDR activation, as they help lower inflammation and improve cognitive function.

Antioxidants:

- **Source:** Antioxidant-rich foods include berries, dark leafy greens, nuts, seeds, and herbs like turmeric and ginger.

- **Function:** Antioxidants help neutralize free radicals and reduce oxidative stress, which is elevated in individuals with chronic CDR activation. Vitamin C, vitamin E, and glutathione are particularly effective in protecting mitochondria from damage and supporting cellular repair.

Magnesium:

- **Source:** Magnesium-rich foods include spinach, almonds, avocados, and dark chocolate.

- **Function:** Magnesium is involved in over 300 biochemical reactions in the body, including those related to energy production, nervous system regulation, and stress reduction. By supporting mitochondrial function and reducing muscle tension, magnesium plays a key role in deactivating the CDR and promoting relaxation.

Coenzyme Q10 (CoQ10):

- **Source:** CoQ10 is found in organ meats and fatty fish and is available as a supplement.

- **Function:** CoQ10 is vital for mitochondrial energy production, facilitating electron transfer in the process of ATP generation. Trauma survivors often experience fatigue and cognitive dysfunction, which CoQ10 can help alleviate by improving cellular energy levels and reducing oxidative stress.

B-Vitamins:

- **Source:** Found in whole grains, eggs, leafy greens, and legumes.

- **Function:** B-vitamins, particularly B6, B9 (folate), and B12, are essential for neurotransmitter production and mitochondrial function. These vitamins help regulate the nervous system and support the body's ability to recover from stress. Supplementation with B-vitamins is essential for trauma survivors experiencing stress-induced nutrient depletion.

Dietary Strategies for Reducing Inflammation and Supporting the CDR

Anti-inflammatory Diet

Overview: An anti-inflammatory diet focuses on whole, nutrient-dense foods that help reduce inflammation and oxidative stress. Foods like fatty fish, dark leafy greens, nuts, seeds, and berries are rich in antioxidants and anti-inflammatory compounds.

Benefits: This diet can help reduce systemic inflammation and promote mitochondrial health, aiding in the deactivation of the CDR. Key anti-inflammatory compounds include omega-3 fatty acids, polyphenols (found in berries and green tea), and flavonoids (found in dark chocolate and citrus fruits).

Nutrition plays a crucial role in activating salugenesis *signalling*, mainly through the use of the anti-inflammatory diet and mitochondrial support. By reducing inflammation and supporting cellular energy production, nutrition helps the body transition from a state of chronic defence (CDR) into one of healing and repair.

Ketogenic Diet

Overview: The ketogenic (keto) diet is high in healthy fats and low in carbohydrates, forcing the body to use ketones instead of glucose for energy. This metabolic shift reduces oxidative stress and enhances mitochondrial function.

Benefits: For trauma survivors with chronic CDR activation, the ketogenic diet may improve cognitive function, reduce brain fog, and restore energy levels by supporting more efficient ATP production in mitochondria.

Fasting and Time-Restricted Eating

Overview: Fasting and time-restricted eating (TRE) help reduce inflammation and promote autophagy—the body's process of cleaning out damaged cells. Autophagy supports cellular repair and regeneration.

Benefits: By promoting cellular renewal, intermittent fasting can help reset the CDR and support long-term health. Periodic fasting reduces oxidative stress and helps the body switch from a defensive mode to one focused on repair.

Pro-inflammatory Cooking Oils and the CDR

Cooking oils high in omega-6 fatty acids, such as soybean, corn, and sunflower oils, are known to contribute to chronic inflammation.

These oils are particularly harmful because they contain polyunsaturated fats that are highly susceptible to oxidation, especially when exposed to heat during cooking. This oxidative damage produces free radicals, which promote inflammation at the cellular level, perpetuating the CDR.

The human body requires both omega-6 and omega-3 fatty acids for various biological processes. Still, the modern Western diet is heavily skewed towards omega-6 fatty acids due to the widespread use of seed oils in processed foods. This imbalance, with omega-6 to omega-3 ratios often as high as 20:1 (instead of the ideal 1:1 ratio), leads to an overproduction of pro-inflammatory eicosanoids derived from omega-6s. These signalling molecules trigger immune responses that, while necessary during acute stress or injury, become harmful when *consistently* activated, as is the case in prolonged CDR.

Prolonged or chronic consumption of these oils disrupts the body's ability to resolve the stress response, keeping it in a heightened state of inflammation. This continuous state of alert interferes with metabolic function and may contribute to a range of chronic health conditions, including cardiovascular disease, diabetes, and gut-related disorders. In particular, omega-6-rich oils have been linked to damage to the gut lining, further exacerbating immune dysregulation and inflammation.

Switching to anti-inflammatory fats can help restore balance and reduce the chronic activation of the CDR. Oils such as extra-virgin olive oil, avocado oil, and flaxseed oil, rich in monounsaturated fats and omega-3s, help reduce inflammation by promoting the production of anti-inflammatory eicosanoids. These oils are more stable during cooking and provide essential nutrients that support mitochondrial function and cellular repair, both crucial for resolving the CDR and promoting overall healing.

The Gut-Brain Axis and the CDR

The gut-brain axis plays a significant role in regulating immune function, mood, and the body's response to stress. Trauma can disrupt the balance of the gut microbiome, leading to inflammation, digestive issues, and chronic CDR activation. Supporting gut health is essential for deactivating the CDR and promoting emotional and physical well-being.

Restoring the Gut Microbiome

Probiotics and Prebiotics

- **Probiotics:** Found in fermented foods like yoghurt, kefir, sauerkraut, and kimchi, probiotics are beneficial bacteria that help balance the gut microbiome and reduce inflammation.

- **Prebiotics:** Prebiotics, found in fibre-rich foods like garlic, onions, bananas, and oats, feed the beneficial bacteria in the gut, promoting a healthy microbiome.

- **Benefits:** A healthy gut microbiome helps regulate immune function and reduce chronic inflammation, which, in turn, helps deactivate the CDR.

Polyphenols

Polyphenols are plant compounds found in foods like berries, dark chocolate, and green tea. Polyphenols promote the growth of beneficial gut bacteria and reduce inflammation. These compounds help restore the gut-brain axis, improving both mental and physical health.

Gut-Immune System Connection

Approximately 70% of the immune system resides in the gut. Trauma often causes the central nervous system to downregulate gut function as the body prioritizes the fight-flight-freeze response. Restoring gut health is vital to balancing immune function and reducing chronic CDR activation.

Key Takeaways

- Targeted nutritional strategies that support mitochondrial function and reduce inflammation can influence the CDR.

- Key nutrients, including omega-3s, antioxidants, magnesium, CoQ10, and B-vitamins, play critical roles in deactivating the CDR and promoting cellular repair.

- Adopting an anti-inflammatory diet or a ketogenic diet can reduce oxidative stress and enhance mitochondrial function, supporting trauma recovery.

- The gut-brain axis is integral to regulating the immune response, and a healthy gut can help deactivate the CDR, mitigating the long-term effects of trauma.

References

Afari, N., & Buchwald, D. (2003). Chronic fatigue syndrome: A review. *American Journal of Psychiatry, 160*(2), 221-236. Available at: https://ajp.psychiatryonline.org/doi/full/10.1176/appi.ajp.160.2.221

Heller, L., & LaPierre, A. (2012). *Healing Developmental Trauma: How early trauma affects self-regulation, self-image, and the capacity for relationship*. North Atlantic Books.

Levine, P. (1997). *Waking the Tiger: Healing trauma*. North Atlantic Books. Available at: https://www.amazon.com/Waking-Tiger-Healing-Peter-Levine/dp/155643233X

Naviaux, R. K. (2014). Metabolic features of the cell danger response. *Mitochondrion, 16*, 7-17. Available at: https://www.sciencedirect.com/science/article/pii/S1567724913002390

Porges, S. (2011). *The Polyvagal Theory: Neurophysiological foundations of emotions, attachment, communication, and self-regulation*. W. W. Norton & Company. Available at: https://www.amazon.com/Polyvagal-Theory-Neurophysiological-Foundations-Communication/dp/0393707008

Siegel, D. J. (2010). *Mindsight: The new science of personal transformation*. Bantam Books. Available at: https://www.amazon.com/Mindsight-New-Science-Personal-Transformation/dp/0553386395

Van der Kolk, B. A. (2015). *The Body Keeps the Score: Brain, mind, and body in the healing of trauma*. Penguin Books. Available at: https://www.amazon.com/Body-Keeps-Score-Healing-Trauma/dp/0143127748

5.

POLLUTION, ENVIRONMENTAL STRESSORS, AND THE CELL DANGER RESPONSE

The modern world introduces us to a wide array of environmental stressors, ranging from air and water pollution to chemical exposure, electromagnetic fields (EMFs), and light pollution. These environmental challenges are not just nuisances in contemporary life; they can have profound impacts on human health, especially for those who are already struggling with trauma. For individuals with trauma-related disorders, these environmental factors may contribute to the persistence of the Cell Danger Response (CDR), making it significantly more challenging for them to heal and recover fully.

Such environmental stressors may act as continuous triggers, keeping the body locked in the protective CDR mode and preventing full recovery. Here's how these factors contribute to this persistent CDR:

Toxins and Chemical Exposure

Air and water pollution, as well as chemical contaminants in food and other products, introduce toxins into the human body. Heavy metals, pesticides, industrial chemicals, and even household pollutants can interfere with normal cellular functions. Cells interpret these toxins as threats, and this perception can maintain the CDR, keeping the body in a heightened state of vigilance.

For trauma survivors, this is particularly harmful. Their cells are already on high alert due to unresolved psychological threats, and the introduction of external toxins can prolong this state. Instead of shifting out of the CDR and into a phase of repair, the body remains defensive, prioritizing survival over healing.

Oxidative Stress and Inflammation

Pollution, especially from particulate matter in the air, can lead to oxidative stress, a condition in which harmful free radicals outweigh the body's antioxidant defences. Oxidative stress is known to drive chronic inflammation, which is a crucial factor in keeping the CDR activated. Trauma itself triggers inflammatory responses as the body reacts to emotional and physical damage. When pollution adds to this inflammation, the result is a prolonged state of cellular stress.

For those in the throes of trauma recovery, this creates a cycle: environmental pollutants exacerbate inflammation, which in turn sustains the CDR, preventing cells from transitioning into a healing phase.

Electromagnetic Field (EMF) Pollution

One of the more insidious environmental factors contributing to CDR is electromagnetic field (EMF) pollution. As technology permeates daily life, we are increasingly exposed to EMFs from mobile phones, Wi-Fi routers, smart devices, and power lines. Although EMF radiation is invisible, emerging research suggests that long-term exposure may negatively affect cellular function and overall health.

For individuals already coping with trauma, chronic exposure to EMF radiation can further destabilize the nervous system. Studies show that EMFs can disrupt sleep patterns, increase oxidative stress, and impair mitochondrial function, which is vital for cellular energy production. Trauma survivors are already prone to heightened stress responses, and prolonged EMF exposure may exacerbate this, keeping the body trapped in a heightened CDR state. The body perceives this radiation as a continuous threat, preventing it from downregulating the CDR and transitioning into recovery.

Light Pollution and Blue Light Exposure

Another often-overlooked factor in maintaining the CDR is light pollution, particularly exposure to artificial blue light. In the 21st century world, people are increasingly exposed to artificial light sources from screens, LED lights, and streetlights, disrupting our natural circadian rhythm. Blue light, which is heavily emitted by electronic devices, can interfere with sleep and suppress the production of melatonin, the hormone responsible for regulating sleep-wake cycles.

For trauma survivors, healthy sleep is critical to healing, as restorative deep sleep is essential for regulating stress and allowing the body to repair itself. Light pollution, especially blue light exposure in the evening, can lead to chronic sleep disturbances. These disturbances not only exacerbate symptoms of trauma but also prolong the CDR by keeping the body in a state of stress. When the body cannot achieve deep, restorative sleep, the central nervous system remains active and defensive, making it harder for trauma survivors to achieve cellular healing.

Endocrine Disruption

Many pollutants, such as endocrine-disrupting chemicals (EDCs), interfere with hormone regulation. These chemicals, found in plastics, pesticides, and other industrial products, can alter the body's delicate hormonal balance. Hormones play a critical role in regulating stress, healing, and recovery from trauma. When environmental pollutants disrupt these systems, it can make it harder for the body to downregulate the CDR.

This is especially relevant for trauma survivors, who often suffer from hormonal imbalances due to prolonged stress. Environmental disruption of hormone function only worsens this condition, making it harder for their bodies to shift out of a defensive posture and into a state of healing.

Psychological Stress from Environmental Factors

It's not only chemical pollutants that impact trauma survivors—noise pollution, overcrowded living conditions, and lack of green spaces also contribute to chronic stress. These environmental factors place a constant burden on the nervous system, keeping it activated and preventing the relaxation and safety needed for recovery from trauma.

Noise pollution, for instance, can disrupt sleep cycles, aggravate anxiety, and keep the brain in a state of hypervigilance. For someone with trauma, whose nervous system is already overwhelmed, these environmental stressors make it even harder to achieve the peace and calm necessary to exit the CDR.

CO2 Levels and Environmental Stress in the CDR

Growing attention has been paid in recent years to the role of carbon dioxide (CO_2) levels in relation to overall health, particularly through the work of researchers like James Nestor. His exploration of how CO_2 affects the body's breathing mechanisms highlights a critical link between environmental factors and physiological stress. Modern lifestyles, marked by shallow breathing and exposure to pollution, often lead to reduced tolerance for CO_2. This can result in poor oxygen exchange and place further strain on the body's cellular systems.

Nestor's work underscores how chronic exposure to poor air quality, particularly in urban environments, exacerbates this problem. With higher CO_2 levels, the body struggles to maintain proper respiration, which can contribute to the prolonged activation of the Cell Danger Response (CDR).

As Nestor suggests, it may be possible to mitigate some of these environmental stressors by addressing CO_2 tolerance and improving breathing patterns. Incorporating breathwork techniques designed to optimize CO_2 levels could support trauma recovery, helping the body deactivate the CDR and promote cellular healing.

Volatile Organic Compounds (VOCs) and Their Impact on the CDR

Volatile Organic Compounds (VOCs) are a class of harmful chemicals found in everyday environments, originating from products like paints, cleaning supplies, building materials, and even furnishings. These compounds off-gas into the air we breathe, contributing to indoor air pollution and posing significant health risks. Prolonged exposure to VOCs can disrupt the body's natural ability to detoxify and regulate cellular functions, often leading to chronic inflammation and immune system overactivation.

In the context of the Cell Danger Response (CDR), VOCs play a critical role in keeping the body in a prolonged state of defence. When VOC levels are elevated in the environment, the body continuously perceives these compounds as toxic threats. This perpetual state of cellular alarm can lead to the chronic activation of the CDR, contributing to a range of health issues such as respiratory problems, fatigue, and systemic inflammation.

Mitigating exposure to VOCs through the use of low-emission products, air purifiers, and adequate ventilation is essential for trauma survivors and individuals dealing with chronic health conditions. Reducing the environmental burden of these pollutants allows the body to shift out of the defence state triggered by the CDR, creating space for cellular repair and recovery.

The Combined Impact of Trauma and Environmental Factors

In essence, pollution, EMF radiation, and light pollution, along with other environmental stressors, can act as continuous, low-level threats that keep the body in a defensive state. For individuals with trauma who are already living with heightened stress responses, these environmental factors can compound the issue, making it exceedingly difficult to exit the CDR. Healing from trauma requires not only psychological support but also a reduction in perceived threats—both internal and external.

Pollution introduces external threats that keep the system on edge, preventing the body from truly resting and healing. The long-term consequence is that many trauma survivors, especially those living in urban or industrial environments, find it much harder to recover, as they are continually bombarded with environmental triggers that sustain the CDR.

Moving Toward Recovery: Reducing Environmental Stress

Addressing the impact of environmental factors on trauma recovery requires both individual and societal action. On an individual level, reducing exposure to toxins—through clean water, air filtration, and organic foods—can help minimize the triggers that keep the CDR activated. Reducing exposure to EMF radiation, such as limiting the use of electronic devices and optimizing sleep environments to reduce blue light exposure, can help the nervous system recover. Detoxification protocols, such as using saunas or increasing antioxidant intake, can also help the body clear out pollutants and reduce oxidative stress.

On a societal level, reducing pollution, regulating EMF exposure, and ensuring access to clean, healthy environments are essential for public health, especially for those recovering from trauma. Advocacy for environmental justice and the reduction of industrial pollution plays a critical role in allowing trauma survivors to move out of the CDR and into a state of healing.

Ultimately, trauma recovery is about more than addressing the psychological aspects of healing; it's about creating a safe, clean environment where the body can stop perceiving *threats* and begin to *heal*.

Key Takeaways

- Environmental stressors, including CO_2 levels and VOCs, play a significant role in activating and perpetuating the Cell Danger Response (CDR).

- Addressing CO_2 tolerance through breathwork and reducing exposure to VOCs can help the body shift out of a state of chronic defence and promote cellular healing.

- Proactive steps to mitigate environmental pollutants are crucial for trauma recovery and long-term health.

Next Steps

- Evaluate the environment for potential sources of pollution, particularly in indoor settings, and consider mitigating strategies such as air purifiers and low-VOC materials.

- Incorporate breathwork techniques that improve CO_2 tolerance to optimize respiratory health and support the resolution of the CDR.

- Work with environmental health specialists to reduce exposure to harmful chemicals, such as VOCs and other air pollutants that can activate the CDR.

References

BioInitiative Report. (n.d.). BioInitiative report: A rationale for a biologically-based public exposure standard for electromagnetic fields (ELF and RF). Available at: https://bioinitiative.org

Environmental Protection Agency (EPA). (n.d.). Volatile organic compounds' impact on indoor air quality. *Environmental Protection Agency.* Available at: https://www.epa.gov/indoor-air-quality-iaq/volatile-organic-compounds-impact-indoor-air-quality

International Agency for Research on Cancer (IARC). (n.d.). IARC classifies radiofrequency electromagnetic fields as possibly carcinogenic to humans. *World Health Organization.* Available at: https://www.iarc.who.int/pressrelease/iarc-classifies-radiofrequency-electromagnetic-fields-as-possibly-carcinogenic-to-humans/

National Institute of Environmental Health Sciences (NIEHS). (n.d.). EMF: Electric and magnetic fields. *National Institute of Environmental Health Sciences*. Available at: https://www.niehs.nih.gov/health/topics/agents/emf

Nestor, J. (2020). *Breath: The new science of a lost art*. Riverhead Books. Available at: https://www.mrjamesnestor.com/breath-book

World Health Organization (WHO). (n.d.). Air pollution and health. *World Health Organization*. Available at: https://www.who.int/health-topics/air-pollution

6.

MITOCHONDRIA AND THE CELL DANGER RESPONSE

Mitochondria, known as the "powerhouses" of cells, do far more than generate energy; they also regulate the body's response to threats through the Cell Danger Response (CDR). When cells detect stressors like infections, toxins, or trauma, mitochondria shift from energy production to defence mode, slowing metabolism to prioritize healing. As we have seen, this transition is crucial but becomes problematic when the healing cycle remains incomplete, leading to chronic conditions.

In trauma, the prolonged activation of the Cell Danger Response (CDR) disrupts mitochondrial function, preventing cells from returning to a state of homeostasis. This dysfunction leads to persistent inflammation, impaired tissue repair, and dysfunction across multiple systems, contributing to long-term physical and mental health issues.

Mitochondrial dysfunction is implicated in a wide range of conditions, including PTSD, chronic fatigue syndrome, autoimmune disorders, anxiety, depression, fibromyalgia, neurodegenerative diseases like Alzheimer's and Parkinson's, metabolic syndrome, cardiovascular disease, and even cancer. The pervasive effects of mitochondrial dysfunction in these conditions underscore its central role in both physical and psychological trauma recovery.

The mitochondria's role in CDR also explains why interventions that target metabolic health—such as ketogenic diets, intermittent fasting, mitochondrial support supplements, and therapies like red light and Frequency Specific Microcurrent (FSM)—are increasingly viewed as crucial for trauma recovery. These interventions aim to restore normal mitochondrial function, allowing the body to complete the healing process and exit the danger mode.

Mitochondria Do More Than Produce Energy

Mitochondria not only generate energy but also act as sensors for environmental changes, a concept termed the **Mitochondrial Information Processing System (MIPS)**. MIPS enables mitochondria to sense both internal and external signals, integrating this information to regulate cellular and systemic physiology. Like a communication network, this process ensures that physiological functions adapt efficiently to changes, helping the body respond to stress and trauma. In CDR, this adaptive ability becomes critical as mitochondria manage the transition between normal function and defence mode.

Repairing Damaged Cell Membranes with Phospholipids

Trauma and chronic stress can damage cellular membranes, including mitochondrial membranes. **Phospholipid therapy**—the use of essential phospholipids like phosphatidylcholine—helps repair these damaged membranes, restoring membrane fluidity and enhancing mitochondrial function. By supporting membrane repair, phospholipids enable better nutrient exchange, detoxification, and cellular communication, all of which are vital for exiting the CDR and returning to normal physiology.

Intermittent Fasting and Mitochondrial Health

Intermittent fasting (IF) is another therapeutic strategy that has gained attention for its role in supporting mitochondrial function. Research shows that IF enhances mitochondrial efficiency, promotes autophagy (the body's natural cell-cleaning process), and reduces oxidative stress. By limiting eating times, the body is able to shift into a state where it uses stored fat for energy, producing ketones that fuel mitochondria more efficiently. This metabolic shift helps regulate the Cell Danger Response and supports cellular repair.

Photobiomodulation and Mitochondrial Health

Photobiomodulation (PBM), also known as red light therapy, has shown significant potential in improving mitochondrial function by enhancing ATP production, reducing oxidative stress, and facilitating mitochondrial repair. Research has demonstrated PBM's effectiveness in mitigating mitochondrial dysfunction, particularly in trauma recovery and enhancing cognitive performance.

By using specific light wavelengths, PBM stimulates mitochondria, helping the body resolve the Cell Danger Response (CDR) and promoting overall healing.

Frequencies and Power for PBM

- **Wavelengths:** PBM typically uses 600–1100 nm, with red light (600–700 nm) and near-infrared (800–1100 nm) penetrating deeper into tissues.

- **Power density:** Effective power densities range between 5 and 50 mW/cm², depending on the condition and tissue depth.

- **Optimal exposure:** 5–20 minutes of exposure, depending on the wavelength and power density, can optimize mitochondrial stimulation and repair processes.

Key Concepts

- **Mitochondrial dynamics:** Mitochondria constantly fuse and divide, responding to cellular needs. Trauma can impair these dynamics, leading to inefficient energy production and cell signalling.

- **Metabolic shifts in CDR:** Mitochondria shift from producing energy (ATP) to creating reactive oxygen species (ROS) in response to stress, initiating the immune and inflammatory response.

- **Therapeutic strategies:** Targeting mitochondria to support their return to optimal function is crucial. Strategies include nutritional approaches like ketogenic diets, intermittent fasting, antioxidant therapy to reduce oxidative stress, and therapies aimed at boosting mitochondrial biogenesis (creating new mitochondria).

Practical Applications

- **Ketogenic (keto) diet:** High in fats and low in carbohydrates, this diet helps restore mitochondrial function by increasing the production of ketones, an alternative fuel source for cells that bypass dysfunctional glucose metabolism.

- **Intermittent Fasting (IF):** IF allows the body to switch to ketone-based energy production and induces autophagy, enhancing mitochondrial repair and efficiency and supporting the resolution of the CDR.

- **Red light therapy (Photobiomodulation):** PBM directly stimulates mitochondrial activity, improving cellular energy production and reducing oxidative stress.

- **Supplements:** Coenzyme Q10, magnesium, and other mitochondrial-supporting supplements can boost mitochondrial efficiency and facilitate the recovery of energy metabolism.

- **FSM therapy:** This emerging therapy targets cellular frequency patterns to restore normal mitochondrial function, which can help reduce the prolonged effects of trauma.

- **Phospholipid therapy:** The use of phospholipids, particularly phosphatidylcholine, helps repair damaged mitochondrial membranes, improving their function and cellular health.

By restoring mitochondrial health, the body can more effectively overcome the prolonged Cell Danger Response, resuming normal cellular function, healing trauma, and preventing the onset of chronic conditions.

Resources

Afari, N., & Buchwald, D. (2003). Chronic fatigue syndrome: A review. *American Journal of Psychiatry, 160*(2), 221-236.

Gorman, G. S., et al. (2016). Mitochondrial diseases: Genetic insights and management strategies. *The Lancet.*

Hamblin, M. R. (2017). Mechanisms and applications of the anti-inflammatory effects of photobiomodulation. *AIMS Biophysics, 4*(3), 337–361. https://doi.org/10.3934/biophy.2017.3.337

Naviaux, R. K. (2014). Metabolic features and regulation of the healing cycle—A new model for chronic disease pathogenesis and treatment. *Mitochondrion, 46,* 278–297

Lim, L. (2023). Traumatic brain injury recovery with photobiomodulation: Cellular mechanisms, clinical evidence, and future potential. *Cells, 13*(5), 385. https://doi.org/10.3390/cells13050385

7.

SALUGENESIS SIGNALING

Unlocking the Body's Innate Healing Power

Introduction to Salugenesis

For millennia, healers have known that the body is not simply a passive victim of disease, but an active participant in its own recovery. In the ancient healing traditions of Ayurveda, Traditional Chinese Medicine, and Indigenous practices, the focus was not merely on eliminating illness but on restoring balance, health, and vitality. This concept—focusing on the origin and promotion of health rather than the origin of disease—has found a modern scientific counterpart in the term salugenesis, coined by Dr. Robert K. Naviaux in 2019. Derived from the Latin *salus* (health) and *genesis* (creation), *salugenesis* describes the biological and cellular processes that guide the body back to a state of homeostasis after stress, illness, or trauma. It represents the body's inherent capacity for self-repair and regeneration, offering a paradigm shift in how we approach healing from trauma and chronic conditions.

Salugenesis signals the biological and cellular processes that guide the body back to a state of homeostasis after stress, illness, or trauma. It represents the body's inherent capacity for self-repair and regeneration, offering a paradigm shift in how we approach healing from trauma and chronic conditions.

Historical and Philosophical Foundations of Healing

Before modern medicine's focus on treating symptoms and pathologies, ancient healers approached health *holistically*. They believed that the body, mind, and spirit were interconnected, and when balanced, these elements allowed the body to heal itself. This idea of an innate healing force—called *vitalism* in early Western medicine—persisted in various cultures. While modern science eventually moved away from the vitalistic framework, it has recently circled back, rediscovering that the body does indeed possess remarkable self-healing abilities guided by complex biological pathways.

The modern concept of salugenesis builds on these ancient principles, but it also embraces cutting-edge science, linking the body's healing to cellular and molecular mechanisms.

Biological Mechanisms of Healing

At the cellular level, salugenesis involves a series of complex processes aimed at repairing damage, restoring balance, and protecting the organism from further harm. Fundamental biological mechanisms include:

- **Cellular repair and regeneration:** Cells can repair themselves after injury. This process is driven by stem cells, which can differentiate into the specific cell types needed to regenerate damaged tissues. In trauma recovery, stem cell activation plays a critical role in repairing muscle, brain tissue, and other affected areas in the body.

- **Inflammation resolution:** While acute inflammation is a vital part of the body's response to injury, chronic inflammation can perpetuate the damage. Salugenesis involves resolving this inflammation once its purpose has been served. Specialized pro-resolving mediators (SPMs) discovered by researchers like Dr. Charles Serhan help terminate inflammation and initiate the healing process.

- **Mitochondrial function and energy:** Mitochondria are central to energy production. Healthy mitochondria are necessary for generating the energy required for cellular repair and immune function. When mitochondrial dysfunction occurs, it can impair the body's ability to heal, making mitochondrial health crucial for trauma recovery.

- **Immune modulation:** The immune system is a double-edged sword. While it protects the body from infection and aids in tissue repair, it can also contribute to chronic stress if over-activated. Modulating the immune response—promoting healing without triggering chronic inflammation—is a critical part of salugenesis signalling.

Salutogenesis: A Public Health Perspective

In 1979, sociologist Aaron Antonovsky introduced the concept of **salutogenesis**, which focuses on the *creation of health* rather than the *prevention of disease*. Antonovsky studied people who remained healthy despite high levels of stress, proposing that factors such as a sense of coherence and the ability to find meaning in life were essential to promoting well-being.

Though focused on psychological and social factors, salutogenesis shares an essential parallel with salugenesis: both prioritize understanding what makes people resilient and healthy rather than what makes them sick. In trauma recovery, this shift in focus—from merely treating symptoms to actively promoting healing—mirrors the role of salugenesis signalling at the cellular level.

Supporting Salugenesis Through Therapeutic Interventions

Modern therapies now focus not just on treating trauma, but on actively supporting the body's healing mechanisms. As mentioned in the previous chapter, several therapeutic interventions have shown promise in activating salugenesis signalling:

- **Nutrition and supplements:** Anti-inflammatory diets, mitochondrial support, and nutritional therapies can enhance the body's capacity to heal. Omega-3 fatty acids, antioxidants, and nutrients like CoQ10 all support mitochondrial health and reduce inflammation, creating the conditions for recovery.

- **Photobiomodulation:** This therapy uses red or near-infrared light to stimulate cellular repair. Photobiomodulation supports mitochondrial function and has been shown to promote healing in tissues affected by injury, inflammation, or trauma.

- **Frequency Specific Microcurrent (FSM):** FSM uses low-level electrical currents to stimulate tissue repair and reduce inflammation. This therapy has been particularly effective in trauma recovery by activating cellular repair processes and modulating the nervous system.

- **Hyperbaric Oxygen Therapy (HBOT):** HBOT enhances oxygen delivery to tissues, promoting healing in cells that have been deprived of oxygen due to injury or trauma. This therapy is beneficial in cases where inflammation or injury has compromised circulation.

- **Heat and cold shock proteins:** Exposure to heat (such as in saunas) or cold (through cryotherapy) induces the production of heat shock proteins (HSPs) and cold shock proteins. These proteins help cells repair damage and protect against future stress, enhancing resilience and recovery.

Trauma, the Nervous System, and Salugenesis

The vagus nerve and the autonomic nervous system play central roles in salugenesis. Trauma often traps the nervous system in a state of hypervigilance or shutdown, inhibiting the body's ability to heal.

Central to the activation and resolution of the CDR is the autonomic nervous system (ANS), which regulates the body's involuntary functions, such as heart rate, digestion, and immune responses. The ANS has two main branches that play vital roles in modulating the CDR and the healing process:

- **Sympathetic nervous system (SNS):** Known as the "fight-or-flight" system, the SNS is activated during times of stress, triggering the CDR. When the body perceives a threat, the SNS ramps up, preparing the body to either confront or flee from danger. In this state, stress hormones like cortisol and adrenaline are released, energy is diverted away from processes like digestion and cellular repair, and inflammation is triggered as a defence mechanism. Prolonged activation of the SNS can keep the body stuck in a defensive mode, preventing the transition to salugenesis.

- **Parasympathetic nervous system (PNS):** Often referred to as the "rest-and-digest" system, the PNS promotes relaxation, recovery, and healing. It plays a crucial role in facilitating salugenesis by calming the stress response and allowing the body to prioritize cellular repair, digestion, and energy restoration. This system is closely linked to the vagus nerve, which regulates the body's ability to switch into a healing mode. The activation of the PNS is essential for moving the body out of the CDR and into a state where it can heal.

Vagus Nerve and Polyvagal Theory

The vagus nerve, as explored in Dr. Stephen Porges's Polyvagal Theory, is integral to calming the nervous system and shifting it into a parasympathetic state. In this state, the body can focus on repair and restoration. Practices such as **Neuroacoustic Sound Therapy** and **Heart Rate Variability (HRV) biofeedback** are designed to support vagal tone and promote recovery.

Forest Bathing (Shinrin-yoku)

Spending time in nature, also known as "forest bathing", has been shown to reduce stress hormones and improve vagal tone, making it another powerful tool in activating the body's healing response.

Balancing the Nervous System for Healing

For the body to transition from the CDR to a state of salugenesis, there must be a rebalancing of the autonomic nervous system, where the parasympathetic nervous system (PNS) can override the prolonged activation of the sympathetic nervous system (SNS). Several therapies can support this rebalancing and help shift the body from a state of defence to one of recovery:

- **Vagus nerve stimulation:** The vagus nerve is vital to the parasympathetic nervous system, calming the body and promoting healing. Techniques like deep breathing exercises, vagal nerve stimulation, and Neuroacoustic Sound Therapy can help activate the vagus nerve and enhance parasympathetic activity.

- **Heart Rate Variability (HRV) Training:** HRV is a measure of the balance between the sympathetic and parasympathetic systems. Higher HRV indicates greater parasympathetic activation, which is associated with better stress resilience and healing capacity. HRV biofeedback techniques can help individuals train their nervous systems to activate the PNS more effectively, promoting the shift toward salugenesis.

- **Mind-Body Practices:** Practices such as yoga, meditation, and forest bathing (spending time in nature–see above) help reduce sympathetic nervous system activation and enhance parasympathetic tone, which supports the body's ability to move into a healing state.

The Sympathetic to Parasympathetic Shift: Key to Salugenesis

The shift from sympathetic dominance to parasympathetic activation is essential for resolving the CDR. Without this shift, the body remains stuck in a defensive state, unable to repair and heal fully. Salugenesis, therefore, is the physiological manifestation of the body moving out of fight-or-flight and into rest-and-repair. It's a process in which the nervous system calms, inflammation resolves, and cellular repair is prioritized, allowing the body to restore balance and function.

Post-Traumatic Growth and Salugenesis

Post-traumatic growth (PTG) is a profound example of the body and mind's ability to heal from trauma and grow stronger. Research suggests that this growth involves a process of rewiring in the brain through **neuroplasticity** and **neurogenesis**. Neuroplasticity allows for the formation of new neural *connections,* while neurogenesis supports the development of *new neurons.* These processes facilitate both cognitive and emotional transformation, enabling individuals to experience personal growth, enhanced mental resilience, and a renewed sense of purpose after trauma.

Key Takeaways

- **Salugenesis represents a shift in healing paradigms:** Rather than focusing solely on treating disease or trauma, salugenesis encourages healing by promoting the body's inherent ability to recover and restore balance at a cellular level. This marks a shift from the pathology-centred model to a health-centred approach.

- **Healing is a cellular process:** Salugenesis involves cellular repair, inflammation resolution, and immune modulation. Critical biological processes like mitochondrial function and stem cell activation are central to the body's ability to regenerate tissues and overcome trauma.

- **The nervous system plays a central role:** The autonomic nervous system, particularly the parasympathetic branch, must be activated for the body to transition from defence (CDR) to healing (salugenesis). Techniques that enhance vagal tone and promote relaxation are key to recovery.

- **Modern therapies can activate salugenesis:** Nutrition, Photobiomodulation, Frequency Specific Microcurrent (FSM), and Hyperbaric Oxygen Therapy (HBOT) are powerful tools in stimulating the body's healing mechanisms. These therapies help resolve chronic inflammation, enhance mitochondrial function, and promote tissue repair.

- **Resolution of the Cell Danger Response (CDR) is essential for healing:** Chronic activation of the CDR keeps the body in a defensive state, blocking healing. Moving out of this state requires balancing the autonomic nervous system, reducing inflammation, and supporting cellular repair through therapeutic interventions.

- **The sympathetic to parasympathetic shift is crucial:** Healing is not possible without the shift from sympathetic dominance (fight-or-flight) to parasympathetic activation (rest-and-repair). Therapies that promote this shift, such as HRV training and vagus nerve stimulation, are essential to trauma recovery.

Next Steps

- **Introduce the concept of salugenesis early in trauma recovery programs:** Begin incorporating the principles of salugenesis into trauma recovery frameworks, ensuring clients understand the body's *natural capacity* for healing. Highlight that recovery isn't just about managing symptoms but actively promoting the body's self-repair processes.

- **Incorporate therapeutic interventions that promote salugenesis:** Develop comprehensive therapeutic plans that integrate interventions proven to stimulate salugenesis, such as anti-inflammatory nutrition, Photobiomodulation, Frequency Specific Microcurrent (FSM), and Hyperbaric Oxygen Therapy (HBOT). Each of these approaches supports the body in moving out of the Cell Danger Response (CDR) and into repair mode.

- **Focus on balancing the autonomic nervous system (ANS):** Emphasize therapies that shift the balance from sympathetic (fight-or-flight) dominance to parasympathetic (rest-and-digest) activation. This includes vagus nerve stimulation, HRV training, yoga, and time in nature (forest bathing).

- **Educate on the role of the nervous system in healing:** Offer resources and training to help people understand how the vagus nerve, parasympathetic nervous system, and Polyvagal Theory contribute to the body's healing process. Encourage practices that strengthen vagal tone and improve resilience to stress.

- **Develop protocols for trauma recovery:** Create trauma recovery protocols that aim for cellular repair and regeneration by addressing mitochondrial health, resolving chronic inflammation, and supporting immune function. Provide clients with personalized strategies that focus on transitioning from CDR to salugenesis.

References

Antonovsky, A. (1979). *Health, stress, and coping: New perspectives on mental and physical well-being.* San Francisco: Jossey-Bass.

Hamblin M. R. (2016) Photobiomodulation or low-level laser therapy, *Journal of Biophotonics, 9*(11–12), https://www.ncbi.nlm.nih.gov/pmc/articles/PMC5215795/

Hansen M. M. (2017) Shinrin-yoku (forest bathing) and nature therapy: A state-of-the-art review. *Int J Environ Res Public Health,* 14(8), 851, https://www.ncbi.nlm.nih.gov/pmc/articles/PMC5580555/

Heart rate variability training. (n.d.) https://www.heartmath.org/resources/heartmath-tools/

Naviaux, R. K. (2014). Metabolic features of the cell danger response. https://pubmed.ncbi.nlm.nih.gov/24759148/

Naviaux, R.K. Mitochondrial and metabolic features of salugenesis and the healing cycle. *Mitochondrion* **70**, 131-163 (2023).

Porges, S. W. (n.d.). *Polyvagal theory.* https://www.stephenporges.com/

8.

SALUTOGENESIS

Fostering Health and Resilience in Trauma Recovery

Introduction to Salutogenesis

In trauma recovery, the focus often centres on understanding and mitigating the factors that contribute to distress and dysfunction. However, an equally vital perspective is offered by the previously mentioned salutogenesis. Unlike pathogenesis, which examines the origins of disease, salutogenesis explores the origins of health. It emphasizes the factors that support human health and well-being, advocating for a proactive approach to developing resilience and promoting recovery.

This chapter delves further into the principles of salutogenesis and their application in trauma recovery.

Understanding Salutogenesis

Salutogenesis seeks to answer the question: **"What keeps people healthy?"**

Components of salutogenesis include:

- **Sense of coherence (SOC):** A core concept that reflects an individual's capacity to perceive life as comprehensible, manageable, and meaningful.

- **General resistance resources (GRRs):** Factors that help individuals cope with stressors and maintain health.

- **Health as a continuum:** Viewing health and illness on a spectrum rather than as binary states.

Sense of Coherence (SOC)

At the heart of salutogenesis lies the SOC, which Antonovsky defines as mixture of optimism combined with a sense of control. The concept seeks to explain why some people get sick under stress while others stay healthy. The SOC has three main components:

- **Comprehensibility:** The degree to which you think that the stimuli deriving from your internal and external environments are structured, predictable, and explicable.

- **Manageability:** The extent to which you feel you have the resources available to meet the demands posed by these stimuli.

- **Meaningfulness:** Your level of acceptance that these demands are challenges worthy of investment and engagement.

There are a number of ways to enhance SOC in trauma recovery:

- **Comprehensibility:** Providing trauma survivors with clear information about their experiences and the healing process helps them make sense of their trauma.

- **Manageability:** Equipping individuals with coping strategies and resources ensures they feel capable of handling their challenges.

- **Meaningfulness:** Helping survivors find purpose and meaning in their recovery journey fosters motivation and resilience.

General Resistance Resources (GRRs)

General resistance resources (GRRs) are a diverse array of factors that help individuals manage stress and maintain health. GRRs can be categorized into:

Personal resources:

- **Intelligence and creativity:** Problem-solving abilities and creative thinking can aid in navigating complex emotional landscapes.

- **Emotional strength:** Resilience and emotional regulation skills help individuals bounce back from adversity.

Social resources:

- **Support networks:** Family, friends, and community provide emotional and practical support.

- **Relationships:** Healthy relationships foster a sense of belonging and security.

Material resources:

- **Financial stability:** Economic security reduces stress and provides access to necessary services.

- **Access to healthcare:** Availability of medical and psychological care supports overall well-being.

There are a number of ways to enhance GRRs:

- **Building strong relationships:** Encouraging the development of supportive relationships and community connections.

- **Promoting personal growth:** Facilitating activities that enhance emotional strength and creativity.

- **Ensuring access to resources:** Advocating for equitable access to healthcare and financial support systems.

Health as a Continuum

Salutogenesis conceptualizes health on a continuum, recognizing that individuals move along a spectrum from wellness to illness based on their experiences and resources. This perspective acknowledges that health and disease are not binary states but exist in a *dynamic* state influenced by various internal and external factors.

This idea has a number of implications for trauma recovery:

- **Dynamic process:** Recovery is viewed as a fluid process where individuals can shift toward greater health and resilience.

- **Holistic approach:** Addressing multiple facets of an individual's life (physical, emotional, social) enhances overall well-being.

- **Personalized interventions:** Tailoring recovery strategies to individual needs and resources promotes effective healing.

Salutogenesis in Practice

Implementing salutogenic principles in trauma recovery involves fostering an environment that enhances SOC and strengthens GRRs. Practical applications include:

- **Trauma-informed mindfulness and meditation:** These practices improve comprehensibility and manageability by promoting present-moment awareness and emotional regulation.

- **Nutrition and physical activity:** A balanced diet and regular exercise support physical health, which in turn bolsters emotional and psychological resilience.

- **Therapeutic interventions:** Approaches such as Cognitive Behavioural Therapy (CBT), Somatic Experiencing, and Equine Therapy can be integrated to address various aspects of trauma.

Foster these qualities in order to create health-promoting environments:

- **Supportive relationships:** Encourage connections with supportive individuals and communities.

- **Safe spaces:** Provide environments where trauma survivors feel secure and empowered to engage in their healing journey.

- **Resource accessibility:** Ensure easy access to necessary resources, including healthcare, education, and social support.

Connection to Trauma and the Cell Danger Response (CDR)

Integrating Salutogenesis with CDR:

- **Resolving CDR:** Salutogenic strategies facilitate the resolution of the CDR by promoting healing and reducing chronic stress.

- **Enhancing cellular repair:** Practices that enhance SOC and strengthen GRRs support the body's transition from a defensive state to one of repair and regeneration.

- **Holistic recovery:** Combining salutogenic principles with cellular healing approaches ensures a comprehensive recovery that addresses both emotional and physical aspects of trauma.

Practical Strategies to Implement Salutogenesis in Trauma Recovery

Developing a Strong Sense of Coherence (SOC):

- Comprehensibility:
    - » **Journaling:** Encourage writing about experiences to organize thoughts and gain clarity.

» **Education:** Provide information about trauma and its effects to demystify symptoms and reactions.

- Manageability:
    - » **Resource-mapping:** Help individuals identify and use available resources (e.g., support groups, therapy).
    - » **Skill-building:** Teach coping strategies such as deep breathing, meditation, and time management.

- Meaningfulness:
    - » **Goal-setting:** Assist in setting personal goals that align with individual values and aspirations.
    - » **Purposeful activities:** Encourage engagement in activities that provide a sense of achievement and purpose.

Enhancing General Resistance Resources (GRRs):

- Personal Growth:
    - » **Emotional regulation exercises:** Practices like trauma-informed mindfulness, cognitive restructuring, and Trauma Release Exercises (TRE) help release tension and trauma stored in the body.
    - » **Creative outlets:** Art Therapy, music therapy, and other creative activities can be used to express emotions.

- Social Support:
    - » **Building relationships:** Facilitate connections with supportive peers, mentors, and community members while being mindful of potential triggers and helping individuals develop the skills to navigate challenging interactions without becoming overwhelmed.

- Access to care:

  - » **Healthcare navigation:** Assist in accessing medical and psychological services.

  - » **Advocacy:** Advocate for policies that improve access to mental health care and support services.

Creating a Salutogenic Environment:

- Daily routines:

  - » **Structured Schedules:** Establishing regular routines to provide stability and predictability.

  - » **Healthy habits:** Promoting balanced nutrition, adequate sleep, and regular physical activity.

- Supportive Spaces:

  - » **Safe zones:** Creating environments where individuals feel safe to express themselves and engage in healing activities.

  - » **Resource centres:** Providing access to educational materials, therapeutic tools, and support services.

Integrating Salutogenic Principles into Daily Life:

- **Trauma-informed mindfulness practices:** Incorporating trauma-informed mindfulness meditation into daily routines to enhance present-moment awareness.

- **Community involvement:** Encouraging participation in community activities to build a sense of belonging and support.

Conclusion

Salutogenesis offers a transformative approach to trauma recovery by emphasizing the enhancement of health-promoting factors rather than solely addressing the roots of distress. By fostering a strong SOC and strengthening GRRs, individuals can cultivate resilience and facilitate holistic healing. Integrating salutogenic principles with cellular healing processes like the Cell Danger Response (CDR) provides a comprehensive framework that addresses both the emotional and physical dimensions of trauma recovery.

As we continue to explore various therapeutic strategies and their impact on healing, embracing salutogenesis empowers trauma survivors to harness their innate strengths and resources, paving the way for sustained well-being and resilience.

Key Takeaways

- Salutogenesis shifts the focus from disease prevention to health promotion, emphasizing factors that support well-being.

- Sense of coherence (SOC)—comprising comprehensibility, manageability, and meaningfulness—is crucial for effective trauma recovery.

- General resistance resources (GRRs) are essential for managing stress and fostering resilience.

- Health as a continuum recognizes that individuals move along a spectrum of health based on their resources and coping abilities.

- Salugenesis signalling leverages salutogenic principles to activate the body's natural healing processes, aiding in the resolution of the Cell Danger Response (CDR).

Next Steps

- Assess your sense of coherence:
    - » Reflect on your ability to make sense of challenges, manage stress, and find meaning in your life.

» Engage in practices that strengthen comprehensibility, manageability, and meaningfulness.

- Evaluate and Strengthen Your Resources:

  » Identify personal, social, and material resources that support your well-being.

  » Take actionable steps to enhance these resources, such as building stronger relationships or accessing new support services.

- Create a Salutogenic Environment:

  » Design your living and working spaces to promote health and well-being.

  » Incorporate daily routines and habits that support physical and emotional health.

- Integrate Salutogenic Practices into Daily Life:

  » Implement mindfulness, meditation, and other health-promoting activities into your daily schedule.

  » Seek out community and support networks that reinforce your resilience and well-being.

Practical Exercises and Reflections

These can be done privately, or with a therapist for feedback.

Exercise 1: Enhancing Comprehensibility

Journaling prompt:

- Write about a recent challenging experience. Describe what happened, how it made you feel, and what you learned from it. This exercise helps organize thoughts and make sense of complex emotions.

Exercise 2: Building Manageability

Resource-mapping:

- Create a list of your current resources, including personal strengths, supportive relationships, and available services. Identify areas where you can seek additional support and develop a plan to access these resources.

Exercise 3: Cultivating Meaningfulness

Purpose exploration:

- Reflect on what gives your life meaning. List activities, relationships, and goals that you find fulfilling. Consider how you can incorporate more of these elements into your daily life to enhance your sense of purpose.

Reflection prompt:

- Assess Your SOC on a scale of 1 to 10. Rate your sense of comprehensibility, manageability, and meaningfulness. Identify specific actions you can take to improve each component.

Implementing strategies:

- **Daily trauma-informed mindfulness practice:** Dedicate 10 minutes each day to trauma-informed mindfulness meditation. Focus on your breath and observe your thoughts without judgement.

- **Strengthening Social Connections:** Reach out to a friend or family member each week. Share your experiences and offer support to foster deeper relationships.

- **Healthy Nutrition Plan:** Incorporate anti-inflammatory foods such as leafy greens, berries, and fatty fish into your meals. Consult a nutritionist if needed to develop a balanced diet plan.

Key Takeaways

- Embracing a salutogenic approach transforms the landscape of trauma recovery by focusing on the positive factors that foster health and resilience.

- By enhancing the SOC and strengthening GRRs, individuals can live on their healing path with greater confidence and purpose.

- As we integrate these principles with cellular healing processes, we pave the way for a holistic and empowered path to recovery.

- I encourage both practitioners and trauma survivors to explore and implement salutogenic strategies, fostering environments and practices that support sustained well-being and resilience.

References

American Psychological Association. (n.d.). *Building resilience*. https://www.apa.org/topics/resilience

Antonovsky, A. (1979). *Health, Stress, and Coping*. San Francisco: Jossey-Bass.

Harvard Health Publishing. (2023). *Quick-start guide to an anti-inflammation diet*. https://www.health.harvard.edu/staying-healthy/quick-start-guide-to-an-antiinflammation-diet

Mindful.org. (n.d.). *What is mindfulness?* https://www.mindful.org/what-is-mindfulness/

Mittelmark, M. B., Sagy, S., Eriksson, M., Bauer, G. F., Pelikan, J. M., Lindström, B., … & Espnes, G. A. (2017). *The Handbook of Ssalutogenesis.* Springer.

Walsh, F. (2016). *Strengthening Family Resilience.* Guilford Press.

World Health Organization (WHO). (2005). *Promoting Mental Health: Concepts, emerging evidence, practice.* World Health Organization.

9.

THE DICHOTOMY OF MEMORY

Autobiographical vs. Traumatic

Introduction

Memory plays an essential role in shaping our identities and experiences. In psychology, a significant distinction exists between autobiographical memory, which allows us to recall past events, and traumatic memory, which often resurfaces in vivid and distressing ways. Understanding this distinction is essential for clinicians working with trauma survivors, as it directly influences therapeutic approaches and recovery processes.

This chapter explores the differences between these memory types, supported by fundamental research, and discusses their implications for the Cell Danger Response (CDR) and salugenesis.

Understanding Autobiographical Memory

Autobiographical memory refers to the ability to recall in your mind specific events from your life. It is often characterized by a coherent narrative and contextual details. This type of memory is typically stored in a way that integrates emotions, sensory information, and personal significance. The hippocampus plays a critical role in this process, helping to contextualize memories and provide a structured narrative that allows individuals to reflect on their past.

Traumatic Memory Characteristics

In contrast, traumatic memory is often characterized by fragmentation and heightened sensory recall. When a traumatic event occurs, the memory is encoded differently, frequently lacking the coherence and narrative structure seen in autobiographical memories. Traumatic memories may be recalled as disjointed images, emotions, or sensations, leading to what individuals often describe as "reliving" the experience.

Key Research Findings

- **Brewin et al. (2010):** This study explores the neuroimaging differences between traumatic and autobiographical memories. It found that heightened sensory details and emotional intensity characterize traumatic memories, whereas autobiographical memories are more coherent and integrated. The research suggests that traumatic memories lack narrative coherence and are primarily processed in the amygdala and sensory cortices rather than the hippocampus.

- **Dual representation theory (Brewin, 2001):** Brewin's theory proposes that traumatic memories are stored in two distinct ways: verbally accessible memories (VAMs), which resemble autobiographical memories, and situationally accessible memories (SAMs), which are more sensory and emotional. SAMs are often challenging to integrate into a coherent narrative, leading to flashbacks where the memory feels immediate and present.

- **Van der Kolk's research (1994; 1995):** Renowned trauma expert Dr. Bessel van der Kolk emphasizes that traumatic memories are often encoded in fragmented forms, relying more on sensory and emotional recall. Individuals may struggle to verbalize these memories, resulting in experiences that feel disjointed and unmanageable.

- **Neurobiology insights (Nadel & Jacobs, 1998):** This study highlights how stress hormones, particularly cortisol, affect the encoding of traumatic memories. Traumatic experiences lead to over-consolidation in the amygdala and under-consolidation in the hippocampus, explaining the vividness of traumatic memories despite their lack of coherent context.

- **Van der Hart et al. (2006):** In *The Haunted Self*, the authors discuss how traumatic memories are stored in sensory and somatic forms, often lacking the temporal coherence of autobiographical memories. This lack of integration leads to experiences of flashbacks or vivid re-experiencing, making it feel as if the trauma is occurring again in the present.

- **Neuroimaging studies (Liberzon & Martis, 2006):** Neuroimaging studies reveal that recalling traumatic memories activates the amygdala while decreasing prefrontal cortex activity, which is responsible for cognitive control and narrative processing. This pattern helps explain the raw emotional experiences tied to traumatic memories.

- **Dr. Ruth Lanius's perspective on traumatic memory:** In a recent perspective article, Dr. Lanius discusses how traumatic memory is marked by sensorimotor fragmentation, where traumatic memories consist of unintegrated sensations and actions. The article argues that current PTSD treatments often overlook these sensorimotor processes, leading to high dropout rates among patients. This highlights the urgent need for interventions that integrate fragmented memories into a coherent narrative.

Implications for Trauma Recovery

Understanding these distinctions between autobiographical and traumatic memory has profound implications for treatment. The fragmented nature of traumatic memories can contribute to the activation of the Cell Danger Response (CDR), a physiological state triggered by stressors, including trauma. When traumatic memories are not fully processed, they can perpetuate the CDR, keeping the individual in a state of fight-or-flight.

Therapies that focus on integrating traumatic memories—such as Somatic Experiencing, EMDR, and **Sensorimotor Therapy**—can help individuals move from a CDR state to one of healing and recovery. This shift is essential for promoting salugenesis, allowing the body to transition from chronic stress to cellular repair and well-being.

Conclusion

The differences between autobiographical and traumatic memory underscore the need for targeted therapeutic approaches in trauma recovery. Recognizing how traumatic memory drives the CDR and hinders healing highlights the importance of addressing these memories in clinical settings.

Key Takeaways

- **Dichotomy of memory:** Autobiographical memories are coherent and contextualized, while traumatic memories are often fragmented and sensory-rich, leading to distressing re-experiencing.

- **Neurobiological distinctions:** Traumatic memories are processed differently in the brain, primarily involving the amygdala and sensory cortices, as opposed to the hippocampus, which is crucial for narrative memory.

- **Dual representation theory:** Traumatic memories can exist as verbally accessible memories (VAMs) and situationally accessible memories (SAMs), with SAMs being harder to integrate and often causing flashbacks.

- **Sensorimotor fragmentation:** Traumatic memories may be characterized by unintegrated sensations and actions, making it difficult for individuals to contextualize and verbalize their experiences.

- **Implications for treatment:** Current PTSD treatments may not adequately address sensorimotor processes, emphasizing the need for interventions that help integrate traumatic memories into a coherent narrative.

- **Connection to CDR and salugenesis:** Understanding the relationship between traumatic memory and the Cell Danger Response (CDR) can inform therapeutic approaches, promoting recovery and health through salugenesis.

References

Brewin, C. R., Dalgleish, T., & Joseph, S. (1996). A dual representation theory of posttraumatic stress disorder. *Psychological Review, 103*(4), 670–686. https://doi.org/10.1037/0033-295X.103.4.670

Brewin, C. R., Gregory, J. D., Lipton, M., & Burgess, N. (2010). Intrusive images in psychological disorders: Characteristics, neural mechanisms, and treatment implications. *Psychological Review, 117*(1), 210–232. https://doi.org/10.1037/a0018113

Kearney, B.E., Lanius, R.A. Why reliving is not remembering and the unique neurobiological representation of traumatic memory. *Nat. Mental Health* **2**, 1142–1151 (2024). https://doi.org/10.1038/s44220-024-00324-z

Liberzon, I., & Martis, B. (2006). Neuroimaging studies of emotional responses in PTSD. *Annals of the New York Academy of Sciences, 1071*(1), 87–109. https://doi.org/10.1196/annals.1364.009

Nadel, L., & Jacobs, W. J. (1998). Traumatic memory is special. *Current Directions in Psychological Science, 7*(5), 154–157. https://doi.org/10.1111/1467-8721.ep10836842

Van der Hart, O., Nijenhuis, E. R. S., & Steele, K. (2006). *The Haunted Self: Structural dissociation and the treatment of chronic traumatization*. Norton.

Van der Kolk, B. A. (1994). The body keeps the score: Memory and the evolving psychobiology of post-traumatic stress. *Harvard Review of Psychiatry, 1*(5), 253–265. https://doi.org/10.3109/10673229409017088

Van der Kolk, B. A., & Fisler, R. (1995). Dissociation and the fragmentary nature of traumatic memories: Overview and exploratory study. *Journal of Traumatic Stress, 8*(4), 505–525. https://doi.org/10.1002/jts.2490080402

10.

BOTTOM-UP THERAPY

Healing Through the Body

Introduction

Trauma isn't just stored in the mind—it leaves lasting imprints on the body. Top-Down Therapy starts by addressing thoughts and beliefs in an effort to influence emotional and physical responses. **Bottom-Up Therapy** begins with the body, focusing on physiological responses and working *upward* to affect emotions and thoughts.

This chapter explores how bottom-up therapy engages the body in the healing process, enabling trauma survivors to release stored tension and move toward recovery.

Top-Down Therapy vs. Bottom-Up Therapy

Top-Down Therapy:

- **Focus:** Primarily addresses cognition and thoughts to influence emotions and bodily responses.

- **Method:** Patients change their thinking patterns to regulate emotions and behaviour.

- **Examples:** Cognitive Behavioural Therapy (CBT) and Talk Therapy.

- **Goal:** Transform thoughts and beliefs first, which trickles down to change emotions and sensations.

Bottom-Up Therapy:

- **Focus:** Begins with physical sensations, targeting how trauma is stored in the body and then influencing emotional and cognitive responses.

- **Method:** Through bodily awareness, trauma survivors release stored stress and tension, which helps shift emotional and mental states.

- **Examples:** Somatic Experiencing (SE), Eye Movement Desensitization and Reprocessing (EMDR), Trauma Releasing Exercises (TRE).

- **Goal:** Heal the body first to facilitate emotional and cognitive recovery.

Types of Bottom-Up Therapies

- Somatic Experiencing (SE)

  » **Overview:** SE focuses on tracking and releasing physical sensations related to trauma. By addressing how the body processes traumatic memories, it helps individuals restore balance in the nervous system.

- Trauma-Releasing Exercises (TRE)

  » **Overview:** TRE involves exercises that activate the body's natural tremoring mechanism, releasing deep muscular tension related to trauma and stress.

- Eye Movement Desensitization and Reprocessing (EMDR)

  » **Overview:** EMDR uses bilateral stimulation (e.g., eye movements) to process traumatic memories by accessing and resolving stored physical responses.

- Brainspotting
  - » **Overview:** Brainspotting identifies points in the visual field that correlate with stored trauma in the body, allowing deep processing of emotional and physical pain.

- Emotional Freedom Techniques (EFT/Tapping)
  - » **Overview:** EFT combines acupressure and cognitive techniques, using tapping to release stored emotional trauma in the body.

- Equine Therapy
  - » **Overview:** Equine Therapy involves non-riding, ground-based interactions with horses, helping trauma survivors process emotions through non-verbal communication and relational experiences.

- Yoga for Trauma Recovery
  - » **Overview:** Trauma-informed yoga emphasizes mindful movement and breathwork, helping individuals reconnect with their bodies and calm their nervous systems.

- Somatic Art Therapy
  - » **Overview:** Somatic Art Therapy combines physical movement and art-making to process trauma, offering an outlet for emotions through creative expression.

- Sandplay Therapy
  - » **Overview:** Sandplay allows clients to express and process trauma through symbolic interaction with sand and miniature figures, facilitating healing through non-verbal, physical expression.

- Family Constellation Therapy
  - » **Overview:** This therapy helps individuals identify and release trauma stored in family dynamics, using a combination of role-play and body-based approaches to heal intergenerational trauma.

- HeartMath and Coherence Training
  - » **Overview:** HeartMath uses biofeedback to regulate heart rate variability (HRV), helping individuals manage stress and trauma responses.

Conclusion

Bottom-Up Therapy offers trauma survivors a pathway to recovery by focusing on how trauma is stored in the body. By accessing these *physical* memories, individuals can heal not just emotionally, but physically and cognitively as well. Whether through movement, sensory stimulation, or interaction with animals, Bottom-Up Therapy engages the body's innate healing capabilities, offering profound results for trauma recovery.

References

Brainspotting therapy. (n.d.). Retrieved from https://brainspotting.com/about-brainspotting/what-is-brainspotting/

Emotional freedom techniques (EFT/tapping). (n.d.). Retrieved from https://www.thetappingsolution.com/what-is-eft-tapping

Eye movement desensitization and reprocessing (EMDR). (n.d.). Retrieved from https://www.emdr.com/what-is-emdr

HeartMath and coherence. (n.d.). Retrieved from https://www.heartmath.com/science/

Sandplay therapy. (n.d.). Retrieved from https://www.sandplay.org/about-sandplay/what-is-sandplay

Somatic art therapy. (n.d.). Retrieved from https://www.arttherapy.org

Somatic experiencing. (n.d.). Retrieved from https://traumahealing.org/se-101

Trauma-informed yoga. (n.d.). Retrieved from https://www.trauma-sensitiveyoga.com

Trauma releasing exercises (TRE). (n.d.). Retrieved from https://traumaprevention.com/what-is-tre

11.

HARNESSING PSYCHONEUROIMMUNOLOGY

The Role of Placebo, Nocebo, and the Therapist's Influence

Introduction

Psychoneuroimmunology (PNI) explores the intricate connection between the mind, nervous system, and immune response. As research continues to reveal how deeply our thoughts, emotions, and beliefs influence physical health, the role of placebo and nocebo effects has come to the forefront of recent medical and psychological discussions.

The placebo effect demonstrates that a person's steadfast belief in the effectiveness of a treatment can lead to tangible, measurable *improvements* in health—even when the treatment itself is *inactive.*

Conversely, the nocebo effect shows that negative expectations or beliefs can worsen symptoms or trigger adverse reactions. Within therapy, a skilled practitioner can harness these effects to support healing, not only by administering evidence-based treatments but also by offering hope and confidence that recovery is possible.

The Power of Belief: Placebo and Nocebo

The placebo effect has long been recognized as a powerful testament to the mind-body connection. Patients given sugar pills, saline injections, or other inert interventions often experience *genuine* improvements in symptoms simply because they believe the treatment will work. This effect is not mere imagination—biochemical processes such as the release of endorphins, changes in brain activity, and modulation of immune function have been observed in placebo responders.

On the flipside, the nocebo effect shows that the anticipation of adverse outcomes can cause real harm. When patients expect a treatment to fail or believe they will experience side effects, those expectations can manifest physically, leading to increased pain, anxiety, or even symptoms unrelated to the treatment.

Psychoneuroimmunology and the Mechanisms Behind Belief

PNI explains the underlying mechanisms of both the placebo and nocebo effects. When a person believes in the efficacy of a treatment, the brain activates pathways that influence the autonomic nervous system and the immune system. This connection is why stress, anxiety, and negative emotions can suppress immune function, while positive emotions, hope, and relaxation can enhance it.

Neurotransmitters like **dopamine** and **serotonin**, which regulate mood and behaviour, are influenced by our expectations. Additionally, the hypothalamic-pituitary-adrenal (HPA) axis, which governs the body's stress response, plays a crucial role in mediating the effects of belief on health. When a person anticipates healing, their body produces a relaxation response, reducing cortisol levels and promoting immune activity.

The Therapist's Influence: A Key Factor in Healing

One of the most critical factors in the placebo effect is the relationship between the patient and the therapist. Studies show that a therapist's confidence in a treatment's success can directly influence client outcomes. A therapist who conveys hope, confidence, and a belief in the strong possibility of healing can trigger positive changes in the client's physiological state, often tipping the balance towards recovery.

This is where psychoneuroimmunology and therapeutic practices intersect. By creating a safe and trusting environment, therapists can help clients engage their parasympathetic nervous system—the "rest-and-digest" state—where the body is primed for healing. In this context, the therapist's well-placed hope and reassurance become part of the treatment, helping to maximize the therapeutic impact.

The Work of Dr. Mario Martinez: Cultural Beliefs and Healing

Dr. Mario Martinez, author of *The MindBody Code*, offers a unique perspective on how cultural beliefs and emotional states shape the immune system and the healing process. He highlights how people's beliefs, particularly those influenced by cultural conditioning, can have profound effects on their health. For example, cultural notions of ageing, worthiness, and illness can affect how a person experiences health challenges or responds to treatments.

Dr. Martinez's bio cognitive model integrates psychoneuroimmunology with cultural beliefs, suggesting that healing is not only a matter of biochemical interventions but also involves challenging and transforming people's deeply held beliefs. For therapists, this means addressing both the conscious and subconscious influences that affect the client's healing process.

Hypothetical: The Therapist's Confidence and Client Outcomes

Consider a therapist working with a client suffering from chronic pain. The client has seen multiple specialists, tried various medications, and has virtually lost hope. When the therapist begins to instil confidence that recovery is possible—using language that suggests past successes and offering reassurance that the client's body can heal—the client begins to relax, lowering their stress hormones and reducing inflammation. Over time, this combination of therapeutic intervention and the therapist's confident belief in healing leads to a gradual reduction in the client's pain levels. This case illustrates the profound impact of placebo and PNI in therapy.

Key Takeaways

- **Belief shapes health outcomes:** Both positive (placebo) and negative (nocebo) expectations can directly affect physical health through psychoneuroimmunological pathways.

- **Therapist influence is crucial:** A therapist's hope, confidence, and belief in healing can positively affect a client's physiological state, leading to improved outcomes.

- **Psychoneuroimmunology explains the mind-body connection:** Neurotransmitters, the autonomic nervous system, and the immune system all play a role in how beliefs influence health.

- **Cultural beliefs matter:** As Dr. Mario Martinez's work shows, cultural conditioning can impact health, and transforming limiting beliefs can aid in recovery.

- **Real-world application:** By fostering a therapeutic alliance grounded in hope and reassurance, therapists can harness the power of the placebo effect, helping clients heal both physically and emotionally.

Conclusion

The growing field of psychoneuroimmunology demonstrates that the mind and body are deeply intertwined. Belief, expectation, and the quality of the therapeutic relationship can profoundly influence health outcomes. For therapists, understanding and applying the principles of placebo, nocebo, and PNI can enhance the efficacy of their treatments, creating an environment in which clients are not just passive recipients of care, but active participants in their healing journey.

References

Ader, R., & Cohen, N. (1993). Psychoneuroimmunology: Conditioning and stress. *Annual Review of Psychology, 44*(1), 53-85. https://doi.org/10.1146/annurev.ps.44.020193.000413

Benedetti, F., Carlino, E., & Pollo, A. (2011). How placebos change the patient's brain. *Neuropsychopharmacology, 36*(1), 339-354. https://doi.org/10.1038/npp.2010.81

Colloca, L., & Miller, F. G. (2011). The nocebo effect and its relevance for clinical practice. *Psychosomatic Medicine, 73*(7), 598-603. https://doi.org/10.1097/PSY.0b013e3182294a50

Martinez, M. (2010). *The MindBody Code: How to change the beliefs that limit your health, longevity, and success.* Sounds True.

Tracey, K. J. (2002). The inflammatory reflex. *Nature, 420*(6917), 853-859. https://doi.org/10.1038/nature01321

Wager, T. D., & Atlas, L. Y. (2015). The neuroscience of placebo effects: Connecting context, learning and health. *Nature Reviews Neuroscience, 16*(7), 403-418. https://doi.org/10.1038/nrn3976

12.

ATTACHMENT THEORY AND THE CELL DANGER RESPONSE

Introduction: The Role of Early Relationships in Trauma

Attachment theory, developed by John Bowlby, emphasizes that the bonds formed between infants and their primary caregivers shape their emotional and psychological development. These early attachment experiences influence how individuals relate to others, regulate emotions, and respond to stress throughout their life.

When children experience trauma or disruptions in these early bonds—such as inconsistent caregiving, neglect, or abuse—it can create insecure attachment patterns. These attachment wounds impact not only emotional health but also the body's physiological responses, particularly the Cell Danger Response (CDR).

This chapter explores the connection between trauma, attachment theory, and the CDR, as well as therapeutic approaches that support healing, such as Brainspotting, Clay Field Therapy, and Family Constellation Work.

Prenatal and Birth Trauma: The Earliest Roots of the Cell Danger Response

Trauma can begin before a child is even born. Prenatal trauma, such as maternal stress, illness, or exposure to environmental toxins, can have profound effects on the developing foetus. Similarly, birth trauma, including complications during delivery, can trigger early activation of the CDR.

When a foetus experiences trauma in the womb or during birth, it disrupts critical cellular signalling pathways. This early activation of the CDR may have long-term consequences for the infant's physical and psychological development, influencing their ability to form secure attachments and increasing their susceptibility to stress.

The Role of Maternal Cortisol in Foetal Development

One of the primary mechanisms through which prenatal trauma impacts the foetus is elevated maternal cortisol levels. Cortisol, a stress hormone, crosses the placental barrier, affecting the developing brain and nervous system. Chronic exposure to maternal cortisol can:

- Alter foetal brain development, particularly in areas responsible for emotional regulation, such as the amygdala and prefrontal cortex.

- Increase the foetus's sensitivity to stress, making the child more likely to experience chronic CDR activation and future attachment challenges.

Birth Trauma and the CDR

Birth itself can be a significant source of trauma, especially in cases of premature birth, emergency C-sections, or difficult labour. This type of trauma immediately activates the CDR, which can alter the development of the child's nervous system, leading to challenges in attachment and emotional regulation. Early trauma primes the infant's body for a heightened stress response, which may affect how they bond with caregivers and process future stress.

The Four Attachment Styles and Trauma

Attachment theory categorizes early relationships into four primary attachment styles, each of which impacts how individuals respond to trauma and regulate emotions:

- **Secure attachment:** Characterized by trust and emotional security, children with secure attachment have caregivers who provide consistent emotional support. Securely attached individuals are better equipped to deactivate the CDR after stress and return to a state of homeostasis.

- **Insecure-avoidant attachment:** In this attachment style, the child learns to suppress their emotional needs because caregivers are emotionally unavailable. Even though these children appear detached, their bodies remain in a heightened state of alert, with the CDR continually activated.

- **Insecure-anxious attachment:** Children with inconsistent caregiving develop anxious attachment, characterized by heightened emotional reactivity and fear of abandonment. The constant fear activates the CDR, leading to prolonged states of hyperarousal.

- **Disorganized attachment:** Often resulting from trauma or abuse, disorganized attachment combines fear and confusion in relationships. These children view their caregivers as both a source of comfort and danger. As a result, the CDR is chronically activated, increasing the risk of PTSD, emotional dysregulation, and physical health issues like chronic inflammation.

The Connection Between Attachment, Trauma, and the CDR

When early attachment is disrupted, it not only affects emotional regulation but also triggers the CDR. As already explored, the CDR, designed to protect cells from threats, remains perpetually activated in cases of unresolved trauma, leading to long-term physiological changes.

For example, when the CDR is chronically engaged, individuals may experience persistent inflammation, immune dysfunction, and mitochondrial damage. These physiological effects, combined with attachment wounds, contribute to the emotional and physical challenges faced by individuals with insecure or disorganized attachment styles.

Therapeutic Approaches to Heal Attachment Wounds and the CDR

Addressing both emotional and physiological trauma requires holistic therapeutic approaches that target both the body and the mind. Below are key therapeutic interventions that can help deactivate the CDR and heal attachment wounds:

- **Brainspotting:** This therapeutic approach focuses on unprocessed trauma stored in the brain's subcortical regions. By targeting specific eye positions, Brainspotting helps individuals access and release stored emotional energy linked to attachment trauma. This method supports the nervous system's regulation and helps deactivate the CDR, allowing for emotional and physiological healing.

- **Clay Field Therapy:** Also known as Sensorimotor Art Therapy, Clay Field Therapy provides a non-verbal way for individuals to process attachment trauma. By working with clay through tactile interaction, individuals release trauma stored in the body, helping to calm the nervous system and reduce chronic CDR activation.

- **Family Constellation Work:** This therapeutic approach explores the transgenerational transmission of trauma, particularly how unresolved trauma from past generations influences current attachment patterns. By mapping out family dynamics, Family Constellation Work helps individuals recognize and release inherited emotional burdens, reducing the activation of the CDR and promoting healing across generations.

- **Somatic Therapies:** Somatic approaches, such as Somatic Experiencing (SE) and Trauma-Releasing Exercises (TRE), help individuals process trauma stored in the body. These therapies focus on releasing physical tension and calming the nervous system, allowing the CDR to deactivate and restoring emotional regulation.

Client/Therapist Alliance and Limited Re-Parenting

In the therapeutic process, the relationship between client and therapist is crucial for healing attachment wounds. The therapist can serve as a "good enough" parent substitute, providing the care and emotional stability that may have been absent during early development. This concept, known as "limited re-parenting", allows the client to experience a secure and nurturing relationship in a safe environment. Over time, this therapeutic relationship becomes a bridge, helping the client develop the capacity to reparent *themselves* and form healthier emotional patterns.

As discussed in the book *A General Theory of Love*, the therapeutic alliance can foster emotional regulation and create the conditions for deep, lasting healing. By building this supportive relationship, therapists help clients repair attachment injuries and deactivate the Cell Danger Response (CDR), moving them toward greater emotional and physiological balance.

Building Secure Attachment in Adulthood Through Targeted Therapies

While early attachment wounds can have lasting effects, therapy and self-awareness can help develop more secure attachment patterns in adulthood. By integrating therapies like Brainspotting, Clay Field Therapy, and Family Constellation Work, individuals can heal deep-seated attachment wounds, deactivate the CDR, and restore balance to their mind and body.

Key Takeaways

- Attachment theory highlights the crucial role of early relationships in shaping emotional and physiological responses to trauma.

- Trauma and attachment disruptions trigger the Cell Danger Response (CDR), leading to chronic physiological and emotional challenges.

- Therapeutic interventions like Brainspotting, Clay Field Therapy, and Family Constellation Work can heal attachment wounds and deactivate the CDR.

- Limited re-parenting within the client/therapist alliance offers a pathway to repairing attachment injuries and developing emotional resilience.

- Prenatal and birth trauma, influenced by factors such as maternal cortisol, can activate the CDR from the earliest stages of life, impacting attachment patterns.

References

Bowlby, J. (1969). *Attachment and Loss: Vol. 1. Attachment.* Basic Books.

Lewis, T., Amini, F., & Lannon, R. (2000). *A General Theory of Love.* Vintage Books.

Naviaux, R. K. (2014). Metabolic features of the cell danger response. *Mitochondrion, 16,* 7-17. https://doi.org/10.1016/j.mito.2013.08.006

Porges, S. W. (2011). *The Polyvagal Theory: Neurophysiological foundations of emotions, attachment, communication, and self-regulation.* W. W. Norton & Company.

Schore, A. N. (2003). *Affect Regulation and the Repair of the Self.* W. W. Norton & Company.

Van der Kolk, B. A. (2014). *The Body Keeps the Score: Brain, mind, and body in the healing of trauma.* Penguin Books.

13.

TRAUMA AND SLEEP DISTURBANCES

Introduction: The Impact of Trauma on Sleep

Sleep is essential for emotional and physical well-being, yet individuals with Post-Traumatic Stress Disorder (PTSD) often struggle with sleep disturbances. Trauma can disrupt standard sleep patterns, leading to insomnia, nightmares, and difficulty staying asleep. These sleep disturbances worsen emotional and cognitive symptoms, and impair physical recovery, as sleep is the time when the body repairs itself.

In this chapter, we will explore the connection between trauma and sleep, focusing on how trauma impacts all four sleep cycles and disrupts the **glymphatic system**, a recently discovered network responsible for clearing waste products from the brain during deep sleep. We will also discuss strategies to restore healthy sleep patterns, including **Cognitive Behavioural Therapy for Insomnia (CBT-I)** and Eye Movement Desensitization and Reprocessing (EMDR).

The Four Sleep Cycles and Their Role in Trauma Recovery

Sleep occurs in a series of repeating cycles, each lasting about 90 minutes. These cycles are divided into four stages, each with a specific role in physical and emotional recovery:

Stage 1: Light Sleep (NREM)

Stage 1 is the transition between wakefulness and sleep. In this phase, the body begins to relax, and the brain slows down. This stage lasts only a few minutes and is crucial for preparing the body for deeper sleep stages.

Stage 2: Deeper Light Sleep (NREM)

Stage 2 is a deeper form of light sleep in which the heart rate slows and the body temperature drops. In this stage, the body prepares for deep sleep, and brain waves become slower with occasional bursts of rapid activity (called sleep spindles). This stage is essential for stabilizing mood and emotional regulation.

Stage 3: Deep Sleep (NREM)

Stage 3, or deep sleep, is crucial for physical recovery, immune system function, and cognitive processes like memory consolidation. During this stage, the body repairs tissues, builds muscle, and strengthens the immune system. Deep sleep is also when the glymphatic system becomes highly active, clearing metabolic waste from the brain.

Many trauma survivors have difficulty entering or maintaining deep sleep due to heightened arousal and hypervigilance. As a result, they miss out on the therapeutic benefits of deep sleep, which can lead to chronic fatigue, weakened immunity, and emotional instability.

Stage 4: REM Sleep

REM sleep is the stage where most dreaming occurs. During REM, the brain processes emotional experiences, helping to integrate them into memory. For trauma survivors, REM sleep is often disrupted by nightmares or fragmented sleep, preventing the brain from fully processing traumatic memories.

Trauma survivors may experience heightened REM activity, leading to vivid, distressing dreams or nightmares. These disturbances can increase anxiety around sleep, contributing to insomnia and avoidance behaviours.

The Glymphatic System: Sleep's Critical Role in Brain Health

The glymphatic system is a recently discovered waste-clearing network in the brain, similar to the lymphatic system in the body. This system is primarily active during deep sleep (Stage 3). It plays a vital role in clearing out toxins, metabolic waste, and proteins like be-ta-amyloid, which have been linked to neurodegenerative diseases.

During deep sleep, cerebrospinal fluid flows through the brain, flushing out toxins and waste products that accumulate during waking hours. This cleansing process is essential for maintaining brain health and cognitive function.

When trauma survivors fail to enter deep sleep, the glymphatic system cannot function effectively, leading to the buildup of metabolic waste in the brain. This accumulation may contribute to brain fog, memory problems, and an increased risk of neurological issues over time.

Common Sleep Disturbances in Trauma Survivors

Insomnia
Insomnia, characterized by difficulty falling asleep or staying asleep, is a common issue among trauma survivors. The hypervigilance and heightened arousal associated with PTSD make it challenging for the body and mind to relax enough to initiate and sustain sleep.

Nightmares
Recurrent nightmares, where individuals re-experience traumatic events, are another hallmark of PTSD. These nightmares can be so distressing that individuals develop anxiety about falling asleep, which further exacerbates insomnia.

Sleep Fragmentation
Trauma survivors often experience sleep fragmentation, where they wake up multiple times throughout the night. This disrupts the natural progression through sleep cycles, particularly REM and deep sleep, preventing the body and brain from fully recovering.

The Link Between Sleep and Emotional Regulation
Sleep is essential for emotional regulation, and sleep deprivation or fragmentation can impair the brain's ability to manage emotions.

Trauma survivors often struggle with mood swings, irritability, and anxiety due to poor sleep quality.

REM sleep is critical for processing emotions and memories. Disrupted REM sleep leaves trauma survivors more vulnerable to emotional distress during the day, as the brain is unable to integrate and process traumatic memories properly.

Deep sleep allows the body to recover from stress by reducing cortisol levels and restoring physical energy. Without adequate deep sleep, trauma survivors may experience chronic stress and fatigue, making emotional regulation even more difficult.

Treating Insomnia

Cognitive Behavioural Therapy for Insomnia (CBT-I)

CBT-I is an effective, non-pharmacological treatment for insomnia. It helps individuals with trauma-related sleep issues by addressing the behaviours and thought patterns that contribute to poor sleep.

The components of CBT-I include:

- **Sleep restriction:** Reducing the time spent in bed to improve sleep efficiency and promote more consolidated, restful sleep.

- **Stimulus control:** Reinforcing the bed as a place for sleep by avoiding activities like watching TV or using devices in bed.

- **Cognitive restructuring:** This involves challenging unhelpful beliefs about sleep, such as worrying about not being able to fall asleep and replacing that with more helpful, sleep-promoting thoughts.

Eye Movement Desensitization and Reprocessing (EMDR) for Nightmares

EMDR is a well-established therapy for processing trauma. It has been shown to reduce the frequency and intensity of nightmares. By reprocessing traumatic memories, EMDR helps the brain integrate these experiences, making them less distressing and reducing their impact on sleep.

Supporting Sleep Through Relaxation Techniques

Trauma-Informed Mindfulness Meditation
Trauma-informed mindfulness meditation helps calm the nervous system, promotes relaxation, and reduces the hyperarousal that interferes with sleep. By focusing on the present moment, trauma-informed mindfulness can help trauma survivors manage intrusive thoughts and anxiety at bedtime.

Progressive Muscle Relaxation
This technique involves tensing and relaxing different muscle groups to release physical tension and promote a sense of calm. Progressive muscle relaxation can help trauma survivors transition from a state of hyperarousal to deep relaxation, improving their ability to fall asleep.

Breathing Techniques
Deep breathing exercises, such as **box breathing** or **4-7-8 breathing**, activate the parasympathetic nervous system, helping the body relax and prepare for sleep.

Advanced Therapies for Insomnia in Trauma Survivors
In addition to traditional approaches like CBT-I and EMDR, advanced therapies such as Hyperbaric Oxygen Therapy (HBOT), Photobiomodulation (PBM), Neuroacoustic Sound Therapy, **CBD**, and **herbal treatments** offer alternative ways to improve sleep quality in trauma survivors. These therapies help regulate the nervous system, promote relaxation, and address underlying physiological imbalances that contribute to insomnia.

Hyperbaric Oxygen Therapy (HBOT)

HBOT involves breathing pure oxygen in a pressurized chamber, which enhances oxygen delivery to the brain and body. HBOT has been shown to reduce inflammation, promote healing, and improve cognitive function. For trauma survivors, HBOT can help alleviate hyperarousal, improve energy levels, and support deeper, more restorative sleep by facilitating brain recovery.

Photobiomodulation (PBM)

Photobiomodulation (PBM) uses low-level red or near-infrared light to stimulate mitochondrial function and reduce inflammation. PBM has shown promise in improving sleep quality by reducing muscle tension, improving circulation, and calming the nervous system. For trauma survivors, incorporating PBM into a bedtime routine can help ease physical discomfort and prepare the body for restful sleep.

Neuroacoustic Sound Therapy

Neuroacoustic Sound Therapy involves listening to sound frequencies that are specifically designed to promote relaxation and entrain brainwave patterns conducive to sleep. This therapy can help synchronize the brain to slower, more relaxed states like **theta** and **delta** brainwaves, which are essential for deep sleep. Regular use of neuroacoustic therapy can reduce insomnia and help trauma survivors regulate their sleep-wake cycles.

CBD (Cannabidiol)

CBD, a non-psychoactive compound found in cannabis, has been shown to help reduce anxiety, inflammation, and pain, all of which can interfere with sleep. CBD can promote relaxation and improve sleep quality in trauma survivors by calming the nervous system and reducing the physical symptoms of hyperarousal. When combined with other therapies, CBD can help ease the transition into sleep and improve overall sleep duration.

Herbal Treatments for Insomnia

Herbal remedies, such as valerian root, passionflower, and chamomile, have long been used to promote relaxation and improve sleep. These herbs have natural sedative properties that can reduce anxiety and promote deeper sleep. Herbal teas or supplements can be integrated into a trauma survivor's nighttime routine to reduce insomnia and enhance sleep quality.

Tapping (EFT) for Sleep

Emotional Freedom Techniques (EFT), also known as tapping, involve gently tapping on specific acupressure points while focusing on emotional distress or anxiety. Tapping can help trauma survivors reduce stress, calm the mind, and release emotional tension, making it easier to fall asleep. By incorporating tapping into a bedtime routine, individuals can create a sense of calm and safety, which is crucial for overcoming insomnia.

Key Takeaways

- Trauma disrupts all four sleep cycles, particularly REM sleep and deep sleep, which are critical for proper emotional and physical recovery.

- The glymphatic system, responsible for clearing waste from the brain during deep sleep, is impaired when trauma survivors fail to achieve REM restorative sleep. This can contribute to cognitive issues like brain fog and memory problems.

- CBT-I and EMDR are effective treatments for improving sleep in trauma survivors, addressing both insomnia and nightmares.

- Advanced therapies, such as HBOT, Photobiomodulation, Neuroacoustic Sound Therapy, CBD, and herbal treatments, offer alternative solutions for addressing insomnia by promoting relaxation and regulating the nervous system.

Resources

Harvey, A. G., & Tang, N. K. (2012). (Mis)perception of sleep in insomnia: A puzzle and a resolution. *Psychological Bulletin, 138*(1), 77-101. https://doi.org/10.1037/a0025730

Lavie, P. (2001). Sleep disturbances in the wake of traumatic events. *New England Journal of Medicine, 345*(25), 1825-1832. https://doi.org/10.1056/NEJMra012893

Naviaux, R. K. (2014). Metabolic features of the cell danger response. *Mitochondrion, 16*, 7-17. https://doi.org/10.1016/j.mito.2013.08.006

Nielsen, T. A., & Levin, R. (2007). Nightmares: A new neurocognitive model. *Sleep Medicine Reviews, 11*(4), 295-310. https://doi.org/10.1016/j.smrv.2007.03.004

Perlis, M. L., Jungquist, C., Smith, M. T., & Posner, D. (2005). *Cognitive Behavioral Treatment of Insomnia: A session-by-session guide.* Springer.

Stickgold, R. (2005). Sleep-dependent memory consolidation. *Nature, 437*(7063), 1272-1278. https://doi.org/10.1038/nature04286

Van der Kolk, B. A. (2014). *The Body Keeps the Score: Brain, mind, and body in the healing of trauma.* Penguin Books.

Walker, M. P. (2017). *Why We Sleep: Unlocking the power of sleep and dreams.* Scribner.

Xie, L., Kang, H., Xu, Q., Chen, M. J., Liao, Y., Thiyagarajan, M., … & Nedergaard, M. (2013). Sleep drives metabolite clearance from the adult brain. *Science, 342*(6156), 373-377. https://doi.org/10.1126/science.1241224

14.

TRAUMA AND THE ENDOCRINE SYSTEM

Introduction: The Stress Response and Hormonal Imbalances

The endocrine system plays a critical role in regulating the body's response to stress, mainly through the **hypothalamic-pituitary-adrenal (HPA)** axis, which controls the release of stress hormones like cortisol. Trauma can severely disrupt the endocrine system, leading to hormonal imbalances that affect emotional regulation, immune function, and physical health.

In this chapter, we'll explore how trauma impacts the HPA axis, blood sugar regulation, and other hormonal systems, leading to conditions like **adrenal fatigue**, **cortisol imbalances**, and **thyroid dysfunction**. We'll also discuss strategies for restoring balance to the endocrine system through nutrition, supplementation, and integrative therapies.

The HPA Axis: Regulating the Body's Stress Response

The hypothalamic-pituitary-adrenal (HPA) axis is the central regulatory system that controls the body's response to stress. When an individual perceives danger, the hypothalamus in the brain sends a signal to the pituitary gland, which then stimulates the adrenal glands to release cortisol and adrenaline. These hormones prepare the body for a "fight-or-flight" response by increasing heart rate, blood pressure, and energy production.

In individuals with Post-Traumatic Stress Disorder (PTSD), the HPA axis is often dysregulated. This dysregulation can lead to either excessive or insufficient cortisol production, both of which have profound effects on mental and physical health.

Cortisol Imbalances and Trauma

Cortisol is the body's primary stress hormone. While it plays a key role in the short-term response to stress, chronic trauma can cause cortisol levels to become imbalanced, leading to a range of physical and emotional symptoms:

- **Chronically high cortisol:** Prolonged elevated cortisol levels can cause muscle breakdown, weight gain (especially around the abdomen), immune suppression, and cognitive impairments. Individuals with PTSD often experience high anxiety, hypervigilance, and difficulty sleeping due to high cortisol levels.

- **Chronically low cortisol:** In cases of adrenal exhaustion, cortisol levels may become too low, leading to symptoms such as chronic fatigue, emotional numbness, and an inability to cope with stress. This can also lead to a weakened immune system and increased susceptibility to illness.

Blood Sugar Regulation and Trauma

Blood sugar regulation is closely linked to the HPA axis and cortisol production. Cortisol helps regulate glucose metabolism by raising blood sugar levels during times of stress to ensure the body has enough energy for the "fight-or-flight" response. However, chronic stress and trauma can lead to **blood sugar dysregulation**, which contributes to mood instability, fatigue, and metabolic disorders.

Trauma disrupts blood sugar regulation in two ways:

- **Insulin resistance:** Chronic stress can cause elevated blood sugar levels, which, over time, may lead to insulin resistance. Insulin resistance occurs when the body's cells become less responsive to insulin, the hormone that helps transport glucose into cells for energy. This can lead to weight gain, fatigue, and an increased risk of developing type 2 diabetes.

- Hypoglycaemia (low blood sugar): Trauma survivors may also experience episodes of low blood sugar (hypoglycaemia), which can result in irritability, anxiety, brain fog, and dizziness. These episodes occur when the body's blood sugar drops too quickly after a cortisol spike.

The Stress-Blood Sugar Cycle

- **Cortisol and blood sugar:** When cortisol levels rise in response to stress, blood sugar also increases. This prepares the body to deal with immediate threats. However, when stress is chronic, this constant elevation in blood sugar can lead to cravings for sugary or high-carbohydrate foods, further destabilizing blood sugar levels.

- **Adrenal fatigue and hypoglycaemia:** When the adrenal glands become exhausted from prolonged stress, they may struggle to produce sufficient cortisol, leading to blood sugar crashes. These crashes can leave trauma survivors feeling drained, anxious, and irritable.

The Impact of Trauma on the Thyroid Gland

The **thyroid gland**, which regulates metabolism, is another part of the endocrine system affected by trauma. Prolonged stress and trauma can disrupt thyroid function, leading to conditions such as **hypothyroidism** (underactive thyroid) or **hyperthyroidism** (overactive thyroid).

The Role of Sex Hormones in Trauma Recovery

Sex hormones, such as **estrogen**, **progesterone**, and **testosterone**, also play a role in how individuals respond to stress and trauma.

Trauma can disrupt the balance of these hormones, leading to mood disturbances, reproductive health issues, and sexual dysfunction.

Adrenal Fatigue: The Aftermath of Chronic Stress

Adrenal fatigue occurs when the adrenal glands are overworked by chronic stress and can no longer produce adequate amounts of cortisol and other stress-related hormones. This condition is common in individuals with PTSD who have been living in a prolonged state of hyperarousal.

Healing the Endocrine System After Trauma

Restoring balance to the endocrine system after trauma requires an integrative approach that includes both lifestyle changes and targeted therapies. Key strategies include:

- Nutrition for hormonal and blood sugar balance:
  - » **Omega-3 fatty acids:** These help reduce inflammation and regulate cortisol levels, supporting healthy metabolism and blood sugar regulation.
  - » **Magnesium:** Magnesium helps calm the nervous system and regulates blood sugar by improving insulin sensitivity.
  - » **Balanced meals:** Eating meals that combine protein, healthy fats, and complex carbohydrates helps stabilize blood sugar levels, preventing spikes and crashes.
- Supplementation for endocrine and blood sugar health
  - » **Adaptogens:** Adaptogenic herbs like ashwagandha and rhodiola help balance cortisol levels and regulate blood sugar by improving the body's response to stress.

- » **Chromium:** This mineral helps improve insulin sensitivity and stabilize blood sugar levels, reducing the risk of hypoglycaemia or insulin resistance.

- » **Vitamin D:** Vitamin D supports overall hormonal balance, including insulin regulation, and reduces inflammation.

Key Takeaways

- Trauma disrupts the HPA axis and cortisol production, leading to imbalances that affect blood sugar regulation, thyroid function, and adrenal health.

- Chronic stress can lead to insulin resistance, causing blood sugar imbalances that contribute to fatigue, mood swings, and metabolic disorders.

- Restoring balance to the endocrine system and blood sugar levels requires a holistic approach, including dietary changes, adaptogens, and supplementation.

- Addressing blood sugar regulation through nutrition, supplements, and lifestyle changes is key to improving mood stability, energy levels, and overall health in trauma survivors.

Resources

Chrousos, G. P. (209). Stress and disorders of the stress system. *Nature Reviews Endocrinology, 5*(7), 374-381. https://doi.org/10.1038/nrendo.2009.106

McEwen, B. S. (2007). Physiology and neurobiology of stress and adaptation: Central role of the brain. *Physiological Reviews, 87*(3), 873-904. https://doi.org/10.1152/physrev.00041.2006

Naviaux, R. K. (2014). Metabolic features of the cell danger response. *Mitochondrion, 16*, 7-17. https://doi.org/10.1016/j.mito.2013.08.006

Sapolsky, R. M. (2004). *Why Zebras Don't Get Ulcers: The acclaimed guide to stress, stress-related diseases, and coping.* Holt Paperbacks.

Smith, S. M., & Vale, W. W. (2007). The role of the hypothalamic-pituitary-adrenal axis in neuroendocrine responses to stress. *Journal of Clinical Investigation, 117*(1), 22-31. https://doi.org/10.1172/JCI97418

15

TRAUMA AND THE IMMUNE SYSTEM

Introduction: How Trauma Affects Immune Function

In this chapter, we will explore how trauma impacts the immune system, the connection between trauma, chronic inflammation, and autoimmune diseases, and how therapies that target the gut and immune health can aid in trauma recovery.

The Immune System's Response to Trauma

The immune system defends the body against pathogens, infections, and disease. However, in the face of trauma, the immune system can become dysregulated. When the CDR is activated in response to trauma, normal immune functions are put on hold as the body focuses on survival. This prolonged activation of the CDR can lead to chronic inflammation, impaired immune function, and susceptibility to illness.

The immune system has two main responses, acute and chronic:

- **Acute trauma response:** In the short term, trauma triggers the immune system to release inflammatory cytokines, which help the body repair damage and fight off infection. This is part of the body's natural response to stress or injury.

- **Chronic trauma response:** When trauma is unresolved, the body remains in a state of chronic alert. The immune system continues to produce inflammatory responses, even in the absence of a real threat. Over time, this can lead to chronic inflammation, which has been linked to a variety of health problems, including heart disease, diabetes, and cancer.

The Connection Between Trauma, Inflammation, and Autoimmune Disorders

Chronic trauma and stress have been shown to increase systemic inflammation, which can have detrimental effects on both mental and physical health. Inflammation is the body's natural defence mechanism, but when it becomes chronic, it can lead to the development of **autoimmune disorders** and other chronic illnesses.

Trauma and Autoimmune Disorders

Autoimmune diseases occur when the immune system mistakenly attacks the body's tissues. Research has shown that individuals who have experienced trauma, particularly early-life trauma, are more likely to develop autoimmune conditions such as **rheumatoid arthritis**, **lupus**, **Crohn's disease**, and **multiple sclerosis**.

The Cell Danger Response plays a central role in this process. When the CDR is chronically activated, the body's immune system becomes hypervigilant, mistaking normal cells or tissues for threats. This can lead to the body attacking itself, resulting in autoimmune conditions.

The Gut-Immune Connection: How Trauma Affects Gut Health

The gut plays a critical role in immune function, and trauma has a direct impact on gut health. In fact, about 70% of the immune system resides in the gut microbiome, which is responsible for regulating immune responses and maintaining a balance between health and disease. When trauma occurs, the central nervous system (CNS) downregulates gut function, as the body prioritizes survival mechanisms like fight, flight, freeze, fawn, or flop.

The Impact of Trauma on the Gut Microbiome

Trauma can disrupt the balance of beneficial and harmful bacteria in the gut, leading to conditions like **leaky gut**, where the intestinal lining becomes permeable, allowing toxins and bacteria to enter the bloodstream. This triggers an immune response, which can lead to chronic inflammation and exacerbate mental health issues, including anxiety, depression, and PTSD.

The CDR, when activated by trauma, shifts the body's focus away from maintaining gut health. This creates an imbalance in the gut microbiome, reducing its ability to regulate the immune system effectively. This disruption can perpetuate both physical and mental health challenges as the immune system remains in a heightened state of activation.

Trauma's Long-Term Effects on Immune Health

Unresolved trauma has lasting effects on the immune system, increasing vulnerability to chronic illnesses and infections. Trauma survivors often experience **immune suppression**, which weakens the body's ability to fight off infections, viruses, and even cancer. At the same time, some trauma survivors experience **immune hyperactivity**, where the immune system becomes overactive, leading to autoimmune conditions and chronic inflammation.

Chronic Inflammation and Disease

- **Heart disease and diabetes:** Trauma survivors are at an increased risk for developing cardiovascular diseases and metabolic disorders due to chronic inflammation. The sustained release of inflammatory cytokines can damage blood vessels, contribute to insulin resistance, and increase the risk of heart attacks and strokes.

- **Mental health and inflammation:** Chronic inflammation also affects the brain, contributing to symptoms of depression, anxiety, and cognitive decline. The neuroinflammatory response triggered by the CDR can impair emotional regulation, memory, and concentration, worsening the psychological effects of trauma.

Supporting Immune Health in Trauma Recovery

Given the profound connection between trauma and immune dysfunction, addressing immune health is an essential part of trauma recovery. Therapies that support gut health, reduce inflammation, and regulate the immune system can help reverse the long-term effects of trauma on the body.

Probiotics and Gut Health

Probiotics, which are beneficial bacteria, play a crucial role in maintaining a healthy gut microbiome. While supporting gut health through probiotics and prebiotics can help restore bacterial balance, improve immune function, and reduce inflammation, not everyone may benefit from certain probiotic-rich foods like sauerkraut and kefir.

Some individuals—particularly those delivered by C-section or exposed to multiple rounds of antibiotics—may lack the requisite gut bacteria to process these foods properly. For them, consuming these probiotics could exacerbate symptoms and increase toxic load.

To determine what's missing in the gut microbiome, a stool test is recommended. Based on the results, a microbiome specialist can guide the individual on how to correct imbalances through targeted probiotic strains or alternative gut-healing strategies, ensuring that the body receives the proper support for recovery without unintended side effects.

Anti-Inflammatory Diets

An anti-inflammatory diet is another critical tool in trauma recovery. Foods rich in omega-3 fatty acids, antioxidants, and polyphenols can reduce inflammation and support immune function. Key components of an anti-inflammatory diet include:

- Fatty fish (like salmon and sardines)

- Leafy greens (avoid oxalates)

- Berries (blueberries, raspberries)

- Nuts and seeds (almonds, flaxseeds)

- Olive oil and green tea

These foods not only help reduce chronic inflammation but also support brain health, promoting emotional regulation and cognitive function.

Integrative Therapies for Immune Support

In addition to diet and stress reduction, integrative therapies can play a critical role in supporting immune function and reducing the long-term effects of trauma on the body. We cover such therapies again here:

Hyperbaric Oxygen Therapy (HBOT)

HBOT involves delivering concentrated oxygen to the body under pressure, which can help reduce inflammation, promote tissue repair, and improve immune function. For trauma survivors, HBOT can help the body shift out of chronic CDR activation and support recovery by promoting cellular repair and reducing oxidative stress. This is also good for the gut and microbiome.

Photobiomodulation (PBM)

PBM uses red and near-infrared light to stimulate cellular repair and reduce inflammation. This therapy can help regulate the immune system and improve mitochondrial function, which is often impaired in trauma survivors due to the chronic activation of the CDR. PBM supports overall immune health and aids in reducing the physical symptoms of trauma. Red light or sunlight on the midsection is good for the gut microbiome.

Herbal Supplements for Immune Health

Herbal supplements such as **turmeric**, **ginger**, and **green tea extract** are powerful anti-inflammatory agents that can help reduce chronic inflammation and support immune regulation. When combined with a healthy diet, these supplements can mitigate the immune dysfunction caused by trauma.

Key Takeaways

- Trauma disrupts immune function by activating the Cell Danger Response (CDR), which can lead to chronic inflammation, immune dysregulation, and autoimmune disorders.

- Chronic inflammation is a hallmark of trauma's impact on the immune system and is linked to conditions like heart disease, diabetes, and mental health disorders.

- Gut health plays a crucial role in immune function, and trauma can impair the gut microbiome, leading to both physical and emotional health challenges.

- Supporting immune health through probiotics, an anti-inflammatory diet, and stress-reduction techniques can help trauma survivors recover from immune dysfunction.

- Integrative therapies, such as HBOT, Photobiomodulation, and herbal supplements, can promote immune regulation and support overall healing from trauma.

References

Dhabhar, F. S. (2014). Effects of stress on immune **function:** The good, the bad, and the beautiful. *Immunologic Research, 58*(2-3), 193-210. https://doi.org/10.1007/s12026-014-8517-0

Dinan, T. G., & Cryan, J. F. (2017). Gut instincts: Microbiota as a key regulator of brain development, ageing and neurodegeneration. *The Journal of Physiology, 595*(2), 489-503. https://doi.org/10.1113/JP273106

Kiecolt-Glaser, J. K., McGuire, L., Robles, T. F., & Glaser, R. (2002). Emotions, morbidity, and mortality: New perspectives from psychoneuroimmunology. *Annual Review of Psychology, 53*(1), 83-107. https://doi.org/10.1146/annurev.psych.53.100901.135217

Miller, G. E., Chen, E., & Parker, K. J. (2011). Psychological stress in childhood and susceptibility to the chronic diseases of aging: Moving toward a model of behavioral and biological mechanisms. *Psychological Bulletin, 137*(6), 959-997. https://doi.org/10.1037/a0024768

Naviaux, R. K. (2014). Metabolic features of the cell danger response. *Mitochondrion, 16*, 7-17. https://doi.org/10.1016/j.mito.2013.08.006

Porges, S. W. (2009). The polyvagal theory: New insights into adaptive reactions of the autonomic nervous system. *Cleveland Clinic Journal of Medicine, 76*(Suppl 2), S86-S90. https://doi.org/10.3949/ccjm.76.s2.17

Rook, G. A., Lowry, C. A., & Raison, C. L. (2013). Microbial 'old friends', immunoregulation and stress resilience. *Evolution, Medicine, and Public Health, 2013*(1), 46-64. https://doi.org/10.1093/emph/eot004

16

THE CELL DANGER RESPONSE AND CANCER

Metabolic and Inflammatory
Pathways to Malignancy

Introduction

Cancer rates in Western countries have been steadily climbing over recent decades, partly due to increased lifespans, but also due to environmental, dietary, and lifestyle factors. Chronic stress, exposure to toxins, and the prevalence of processed, pro-inflammatory diets have all been associated with cancer risk. These factors can also trigger or perpetuate the CDR, creating a biological environment conducive to the development of cancer. Understanding how prolonged CDR contributes to this growing epidemic is crucial for developing new prevention and treatment strategies.

Mitochondrial Dysfunction and Cancer Metabolism

In the early stages of the CDR, mitochondrial function shifts to a state where energy production is reduced. Mitochondria, which typically produce energy through oxidative phosphorylation, switch to glycolysis, a less efficient form of energy production. This metabolic shift, known as the **Warburg effect**, is a hallmark of cancer cells, which prefer glycolysis even in the presence of oxygen. By using glycolysis, cancer cells create an environment conducive to rapid growth, survival, and immune evasion.

In prolonged CDR, mitochondrial dysfunction persists, preventing the normal return to oxidative metabolism. This ongoing shift supports the metabolic needs of cancer cells, allowing them to thrive and resist apoptosis (programmed cell death). As a result, chronic CDR is implicated in several cancers that rely on glycolysis for energy production.

Chronic Inflammation and Cancer

Inflammation is a significant component of the CDR, designed to protect the body from harm by eliminating pathogens and initiating tissue repair. However, when inflammation becomes chronic, it creates a pro-tumour environment. Chronic inflammation, sustained by unresolved CDR, leads to the release of inflammatory cytokines and reactive oxygen species (ROS), which can damage DNA, promote mutations, and support tumour growth.

Inflammation also promotes angiogenesis, the formation of new blood vessels, which tumours need to grow and metastasize. Furthermore, the constant activation of immune cells in an inflamed environment can lead to immune exhaustion, allowing cancer cells to evade destruction.

Immune Evasion in Chronic CDR

Under normal conditions, the immune system detects and eliminates cancerous cells. However, chronic CDR disrupts immune surveillance, impairing the body's ability to recognize and destroy cancer cells. In this prolonged state, immune cells like tumour-associated macrophages (TAMs) may even support tumour growth by promoting inflammation rather than attacking cancer cells.

The suppression of key immune responses during chronic CDR allows tumours to grow unchecked, leading to the progression and spread of cancer. This immune dysregulation is a crucial link between chronic CDR and cancer, as it helps cancer cells evade destruction while fostering an environment that supports their survival.

Fibrosis, Tissue Repair, and Cancer Risk

Fibrosis, or the thickening and scarring of tissue, is a common consequence of unresolved CDR. During routine healing, the CDR promotes tissue repair, but prolonged activation leads to excessive fibrosis. Chronic fibrosis alters the tissue microenvironment in ways that increase cancer risk. For example, liver fibrosis, which occurs in response to chronic inflammation or damage, can lead to liver cancer. Similarly, lung fibrosis caused by chronic lung inflammation is a known risk factor for lung cancer.

Fibrotic tissue is more prone to mutations, and the disrupted tissue architecture creates an environment where cancer cells can take root and proliferate.

Cellular Senescence and Carcinogenesis

One of the CDR's protective mechanisms is cellular senescence, where cells stop dividing to prevent the replication of damaged DNA. While this halts the spread of potentially harmful mutations, it also creates a microenvironment rich in inflammatory signals, which can promote cancer. Senescent cells release pro-inflammatory factors that contribute to a cancer-promoting environment, while their inability to die (apoptosis resistance) means they persist in tissues, further driving chronic inflammation.

The Metabolic Environment in CDR and Cancer

Chronic CDR induces metabolic changes, including insulin resistance, oxidative stress, and altered lipid metabolism, all of which contribute to cancer risk. Prolonged CDR affects glucose metabolism and promotes the Warburg effect in cancer cells, giving them a survival advantage. Oxidative stress, caused by the accumulation of ROS, can damage DNA and cellular structures, increasing the likelihood of malignant transformation.

Cell Cycle Arrest, DNA Repair, and Cancer

During the CDR, cells enter a state of cell cycle arrest to prevent damaged DNA from being replicated. While this is protective in the short term, prolonged cell cycle arrest without proper resolution increases the risk of mutations. Chronic CDR can impair DNA repair mechanisms, allowing genetic errors to accumulate, which promotes the development of cancer.

Therapeutic Implications: Targeting CDR in Cancer

Given the strong links between chronic CDR and cancer, targeting its metabolic and inflammatory components presents a promising therapeutic strategy. Therapies aimed at restoring mitochondrial function, resolving inflammation, and supporting proper immune function could help prevent or treat cancer:

- Mitochondrial-targeted therapies, such as metabolic agents, mitochondrial antioxidants, or Hyperbaric Oxygen Therapy (HBOT), could help restore proper cellular metabolism.

- Anti-inflammatory approaches that resolve chronic inflammation without suppressing immune function could support cancer prevention and improve outcomes.

- Immunotherapies that reverse immune suppression and restore normal immune surveillance may help the body fight off cancerous cells.

Conclusion

The prolonged Cell Danger Response (CDR) plays a significant role in cancer development and progression by promoting mitochondrial dysfunction, chronic inflammation, immune suppression, and metabolic changes. Understanding this connection opens new pathways for preventing and treating cancer by targeting the root causes of these metabolic and inflammatory imbalances. Future therapies could aim to resolve chronic CDR, potentially offering a new approach to cancer treatment.

Key Takeaways

- Chronic CDR disrupts mitochondrial function and promotes the Warburg effect, a metabolic condition favoured by cancer cells.

- Prolonged inflammation during CDR creates a tumour-promoting environment, leading to DNA damage and immune system evasion.

- Immune suppression and fibrosis caused by unresolved CDR foster cancer growth and metastasis.

- Therapeutic strategies targeting CDR could include mitochondrial support, anti-inflammatory approaches, and immunotherapies aimed at reversing immune suppression.

Next Steps

- Further research is needed to understand how therapies targeting the resolution of CDR could be integrated into cancer prevention and treatment protocols.

- Clinical trials involving mitochondrial and metabolic therapies should be explored to determine their efficacy in reducing cancer risk in individuals with chronic CDR.

- Holistic approaches that address both metabolic health and immune function may offer additional benefits in cancer therapy.

References

Hanahan, D., & Weinberg, R. A. (2011). Hallmarks of cancer: The next generation. *Cell, 144*(5), 646-674. https://doi.org/10.1016/j.cell.2011.02.013

Mantovani, A., Allavena, P., Sica, A., & Balkwill, F. (2008). Cancer-related inflammation. *Nature, 454*(7203), 436-444. https://doi.org/10.1038/nature07205

Multhoff, G., Molls, M., & Radons, J. (2011). Chronic inflammation in cancer development. *Frontiers in Immunology, 2*, 98. https://doi.org/10.3389/fimmu.2011.00098

Naviaux, R. K. (2014). Metabolic features of the cell danger response. *Mitochondrion, 16*, 7-17. https://doi.org/10.1016/j.mito.2013.08.006

Warburg, O. (1956). On the origin of cancer cells. *Science, 123*(3191), 309-314. https://doi.org/10.1126/science.123.3191.309

17.

THE CELL DANGER RESPONSE AND METABOLIC PSYCHIATRY

Introduction to Metabolic Psychiatry and the CDR

Metabolic psychiatry is an emerging field that challenges traditional views of mental health, focusing on how metabolic dysfunctions—such as insulin resistance, mitochondrial issues, and chronic inflammation—contribute to psychiatric conditions like depression, anxiety, schizophrenia, and bipolar disorder. The Cell Danger Response (CDR) is a central concept in this model.

Recent advancements suggest that, by targeting metabolic dysfunction and resolving chronic CDR activation, we can address the root causes of many mental health disorders. This chapter highlights researchers and institutions exploring the metabolic roots of psychiatric disorders, from dietary interventions to cutting-edge metabolic therapies.

Stanford University: Shebani Sethi's Work

At Stanford University's Metabolic Psychiatry Clinic, Dr. Shebani Sethi leads research into how addressing metabolic dysfunction improves mental health outcomes. One of the clinic's main focuses is the ketogenic diet, a low-carbohydrate, high-fat diet that shifts the body's energy source from glucose to ketones. This metabolic shift can reduce inflammation, improve mitochondrial function, and reverse insulin resistance, key factors in stabilizing psychiatric symptoms like depression and bipolar disorder.

In one pilot study, patients with schizophrenia and bipolar disorder who followed a ketogenic diet experienced significant improvements in both metabolic and psychiatric symptoms, including weight loss, reduced insulin resistance, and improved mood.

Dr. Sethi's research at Stanford continues to explore the profound connection between metabolic health and mental wellness.

Harvard University: Christopher Palmer's Research

At Harvard Medical School, Dr. Christopher Palmer has been pioneering research that reframes mental disorders as metabolic disorders of the brain. His work focuses on mitochondrial dysfunction and neuroinflammation as central components of the CDR that contribute to psychiatric conditions. Palmer's research supports the theory that improving mitochondrial function through metabolic interventions, such as the ketogenic diet, can lead to significant improvements in patients with severe mental illness.

For example, Palmer's patients with treatment-resistant mental illnesses, such as schizophrenia and bipolar disorder, have responded well to metabolic therapies. By targeting the brain's energy systems and reducing inflammation, these treatments have shown remarkable improvements in cognition, mood regulation, and overall mental health.

UK Metabolic Psychiatry Hub

In the UK, the Metabolic Psychiatry Hub—a collaboration between the University of Edinburgh, King's College London, the University of Bristol, and the University of Exeter—is advancing the field by focusing on the bi-directional relationship between metabolic health and severe mental illness (SMI). Their research explores how conditions like obesity, type 2 diabetes, and insulin resistance contribute to psychiatric disorders and how metabolic-based treatments, such as ketogenic diets and diabetes medications like metformin, can improve both metabolic and mental health.

This multidisciplinary approach is uncovering new treatments and therapies that integrate metabolism and mental health, offering new hope for individuals with treatment-resistant psychiatric conditions.

Metabolic Mind: Non-Profit Advocacy

Founded by David Baszucki, Metabolic Mind is a non-profit organization dedicated to promoting the use of metabolic therapies for treating mental illness. The organization is based on the success of using nutritional ketosis to manage psychiatric disorders, inspired by Baszucki's personal experience with his son's recovery from mental illness. Dr. Bret Scher, the medical director of Metabolic Mind, advocates ketogenic therapies, low-carbohydrate diets, and lifestyle changes as potential treatments for psychiatric disorders.

Metabolic Mind aims to educate families and clinicians about how addressing metabolic dysfunction through dietary interventions can lead to improvements in psychiatric conditions such as bipolar disorder, schizophrenia, and major depression.

Food and Mood Centre, Melbourne

At the forefront of **nutritional psychiatry**, the Food and Mood Centre in Melbourne, led by Professor Felice Jacka, is researching how diet impacts mental health. Their pioneering work explores the links between diet, inflammation, and mental health disorders such as depression, anxiety, and schizophrenia. Jacka's team has found that addressing nutritional deficiencies and improving gut health through dietary changes can reduce inflammation and improve brain function, leading to better mental health outcomes.

This research aligns with the metabolic psychiatry model, showing how diet-driven metabolic improvements can alleviate psychiatric symptoms and contribute to long-term mental health.

Julia Rucklidge's Work, Christchurch, NZ

Dr Julia Rucklidge, at the Te Puna Toiora Research Lab at the University of Canterbury in Christchurch, New Zealand, focuses on the role of **micronutrient supplementation** in treating mental health disorders such as ADHD, anxiety, and mood disorders. Her research demonstrates that correcting nutritional deficiencies can dramatically improve brain function and mental health, further supporting the idea that addressing metabolic dysfunction is key to treating psychiatric conditions.

Rucklidge's work provides strong evidence that dietary interventions and micronutrient supplementation can be effective treatments for a wide range of mental health disorders.

Conclusion

The field of metabolic psychiatry is rapidly growing, with research from Stanford, Harvard, the UK Metabolic Psychiatry Hub, the Food and Mood Centre, and Te Puna Toiora all demonstrating that addressing metabolic dysfunction can significantly improve mental health outcomes. By resolving chronic activation of the Cell Danger Response through dietary, lifestyle, and metabolic therapies, this approach offers a promising path for treating psychiatric disorders.

As more research confirms the connection between metabolic health and mental illness, metabolic psychiatry may reshape the future of mental health treatment, offering hope for those struggling with long-term, treatment-resistant conditions.

Food and Mood Centre, Melbourne:

- The Food and Mood Centre at Deakin University, led by Professor Felice Jacka, focuses on the impact of diet on mental health.

- Deakin University https://www.deakin.edu.au/faculty-of-health/research/food-and-mood-centre.

Harvard University, Christopher Palmer's Research:

- Dr. Christopher Palmer's research on the connection between metabolism and mental health, including his theory that mental disorders are metabolic disorders of the brain.

- Dr Palmer's website: https://www.chrispalmermd.com.

- MindHealth360 podcast: https://www.mindhealth360.com/podcast/metabolic-psychiatry-a-unifying-theory-of-mental-illness/.

Julia Rucklidge's Work, Christchurch, NZ:

- Julia Rucklidge's research at Te Puna Toiora focuses on the role of micronutrients in mental health treatment.

- Te Puna Toiora, University of Canterbury: https://www.canterbury.ac.nz/research/about-uc-research/research-groups-and-centres/te-puna-toiora-mental-health-and-nutrition-research

Metabolic Mind:

- Metabolic Mind, a non-profit founded by David Baszucki, promotes the use of ketogenic diets and metabolic interventions for psychiatric disorders.

- Metabolic Mind: https://www.metabolicmind.org.

Stanford University's Metabolic Psychiatry Clinic:

- Dr. Shebani Sethi's work on metabolic dysfunction and the ketogenic diet for psychiatric disorders.

- Stanford Medicine News Center: https://med.stanford.edu/news/all-news/2022/11/metabolic-psychiatry.html.

UK Metabolic Psychiatry Hub:

- The UK Metabolic Psychiatry Hub is a collaboration between several universities, advancing metabolism-based treatments for severe mental illness.

- The McPin Foundation: https://mcpin.org/project/hub-for-metabolic-psychiatry/

18.

CHRONIC PAIN AND TRAUMA

Introduction: The Link Between Trauma and Chronic Pain

For many individuals with Post-Traumatic Stress Disorder (PTSD), trauma manifests not only as emotional distress but also as chronic *physical* pain. Trauma survivors often experience musculoskeletal pain, headaches, and conditions like fibromyalgia or chronic fatigue syndrome. The mind-body connection is integral to understanding how trauma affects pain perception, as the nervous system remains in a state of heightened arousal, causing ongoing tension and discomfort.

This chapter explores the relationship between trauma and chronic pain, focusing on how trauma can disrupt pain perception, amplify physical symptoms, and lead to chronic pain syndromes. We will also discuss effective treatment strategies, including **somatic therapies**, **mind-body approaches**, and integrative pain management techniques, such as the **Stellate Ganglion Block (SGB)** procedure.

How Trauma Affects Pain Perception

Trauma alters the body's response to pain through the nervous system's regulation of pain signals. When trauma occurs, the fight-or-flight response becomes activated, leading to a flood of stress hormones like cortisol and adrenaline. This state of hyperarousal can increase pain sensitivity and lead to persistent pain, even in the absence of injury.

The central nervous system (CNS) has two main roles here:

- **Hypervigilance and pain sensitivity:** Individuals with PTSD often experience heightened sensitivity to pain, a condition known as hyperalgesia. This occurs because the CNS remains hypervigilant, scanning for potential threats, which amplifies the body's perception of pain.

- **Central sensitization:** In cases of chronic pain, the CNS becomes sensitized to pain signals, resulting in an exaggerated response to even minor stimuli. This process, known as central sensitization, is typical in individuals with trauma and contributes to the persistence of pain over time.

Chronic Pain Syndromes Linked to Trauma

Chronic pain syndromes are common among trauma survivors, and the connection between physical pain and psychological trauma is well-documented. Trauma can contribute to the development of conditions like fibromyalgia, chronic fatigue syndrome (CFS), and irritable bowel syndrome (IBS), all of which involve physical pain.

The Stellate Ganglion Block (SGB): From Pain Treatment to PTSD Relief

The **Stellate Ganglion Block (SGB)** procedure was initially developed as a treatment for chronic pain, particularly in conditions like **complex regional pain syndrome**. The procedure involves injecting an anaesthetic into the **stellate ganglion**, a group of nerves in the neck that are involved in regulating the body's stress response and pain signals.

When veterans who suffered from chronic pain underwent the SGB procedure, doctors noticed a significant reduction in their PTSD symptoms, including improvements in anxiety, hypervigilance, and emotional regulation. This unexpected outcome led to further exploration of SGB as a potential treatment for PTSD.

The SGB procedure interrupts the sympathetic nervous system's "fight-or-flight" response, helping the body transition into a more relaxed state. By calming the overactive stress response, SGB helps reduce both pain and PTSD symptoms, making it a promising dual-purpose treatment for trauma survivors.

Muscle Tension and Trauma

One of the most common physical symptoms of trauma is muscle tension, particularly in the neck, shoulders, and back. Trauma survivors often carry stress in their muscles, leading to chronic pain and tightness. The central nervous system (CNS), which remains in a heightened state of alertness after trauma, sends signals to the muscles to remain tense, creating a cycle of discomfort.

The central nervous system affects muscle tightness in two ways:

- **Fight-or-flight response:** The CNS activates the fight-or-flight response in the presence of perceived danger, which causes muscles to tighten in preparation for action. For trauma survivors, this response can become chronic, leading to persistent muscle tension even in the absence of immediate threats.

- **Lactate buildup:** Prolonged muscle tension can lead to the buildup of lactate in the muscles, causing soreness, stiffness, and fatigue. Trauma survivors who experience chronic muscle tension often have difficulty relaxing, which exacerbates their pain.

Trauma, Inflammation, and Chronic Pain

Chronic inflammation is a key factor in the development of chronic pain, and trauma is a significant contributor to systemic inflammation. When the body remains in a state of heightened stress, inflammatory markers such as **C-reactive protein (CRP)** and **cytokines** increase, leading to pain and stiffness in the joints and muscles.

The Role of the Immune System in Inflammation

Trauma can dysregulate the immune system, leading to an overactive immune response and chronic inflammation. This inflammation exacerbates conditions like arthritis, fibromyalgia, and IBS.

Inflammation amplifies pain signals in the body, leading to increased sensitivity to pain and discomfort. Trauma survivors may experience chronic joint pain, muscle aches, and other inflammatory symptoms.

Healing Chronic Pain in Trauma Survivors

Healing chronic pain in trauma survivors requires a holistic approach that addresses both the physical and emotional components of pain. Integrating mind-body therapies with conventional pain management techniques can help trauma survivors reduce pain, improve mobility, and enhance their quality of life.

Somatic Therapies for Pain Relief

Somatic therapies focus on the connection between the body and mind, helping trauma survivors release tension and trauma stored in their muscles. Approaches such as Somatic Experiencing (SE) and Trauma Releasing Exercises (TRE) help individuals become more aware of their physical sensations and release pent-up energy from the body.

Mind-Body Approaches to Pain Management

Mind-body approaches, such as yoga, trauma-informed mindfulness meditation, and biofeedback, can help trauma survivors manage chronic pain by reducing stress and improving body awareness.

Integrative Pain Management Techniques

In addition to somatic and mind-body approaches, several integrative therapies can help trauma survivors manage chronic pain. As previously introduced in other chapters, two of these therapies are relevant here:

Photobiomodulation (PBM) for Pain Relief

Photobiomodulation (PBM) therapy uses low-level red or near-infrared light to stimulate cellular repair and reduce inflammation.

Hyperbaric Oxygen Therapy (HBOT)

HBOT enhances oxygen delivery to tissues, promoting healing and reducing oxidative stress.

Key Takeaways

- Trauma disrupts the body's pain regulation mechanisms, leading to chronic pain conditions such as fibromyalgia, chronic fatigue syndrome, and irritable bowel syndrome.

- The Stellate Ganglion Block (SGB) procedure, initially used for pain treatment, has shown promising results in reducing PTSD symptoms by calming the overactive stress response.

- Healing chronic pain requires a combination of somatic therapies, mind-body approaches, and integrative pain management techniques like Photobiomodulation (PBM) and HBOT.

References

Afari, N., & Buchwald, D. (2003). Chronic fatigue syndrome: A review. *American Journal of Psychiatry, 160*(2), 221-236. https://doi.org/10.1176/appi.ajp.160.2.221

Clauw, D. J. (2014). Fibromyalgia: A clinical review. *JAMA, 311*(15), 1547-1555. https://doi.org/10.1001/jama.2014.3266

Lipov, E., & Ritchie, E. C. (2015). A review of the use of stellate ganglion block in the treatment of PTSD. *Current Psychiatry Reports, 17*(6), 599. https://doi.org/10.1007/s11920-015-0599-4

Naviaux, R. K. (2014). Metabolic features of the cell danger response. *Mitochondrion, 16*, 7-17. https://doi.org/10.1016/j. mito.2013.08.006

Schleip, R., & Jäger, H. (2015). *Fascia in Sport and Movement*. Handspring Publishing.

Van der Kolk, B. A. (2014). *The Body Keeps the Score: Brain, mind, and body in the healing of trauma*. Penguin Books.

19.

TRAUMA, ADDICTION, AND SELF-DESTRUCTIVE BEHAVIOURS

Introduction: The Connection Between Trauma and Addiction

There is a strong link between trauma and addiction. Many individuals who have experienced trauma, especially early in life, turn to substances or self-destructive behaviours as a way to cope with their overwhelming emotional pain. This can lead to addiction, disordered eating, self-harm, and other harmful coping mechanisms. Trauma survivors may use these behaviours to numb their emotions, avoid painful memories, or regain a sense of control over their lives.

In this chapter, we will explore how trauma contributes to the development of addiction and self-destructive behaviours, focusing on the psychological and physiological mechanisms at play. We will also discuss strategies for breaking the cycle of addiction and promoting healing through trauma-informed care, holistic therapies, and integrative approaches.

The Cycle of Trauma and Addiction

Trauma creates a state of emotional dysregulation, where individuals struggle to manage overwhelming feelings of fear, anxiety, sadness, or anger. To cope with this emotional turmoil, trauma survivors may turn to substances like alcohol and drugs, or engage in self-harming behaviours, to temporarily relieve their distress.

The Role of the Brain's Reward System

Addiction is driven by the brain's reward system, particularly the release of dopamine in response to pleasurable activities. Substances like alcohol, opioids, or stimulants trigger significant releases of dopamine, providing a temporary sense of relief or euphoria. For trauma survivors, this relief can become a way to escape from painful emotions or traumatic memories.

Many trauma survivors use substances to numb their emotions and avoid confronting the pain of their trauma. This avoidance strategy creates a cycle in which addiction takes over as a primary coping mechanism.

Over time, the brain becomes less sensitive to dopamine, requiring higher doses of substances to achieve the same effect. This escalation increases the risk of addiction and makes it harder to stop using substances without professional help.

Trauma and Self-Destructive Behaviours

Self-destructive behaviours are often rooted in trauma and can manifest as disordered eating, self-harm, reckless behaviours, or abusive relationships. These behaviours are a way for individuals to gain a sense of control over their bodies or emotions when they feel powerless due to their trauma.

Disordered Eating and Trauma

Disordered eating behaviours, such as **binge eating**, **anorexia**, or **bulimia**, are common among trauma survivors. For many, controlling their food intake or weight provides a sense of control that they may have lost during the traumatic experience.

Trauma survivors may use food as a way to regulate emotions, either by overeating to numb their feelings or restricting food to feel a sense of mastery over their bodies. This cycle can lead to serious health issues and perpetuate the emotional pain they are trying to avoid.

Self-Harm and Trauma

Self-harm, such as cutting, burning, or hitting oneself, is another self-destructive behaviour that trauma survivors may use to cope with overwhelming emotions. For some, self-harm provides a temporary release of emotional pain or serves as a method to express feelings they cannot put into words.

In some cases, inflicting physical pain on themselves allows trauma survivors to temporarily distract themselves from emotional pain or regain a sense of control over their bodies. However, this behaviour can become a dangerous coping mechanism, leading to further emotional and physical harm.

How Trauma Impacts the Brain and Contributes to Addiction

Trauma has a profound impact on the brain, particularly in areas that regulate stress, emotions, and reward processing. Understanding how trauma affects the brain is key to understanding the development of addiction and self-destructive behaviours.

The amygdala and the prefrontal cortex both have important roles in addiction:

- **Amygdala:** The amygdala is the brain's fear centre and is hyperactive in trauma survivors. This overactivity makes it difficult for individuals to feel safe, leading them to seek out substances or behaviours that provide temporary relief by calming the amygdala.

- **Prefrontal cortex:** The prefrontal cortex, which is responsible for decision-making, impulse control, and emotional regulation, becomes less active in trauma survivors. This impairment makes it harder for individuals to resist addictive behaviours or make healthy decisions.

Stress and the HPA Axis

Trauma also affects the **hypothalamic-pituitary-adrenal (HPA) axis**, which controls the body's stress response. Chronic stress from unresolved trauma leads to dysregulation of the HPA axis, causing an overproduction of stress hormones like cortisol. This state of chronic stress increases cravings for substances or harmful behaviours as a means of alleviating the emotional burden.

Breaking the Cycle of Addiction: Trauma-Informed Care

Treating addiction and self-destructive behaviours in trauma survivors requires a trauma-informed approach that addresses both the physical and emotional aspects of trauma. Traditional addiction treatment alone may not be sufficient, as it often focuses on the behaviour without addressing the underlying trauma.

Trauma-Informed Addiction Treatment

Trauma-informed care recognizes the connection between trauma and addiction and focuses on creating a safe, supportive environment for healing. Key principles include:

- **Safety:** Ensuring that trauma survivors feel physically and emotionally safe in the treatment environment.

- **Empowerment:** Helping individuals regain a sense of control and autonomy over their lives.

- **Collaboration:** Working with trauma survivors as partners in their recovery process rather than imposing a top-down approach.

Integrated Therapies for Trauma and Addiction

Integrating trauma-focused therapies into addiction treatment can help individuals process their trauma and develop healthier coping mechanisms. Some effective approaches include:

- **Eye Movement Desensitization and Reprocessing (EMDR):** EMDR helps trauma survivors reprocess traumatic memories, reducing the emotional intensity of those memories and breaking the link between trauma and addictive behaviours.

- **Somatic Experiencing (SE):** Somatic Experiencing focuses on body awareness and helps trauma survivors release pent-up energy from their bodies, reducing the need for addictive behaviours to cope with emotional pain.

Holistic Approaches to Addiction Recovery

Holistic approaches to addiction recovery address the whole person—mind, body, and spirit—offering a more comprehensive path to healing. These approaches can be particularly beneficial for trauma survivors who need support in regulating their emotions, calming their nervous systems, and restoring balance to their lives.

Trauma-Informed Mindfulness and Meditation

Trauma-informed mindfulness practices, such as meditation and breathwork, help trauma survivors become more aware of their emotions and physical sensations without judgement. This awareness allows them to respond to cravings or emotional triggers in healthier ways.

Mindfulness-Based Relapse Prevention (MBRP) combines trauma-informed mindfulness practices with traditional relapse prevention techniques to help individuals manage cravings and emotional distress without resorting to addictive behaviours.

Yoga and Movement Therapies

Trauma survivors often carry emotional pain in their bodies, leading to chronic tension and discomfort. Trauma-informed yoga and other movement therapies help individuals reconnect with their bodies, release tension, and develop healthier ways of coping with stress.

Trauma-informed yoga focuses on gentle, mindful movement and breath awareness. This practice helps trauma survivors build body awareness and reduce physical and emotional tension that contributes to addiction.

Herbal and Nutritional Support

Certain herbs and nutritional supplements can support trauma survivors in regulating their mood, reducing cravings, and restoring balance to the body's stress response:

- **Adaptogenic herbs:** Herbs like ashwagandha, Rhodiola, and holy basil help regulate cortisol levels and reduce stress, which can be beneficial in managing cravings and reducing the emotional distress that drives addiction.

- **Omega-3 fatty acids:** Omega-3 fatty acids, found in fish oil and flaxseeds, help reduce inflammation and improve brain function, supporting emotional stability during recovery.

Building Resilience and Preventing Relapse

Recovery from trauma and addiction is an ongoing process that requires building emotional resilience and developing strategies to prevent relapse. Trauma survivors benefit from learning how to manage stress, regulate their emotions, and develop healthy coping mechanisms that support long-term recovery.

Two helpful ways of building emotional resilience include:

- **Cognitive Behavioural Therapy (CBT):** CBT helps individuals identify and challenge negative thought patterns that contribute to addictive behaviours. By reframing these thoughts, trauma survivors can develop healthier coping strategies and build resilience in the face of stress.

- **Emotional regulation skills:** Teaching trauma survivors how to regulate their emotions through techniques like deep breathing, grounding exercises, and self-compassion can reduce the risk of relapse and promote long-term recovery.

Key Takeaways

- Trauma is strongly linked to addiction and self-destructive behaviours, as trauma survivors often turn to substances or harmful behaviours to cope with emotional pain.

- Addiction is driven by the brain's reward system and is compounded by the emotional dysregulation caused by trauma.

- Breaking the cycle of addiction requires a trauma-informed approach that integrates traditional addiction treatment with trauma-focused therapies such as EMDR and Somatic Experiencing.

- Holistic approaches, including mindfulness, yoga, and herbal support, offer additional tools for trauma survivors to manage cravings, reduce stress, and restore balance.

- Building emotional resilience and learning to regulate emotions are critical components of preventing relapse and promoting long-term recovery.

References

Bremner, J. D. (2006). Traumatic stress: Effects on the brain. *Dialogues in Clinical Neuroscience, 8*(4), 445-461. https://doi. org/10.31887/DCNS.2006.8.4/jbremner

Felitti, V. J., Anda, R. F., Nordenberg, D., Williamson, D. F., Spitz, A. M., Edwards, V., … & Marks, J. S. (1998). Relationship of childhood abuse and household dysfunction to many of the leading causes of death in adults: The adverse childhood experiences (ACE) study. *American Journal of Preventive Medicine, 14*(4), 245-258. https://doi.org/10.1016/S0749-3797(98)00017-8

Khantzian, E. J. (1997). The self-medication hypothesis of substance use disorders: A reconsideration and recent applications. *Harvard Review of Psychiatry, 4*(5), 231-244. https://doi.org/10.3109/10673229709030550

Miller, W. R., & Rollnick, S. (2013). *Motivational Interviewing: Helping people change* (3rd ed.). Guilford Press.

Ogden, P., Minton, K., & Pain, C. (2006). *Trauma and the Body: A sensorimotor approach to psychotherapy.* W. W. Norton & Company.

Shapiro, F. (2017). *Eye Movement Desensitization and Reprocessing (EMDR) Therapy: Basic principles, protocols, and procedures* (3rd ed.). Guilford Press.

Sinha, R. (2008). Chronic stress, drug use, and vulnerability to addiction. *Annals of the New York Academy of Sciences, 1141*(1), 105-130. https://doi.org/10.1196/annals.1441.030

Van der Kolk, B. A. (2014). *The Body Keeps the Score: Brain, mind, and body in the healing of trauma.* Penguin Books.

20

FAMILY CONSTELLATION THERAPY, DYNAMIC THERAPY, AND THE CELL DANGER RESPONSE

Introduction: Healing Beyond the Individual

Trauma is often seen as a profoundly personal experience, but its effects extend far beyond the individual, rippling through families, communities, and down the even generations. In the context of trauma recovery, it's essential to recognize the broader dynamics that contribute to suffering. **Family Constellation Therapy** and **Dynamic Therapy** are two approaches that focus on these extended dynamics, shedding light on how unresolved traumas from previous generations can become embedded in family systems, contributing to individual distress and chronic activation of the Cell Danger Response (CDR).

In this chapter, we will explore how these therapeutic approaches help address inherited trauma and systemic emotional burdens, and how they interact with the CDR to promote healing at both the individual and family levels.

The Role of Inherited Trauma in Chronic Stress

Trauma is not only personal; it can be inherited across generations. Family systems theory suggests that trauma, unresolved emotional conflicts, and dysfunctional patterns within a family can be passed down from one generation to the next. This phenomenon is sometimes referred to as "transgenerational trauma". While individuals may not consciously remember the events that affected their ancestors, the emotional and physical imprints of these traumas can remain active within the family system.

When transgenerational trauma remains unresolved, it can perpetuate patterns of chronic stress, emotional dysfunction, and illness. The CDR becomes an essential concept in this context, as the body's cells may continue to interpret these inherited emotional burdens as threats, keeping individuals stuck in a state of chronic defence, even if it was their ancestors who experienced the original trauma.

Family Constellation Therapy: Unravelling Generational Trauma

Bert Hellinger developed Family Constellation Therapy, which is based on the idea that unresolved family traumas, emotional entanglements, and imbalances in the family system can lead to mental, emotional, and physical problems in the present generation. This therapy allows individuals to explore how their suffering may be connected to the unresolved traumas of their ancestors.

During a Family Constellation session, a group of people or stand-in representatives are used to recreate and represent the family system. This process brings hidden dynamics and unresolved traumas to the surface, allowing the client to see how certain emotional burdens may not actually be their own, but part of a more considerable family legacy. By acknowledging these dynamics and giving them space to be witnessed, individuals often experience a release of emotional tension and begin to heal.

Family Constellation and the CDR

From a CDR perspective, the unresolved traumas carried within a family system can keep an individual in a heightened state of cellular defence. The body perceives these inherited emotional burdens as ongoing threats, which lead to chronic activation of the CDR, manifesting in symptoms such as chronic fatigue, anxiety, depression, and even physical illness. Family Constellation Therapy helps break this cycle by identifying and acknowledging these transgenerational traumas, giving the body and cells the signal that the danger has passed, and allowing the CDR to deactivate.

Family Constellation Therapy and Dynamic Therapy work on both emotional and cellular levels, helping to resolve trauma by supporting the body's transition from the CDR into salugenesis (see Chapter 7). These therapies play a pivotal role in allowing the body to let go of defence mechanisms and engage its natural healing processes.

An Illustrative Example: Generational Healing Through Family Constellation

Consider the case of a woman named Sarah, who experienced chronic anxiety and an overwhelming sense of guilt, even though she had no apparent reason to feel this way based on her personal experiences. Through Family Constellation Therapy, Sarah discovered that her grandmother had endured significant trauma during World War II and that this trauma had not been processed or resolved. The weight of this unresolved grief had been passed down to Sarah, manifesting as anxiety and guilt. After engaging in Family Constellation Therapy, Sarah experienced a profound emotional release, and her chronic anxiety subsided as her body no longer perceived the inherited trauma as an immediate threat.

Dynamic Therapy: Addressing the Flow of Emotional Energy

Dynamic Therapy is another therapeutic approach that focuses on the underlying emotional processes and patterns that contribute to mental and physical health problems. This approach is based on the idea that emotional energy needs to flow freely for optimal well-being. When emotional energy is blocked—often due to trauma or emotional suppression—this blockage can manifest as emotional distress, psychological symptoms, and even physical illness.

Dynamic Therapy aims to help individuals recognize and release these emotional blockages by exploring unconscious patterns, unresolved conflicts, and repressed emotions. Through this process, clients can restore the flow of emotional energy, allowing for more profound healing.

Dynamic Therapy and the CDR

Dynamic Therapy is highly relevant to the CDR because it helps address the emotional stagnation that keeps the body in a state of defence. When trauma remains unresolved, or emotions are suppressed, the body continues to perceive a threat at the cellular level. This chronic emotional blockage can lead to prolonged CDR activation, as the cells remain on high alert, unable to return to normal functioning.

By addressing these underlying emotional blockages, Dynamic Therapy helps individuals restore their emotional balance, which signals to the body that it is safe to deactivate the CDR. As a result, the individual's physical symptoms, such as chronic inflammation, fatigue, and immune dysfunction, often improve.

An Illustrative Example: Releasing Emotional Blockages with Dynamic Therapy

John was a successful professional who struggled with chronic pain, migraines, and digestive issues that had no apparent medical cause. Despite seeing numerous specialists, he couldn't find relief. Through Dynamic Therapy, John explored his suppressed emotions, particularly unresolved grief over the loss of his father during his teenage years. By addressing these emotions and allowing himself to feel and express his grief, John experienced a significant reduction in his physical symptoms, as his body no longer needed to maintain its chronic defence posture.

The Connection Between Family Constellation Therapy, Dynamic Therapy, and the CDR

Both Family Constellation Therapy and Dynamic Therapy are deeply connected to the CDR, as they address different aspects of how emotional trauma and unresolved stress contribute to the chronic activation of this cellular defence mechanism:

- Family Constellation Therapy helps release inherited traumas and emotional burdens that perpetuate the chronic activation of the CDR across generations.

- Dynamic Therapy focuses on releasing emotional blockages that occur within an individual's lifetime, helping the body deactivate the CDR by restoring the flow of emotional energy.

By addressing both the transgenerational *and* individual levels of trauma, these therapies help individuals break free from the chronic activation of the CDR, promoting healing—not only for themselves but also for future generations.

Integrating Family Constellation and Dynamic Therapy into Trauma Recovery

To fully integrate these approaches into trauma recovery, it's important to:

- **Acknowledge the role of family history:** It is crucial to recognize that certain emotional burdens may not originate from the individual but from the family system around them when resolving transgenerational trauma.

- **Explore unconscious patterns:** Dynamic Therapy encourages individuals to become aware of unconscious emotional patterns that may be keeping them stuck in a state of chronic stress.

- **Restore the flow of emotional energy:** Both therapies work to release emotional blockages, signalling to the body and cells that it is safe to deactivate the CDR.

Key Takeaways

- Trauma is not only personal; it can be passed down through family systems, contributing to chronic stress and CDR activation in individuals.

- Family Constellation Therapy addresses inherited trauma and helps individuals release emotional burdens that have been carried across generations.

- Dynamic Therapy focuses on releasing emotional blockages and unresolved conflicts, allowing the body to deactivate the CDR and return to a state of healing.

- Integrating these therapies into trauma recovery helps individuals break free from chronic CDR activation and promotes healing at both the personal and generational levels.

References

Hellinger, B. (1999). *Love's Hidden Symmetry: What makes love work in relationships*. Zeig, Tucker & Theisen.

Levine, P. A. (2011). *In an Unspoken Voice: How the body releases trauma and restores goodness*. North Atlantic Books.

Naviaux, R. K. (2014). Metabolic features of the cell danger response. *Mitochondrion, 16*, 7-17. https://doi.org/10.1016/j.mito.2013.08.006

Porges, S. W. (2011). *The Polyvagal Theory: Neurophysiological foundations of emotions, attachment, communication, and self-regulation*. W. W. Norton & Company.

Ruppert, F. (2008). *Trauma, Bonding & Family Constellations: Understanding and healing injuries of the soul*. Green Balloon Publishing.

Van der Kolk, B. A. (2015). *The Body Keeps the Score: Brain, mind, and body in the healing of trauma*. Penguin Books.

21.

SOMATIC EXPERIENCING: TAPPING INTO THE BODY'S WISDOM

Introduction

Somatic Experiencing (SE), developed by Dr. Peter Levine, is based on the idea that trauma disrupts the natural self-regulation processes of the nervous system. Trauma can leave the body stuck in fight, flight, freeze, fawn or flop responses, leading to chronic tension, anxiety, or shutdown. SE helps restore balance by assisting individuals to reconnect with the body's innate healing abilities, allowing the body to release stored trauma energy and transition into salugenesis—the body's process of cellular repair and restoration.

The Theory Behind Somatic Experiencing

The foundation of SE comes from the observation of animals in the wild. After a life-threatening event, animals naturally discharge the excess energy through shaking or trembling, allowing them to return to a calm state. Humans, however, tend to suppress these natural physical responses, causing trauma to become "stuck" in the body. SE seeks to resolve this incomplete self-protective response.

By guiding trauma survivors through an awareness of their bodily sensations, SE helps complete these unresolved responses and discharge the stored energy. This process is gradual and works by slowly introducing elements of the trauma while ensuring that the client remains in a safe and controlled environment.

Key Components of Somatic Experiencing

- **Pendulation:** The practice of moving back and forth between sensations of distress and sensations of calm or safety. This helps the body release trauma in small, manageable doses.

- **Titration:** SE avoids overwhelming the nervous system by breaking down the trauma experience into small pieces. The idea is to gently and gradually introduce traumatic sensations, allowing the nervous system to process the experience without becoming overwhelmed.

- **Discharge and completion:** The goal of SE is to allow the body to complete the self-protective responses that were halted during the traumatic event. Once the stored energy is released, clients often experience sensations of warmth, tingling, or trembling, indicating that the body has begun to return to a state of balance.

- **Body awareness:** Instead of focusing on the cognitive story of trauma, SE emphasizes body sensations. Clients are encouraged to track subtle bodily cues like tightness, tingling, heat, or coldness, which may represent the body's attempt to release the trauma.

How Somatic Experiencing Works

In a typical session, the therapist helps the client tune into their body sensations, such as muscle tension, tightness, or changes in temperature, rather than focusing on the traumatic event itself. The therapist guides the individual through the process of observing and releasing these sensations, helping to restore the body's natural rhythm.

Rather than focusing on "talking through" trauma, SE engages with the physiological processes behind trauma reactions. Clients might begin by discussing the trauma briefly, but the emphasis will shift toward tracking the body's responses to memories or stress. The therapist helps clients learn to notice how the body stores trauma and works to release it.

Somatic Experiencing and Salugenesis

Salugenesis is the process of the body shifting from a state of defence and survival (the Cell Danger Response) into a state of cellular repair and healing (see Chapter 7). Somatic Experiencing plays a crucial role in facilitating this transition by helping the body resolve its stuck fight-flight-freeze-fawn-flop responses. Through the gradual release of stored trauma energy, SE helps the nervous system return to homeostasis, reducing chronic stress and inflammation. This allows the body to move into salugenesis, where healing and repair occur at the cellular level. The discharge of stored tension facilitates more profound biological healing, supporting the body's ability to enter a state of regeneration and resilience.

Applications of Somatic Experiencing

- **PTSD:** SE is particularly effective for those who have Post-Traumatic Stress Disorder (PTSD), where individuals often remain in a heightened state of arousal or hypervigilance. SE helps them discharge this accumulated energy and reduce symptoms like anxiety, flashbacks, and hypervigilance.

- **Developmental trauma:** Individuals who have experienced ongoing stress or trauma during childhood can benefit from SE, which helps address attachment wounds and chronic stress responses stored in the body.

- **Chronic pain:** SE has also been shown to alleviate chronic pain, particularly when pain is connected to unresolved trauma stored in the body.

Scientific Support

Research supports SE as an effective intervention for reducing trauma symptoms, restoring the nervous system to balance, and facilitating long-term emotional and physical recovery. The slow, intentional nature of SE allows clients to heal *without* becoming overwhelmed by re-experiencing traumatic events.

Key Takeaways

- **Body-based healing:** SE helps trauma survivors heal by releasing stored trauma energy in the body, emphasizing physical sensations over cognitive processing.

- **Safe, gradual exposure:** Through pendulation and titration, SE prevents overwhelm by gradually helping clients process trauma in small doses.

- **Restoring balance:** SE helps the nervous system return to homeostasis, facilitating salugenesis—the body's transition from defence to healing.

- **Applications:** SE is particularly effective for treating PTSD, developmental trauma, and chronic pain, supporting deep, body-based healing.

Next Steps

If you are considering Somatic Experiencing as a therapy for trauma recovery, here's how to get started:

- **Find a certified SE practitioner:** Make sure the therapist is trained and certified in SE. The Somatic Experiencing Trauma Institute can help you find practitioners.

- **Engage in body awareness exercises:** Begin by practicing trauma-informed mindfulness of your body's sensations during moments of stress. Track tightness, heat, or tingling, and notice how your body responds to different stimuli.

- **Combine SE with other therapies:** SE works well when integrated with other trauma therapies, such as EMDR or talk therapy, offering a full-body approach to trauma recovery.

- **Attend to self-care:** Alongside SE, engage in restorative practices like meditation, yoga, and breathwork to continue the body's healing process outside of therapy.

Resources

Peter Levine on Somatic Experiencing. (n.d.). Explore the work of Dr. Peter Levine, the creator of Somatic Experiencing, and how this therapy addresses trauma. Retrieved from https://www.somaticexperiencing.com/about-peter

Somatic Experiencing® Trauma Institute. (n.d.). Learn more about the principles of Somatic Experiencing and its applications in trauma healing. Retrieved from https://traumahealing.org/se-101

The science behind Somatic Experiencing. (2020). A detailed look into the science and biological mechanisms that make SE effective. *Frontiers in Psychology.* https://doi.org/10.3389/fpsyg.2020.00553/full

22.

BRAINSPOTTING

Unlocking the Brain's Trauma
Capsules for Deep Healing

Introduction

Brainspotting (BSP), developed by Dr. David Grand, evolved from his work in refining and slowing down Eye Movement Desensitization and Reprocessing (EMDR), making it a more gentle and less triggering method for trauma survivors. Dr. Grand referred to this as **EMDR: Natural Flow**.

Dr. Peter Levine, the founder of Somatic Experiencing (SE) (see previous chapter), once encouraged Grand to "slow the eye movements down even more—much, much more". Around that time, Grand was working with elite athletes, using his Natural Flow method to enhance their performance. A breakthrough moment came during a session with a teenage ice skater who had struggled to master a particular move, the triple loop, for over a year. While tracking Grand's fingers as they moved slowly in front of her, her eyes wobbled and froze at a particular point in her field of vision. Grand paused his finger at this position, and as the young skater focused on this "still point", a flood of deep, unresolved relational traumas surfaced—issues that had not emerged during their year of therapy together.

The following day at practice, she completed a flawless triple loop and never had a problem executing the manoeuvre again. This was a pivotal moment for Grand. He began exploring this method with his supervisees and encouraged them to apply it with their own clients. The results were remarkable.

Thus, Brainspotting was born, blending elements of Natural Flow EMDR and Somatic Experiencing. The guiding principle, encapsulated by the tagline *"Where you look affects how you feel"*, indicates that when a client's issue is linked to a body sensation and an external eye position, the brain seems to locate the underlying trauma, unlock it, and process it at a deeper level than was previously possible, often without the client needing to verbalize the specifics.

Over time, Brainspotting gained global traction. Therapists reported profound and lasting healing in their clients, particularly those dealing with trauma. Dr. Grand identified these eye positions as "brain spots", areas of unresolved trauma stored in the brain. In the years since its inception, Brainspotting has been successfully integrated with a wide range of therapeutic modalities, including Internal Family Systems (IFS), Narrative Therapy, Somatic Therapies, Cognitive Behavioural Therapy (CBT), Gestalt Therapy, Equine Therapy, and even Performance Coaching for athletes and artists.

This therapeutic method has shown success within a broad spectrum of issues, including addiction recovery, perinatal trauma, and physical syndromes like chronic pain. Brainspotting is even adaptable for clients with limited interoception (the awareness of internal body sensations, like heartbeat, breathing and hunger), visual impairments, and neurodivergent conditions such as autism and pathological demand avoidance (PDA). Its client-driven approach makes it particularly suited for those who struggle with talk-based therapies, such as teenagers and those who prefer a non-verbal, deeply attuned method.

The Science Behind Brainspotting

At the core of Brainspotting is the understanding that trauma is often stored in the brain's **subcortical regions**, particularly the **limbic system**, which governs survival instincts and emotional regulation. Unlike the **neocortex**, which manages cognitive processes, the subcortical brain holds implicit memories and emotions—those often inaccessible through conventional talk therapy.

By focusing on **brain spots**, Brainspotting bypasses the thinking brain and accesses these deeper layers of trauma. This allows for the release of unresolved trauma and paves the way for healing, not just on an emotional level but also at the physical level, where trauma may manifest as chronic pain or other somatic symptoms.

How Brainspotting Works

In a typical Brainspotting session, the client brings forward an issue they wish to explore. The therapist helps the client find a "brain spot", a point in the visual field that triggers an emotional or physical response. Once the brain spot is located, the therapist holds that position with a pointer, or the client simply keeps their focus on that spot while the brain naturally begins to process the trauma. The therapist remains highly attuned but in a non-directive role, allowing the client's brain to lead the way.

The therapist's role in Brainspotting is defined by **Dual Attunement**: the therapist provides both relational attunement (through deep empathetic presence) and neurological attunement (by guiding the client to the brain spot). This approach creates a safe environment for trauma processing, with the therapist metaphorically "staying in the tail of the comet", following the client's lead.

Clients are encouraged to remain in a state of mindful awareness, noticing any emotions, sensations, or thoughts—without needing to analyse or change them. This focused mindfulness helps the brain to naturally heal unresolved trauma without unnecessary cognitive interference.

Brainspotting and Salugenesis

Brainspotting aligns with the concept of salugenesis—the process by which the body moves from a state of survival into one of cellular healing and repair. By accessing and resolving deeply stored trauma in the subcortical brain, Brainspotting helps release the trapped energy associated with survival responses, allowing the nervous system to reset. This shift moves the body out of chronic defence mode and into a state where healing and regeneration can occur, supporting salugenesis on a cellular level.

Applications of Brainspotting

- **Post-Traumatic Stress Disorder (PTSD) and Complex Trauma:** Brainspotting is highly effective for clients with severe trauma, especially those who struggle with repressed or dissociated memories. It reaches layers of trauma that other therapies may not be able to access.

- **Anxiety and Panic Disorders:** By locating the brain spot associated with anxiety, Brainspotting helps clients reduce anxiety at its root. Panic attacks, often a combination of flight and freeze responses, are addressed by resolving the underlying cause.

- **Physical pain:** Chronic pain linked to trauma stored in the nervous system can be alleviated through Brainspotting, which helps release both the emotional and physical tension held within the body.

- **Performance expansion:** Brainspotting is used to unlock mental blocks and enhance performance in athletes, artists, and professionals. By resolving performance-related anxieties and subconscious obstacles, it allows individuals to reach new heights in their work.

Scientific Support

Research demonstrates that Brainspotting effectively targets the limbic system, where trauma is stored, allowing for deep emotional and physical healing. Studies comparing Brainspotting with EMDR show comparable results, particularly in treating trauma and PTSD.

Leading trauma experts, including Bessel van der Kolk, Peter Levine, and Gabor Maté, emphasize the need for somatic approaches, as trauma is stored in the body's tissues, not just in the brain. Brainspotting's ability to combine mental, emotional, and somatic processing in one method aligns with these insights, offering a holistic approach to trauma resolution.

Key Takeaways

- **Subcortical healing:** Brainspotting accesses deep regions of the brain where trauma is stored, facilitating healing at multiple levels—emotional, mental, and physical.

- **Non-verbal trauma processing:** By bypassing cognitive processes, Brainspotting is ideal for clients who find it difficult to verbalize trauma.

- **Facilitating salugenesis:** Brainspotting supports the body's shift from survival mode to cellular repair, promoting lasting recovery.

- **Versatility:** Brainspotting can be used for trauma, anxiety, chronic pain, and performance issues, making it a versatile tool in therapeutic settings.

Next Steps

If you're considering Brainspotting for trauma recovery:

- **Find a certified practitioner:** Ensure the therapist is trained and certified in Brainspotting. You can search through the *Brainspotting International Directory* or find practitioners on *Psychology Today*.

- **Prepare with mindfulness:** Engage in body-centered mindfulness practices to increase awareness of bodily sensations, which will aid in Brainspotting sessions.

- **Combine with other therapies:** Brainspotting can be combined with other trauma therapies like Gestalt Therapy, Somatic Experiencing, or Internal Family Systems (IFS) for a more comprehensive approach.

- **Practice self-care:** Support your healing process by maintaining regular self-care activities such as yoga, meditation, or journaling.

Resources

Brainspotting International. (n.d.). Learn more about Brainspotting, its applications, and how to find a certified practitioner. https://brainspotting.com/about-brainspotting/what-is-brainspotting/

D'Antoni, F., Matiz, A., Fabbro, F., & Crescentini, C. (2022). Eye movement desensitization and reprocessing (EMDR) and mindfulness for chronic post-traumatic stress symptoms: A pilot randomized controlled trial. International Journal of Environmental Research and Public Health, 19(3), 1142. https://doi.org/10.3390/ijerph19031142

23.

MENTAL HEALTH INCORPORATING HORSES

Introduction

Equine Therapy provides a unique, experiential approach to addressing mental health challenges, particularly trauma, through interactions with horses. Unlike traditional talk therapies, equine therapy is often ground-based. It allows clients to interact with horses in a reflective, nonverbal environment that promotes self-awareness, emotional regulation, and healing. Horses' sensitivity to non-verbal cues helps them mirror clients' internal states, facilitating insights that foster emotional growth.

Exploring Models of Equine Therapy

Multiple Equine Therapy models exist, each offering a unique approach to therapeutic and personal development. These models leverage horses' natural characteristics to support mental health recovery, encouraging clients to process emotions, improve interpersonal skills, and explore behaviours in a safe and reflective setting.

Equine-Facilitated Psychotherapy (EFP)

Equine-Facilitated Psychotherapy (EFP) is a ground-based therapy that focuses on helping clients explore emotions, behaviours and relational patterns through direct interaction with horses. Horses, with their sensitivity to non-verbal cues, mirror a client's emotional state, allowing for powerful insights that aid in self-awareness and emotional processing. EFP is effective for addressing issues such as anxiety, depression, trauma, and behavioural challenges (Dell et al., 2011).

Equine-Assisted Learning (EAL)

Equine-assisted learning (EAL) focuses on skill-building and personal development. It uses structured activities with horses to enhance communication, leadership, teamwork and problem-solving abilities. EAL is primarily educational rather than therapeutic, making it ideal for youth development, corporate training and other growth-focused settings (Hallberg, 2008).

The HEAL Model™ (Human-Equine Alliances for Learning)

The HEAL Model integrates principles of social-emotional learning with equine interactions, promoting resilience and emotional intelligence. It is built around the "Six Keys to Relationship", which guides clients in managing emotions and improving interpersonal skills. HEAL is suitable for both therapeutic and educational settings, fostering personal growth and emotional healing (Kaiser et al., 2006).

Arenas for Change (ARCH)

ARCH combines equine interactions with structured storytelling. This facilitation process provides a supportive, non-directive environment for clients to explore their personal narratives. Framing clients as heroes on a journey encourages emotional breakthroughs, resilience and self-discovery. ARCH is well-suited for clients looking to reflect on their stories within a safe, non-analytical space (Oli and Alex, n.d.).

Therapeutic Riding and Hippotherapy

These approaches involve mounted activities that focus on physical, emotional and cognitive development. Therapeutic riding builds confidence, coordination and social engagement, while hippotherapy uses the horse's movement as a treatment strategy managed by a physical, occupational or speech therapist. These approaches benefit individuals with physical disabilities, developmental disorders and neurological conditions, supporting both physical and emotional growth (Sterba, 2007).

The Science Behind Equine Therapy

Horses' sensitivity to non-verbal cues makes them powerful therapeutic partners. They often reflect the client's internal state through their own behaviour. This immediate feedback allows clients to process emotions and behaviour patterns in a non-verbal, supportive environment. For individuals who struggle with verbal expression, Equine Therapy offers an accessible pathway to deeper self-awareness and emotional release (Pendry & Roeter, 2013).

Equine Therapy and Salugenesis

Equine Therapy promotes salugenesis by guiding clients from a defensive state into a healing state. Through non-verbal interaction with horses, clients process stored trauma energy, facilitating the transition from the Cell Danger Response (CDR) to recovery. This shift encourages emotional and physical regulation, which is essential for sustainable healing (Levinson & Mallon, 1997).

Integrating Trauma-Focused Therapies

Layering Equine Therapy with trauma-specific modalities deepens emotional processing, allowing clients to address trauma from multiple angles.

- **Brainspotting:** This modality focuses on specific eye positions to access deeply stored emotional material. When layered with Equine Therapy, Brainspotting enables clients to safely process difficult memories, with the calming presence of horses providing added emotional support.

- **Somatic Art:** Somatic art integrates creative expression with body awareness, helping clients explore trauma through both physical and artistic channels. Horses enhance this process by mirroring non-verbal cues, encouraging clients to release stored emotions in a grounded, responsive environment (Malchiodi, 2005).

- **Combining Equine Therapy with Family Constellation Therapy:** The integration of Equine Therapy and Family Constellation Therapy offers a powerful dual approach to trauma healing. Horse assisted therapy provides an experiential, non-verbal pathway for clients to process emotions with the aid of horses, while Family Constellation Therapy addresses hidden family dynamics and systemic issues. Together, these therapies allow clients to explore personal trauma and uncover ancestral patterns, creating a holistic space for emotional resolution and profound healing.

These layered therapies promote multi-sensory healing and address trauma across emotional, cognitive and somatic dimensions, supporting clients on a holistic path to recovery.

Applications of Equine Therapy

Equine Therapy can support various mental health needs, particularly for trauma survivors. Key applications include:

- **Trauma and PTSD:** Non-verbal processing in equine therapy allows trauma survivors, especially those with PTSD, to engage with traumatic memories and emotions indirectly (Schultz et al., 2007).

- **Emotional Regulation:** Clients with emotional regulation challenges benefit from observing how horses respond to their cues, fostering self-awareness and emotional control (Pendry et al., 2018).

- **Building Trust and Relationships:** Equine Therapy provides a safe space for clients to explore trust and develop interpersonal skills, which is beneficial for those working to rebuild relational stability (Yorke et al., 2008).

Key Takeaways

- **Non-verbal feedback:** Horses provide immediate, non-verbal insights, helping clients process emotions and trauma.

- **Experiential learning:** The ground-based, non-riding nature of equine therapy offers clients real-time reflection and emotional awareness.

- **Facilitating salugenesis:** Equine Therapy encourages the body's shift from a defensive to a healing state, enabling profound emotional and physical recovery.

- **Versatile applications:** This therapy is valuable for trauma survivors, individuals with emotional regulation needs, and those rebuilding trust.

Next Steps

To get started with equine therapy:

1. **Find a certified practitioner:** Seek qualified practitioners in the model that best suits your needs.

2. **Engage in reflective practices:** Journaling before and after sessions can enhance the benefits.

3. **Integrate with other therapies:** Equine Therapy complements trauma-focused therapies such as Brainspotting, Somatic Art and Clay Field Therapy.

4. **Explore nature-based practices:** Complementary practices like forest bathing or walking meditations can enhance the grounding effects of equine therapy.

References

Dell, C., Chalmers, D., Dell, D., Sauve, E., & MacKinnon, T. (2011). Horse as healer: Equine-assisted learning in the healing of First Nations youth from solvent abuse. *Pimatisiwin: A Journal of Aboriginal and Indigenous Community Health, 9*(1), 81–106.

Hallberg, L. (2008). *Walking the Way of the Horse: Exploring the power of the horse-human relationship.* iUniverse.

Kaiser, L., Spence, L. J., Lavergne, A. G., & Bosch, K. (2006). *Can a week of therapeutic riding make a difference? – A pilot study.* Anthrozoös, *19*(1), 63-74.

Levinson, D. J., & Mallon, G. P. (1997). *Pet-oriented child psychotherapy.* Charles C. Thomas.

Malchiodi, C. A. (2005). *Expressive Therapies.* Guilford Press.

Oli and Alex. (2024, January 10). *EAGALA: The equine-assisted therapy model.* Retrieved from https://www.oliandalex.com

Pendry, P., & Roeter, S. (2013). Experimental trial demonstrates positive effects of equine facilitated learning on child social competence. *Human-Animal Interaction Bulletin, 1*(1), 1-19.

Schultz, P. N., Remick-Barlow, G. A., & Robbins, L. (2007). Equine-assisted psychotherapy: A mental health promotion/intervention modality for children who have experienced intra-family violence. *Health & Social Care in the Community, 15*(3), 265-271.

Sterba, J. A. (2007). Does horseback riding therapy or therapist-directed hippotherapy rehabilitate children with cerebral palsy? *Developmental Medicine and Child Neurology, 49*(1), 68-73.

Yorke, J., Adams, C., & Coady, N. (2008). Therapeutic value of equine-human bonding in recovery from trauma. *Anthrozoös, 21*(1), 17-30.

24

CLAY FIELD THERAPY

Exploring Trauma Through Touch

Introduction

Clay Field Therapy is a form of sensorimotor therapy that uses the tactile experience of shaping and moulding clay to help individuals process and release trauma. Through the physical manipulation of clay, clients can access deep, unconscious emotions and experiences stored in the body. This therapy is especially effective for individuals who struggle to express trauma verbally, as it engages the body's **haptic perception** (sense of touch) to facilitate healing.

History of Clay Field Therapy

Clay Field Therapy was developed in the 1980s by Heinz Deuser, a German art therapist who recognized the power of tactile engagement as a therapeutic tool. Drawing from principles of sensorimotor therapy, Deuser saw the potential for clay to act as a bridge between the body's sensory system and emotional processing. His work expanded the use of clay as a healing tool for trauma, developmental challenges, and emotional regulation, particularly for clients who found verbal communication difficult. Over the past few decades, Clay Field Therapy has gained recognition for its unique ability to engage both the mind and body in trauma recovery.

The Science Behind Clay Field Therapy

Clay Field Therapy is based on the principle that trauma is often stored in the body and can be accessed through **tactile engagement**. The act of manipulating clay provides clients with a non-verbal way to express emotions that may be difficult to articulate. The physical resistance of the clay offers feedback to the hands, helping clients explore and work through stored tension, trauma, and unresolved emotional experiences.

Clay is a unique medium because it provides both resistance *and* flexibility, allowing individuals to create and destroy forms as part of the therapeutic process. This interaction helps release physical tension and emotional blockages that may have been held in the body for years.

How Clay Field Therapy Works

In a typical Clay Field Therapy session, clients are provided with a field of clay (a flat box filled with clay) and are encouraged to explore the material with their hands. The therapist guides the client to notice their physical sensations and emotional responses as they work with the clay.

The focus of Clay Field Therapy is on how the client physically interacts with the clay, paying attention to sensations of resistance, pressure, and tension. Clay provides a non-verbal way to process trauma, allowing individuals to work through emotions without the need for words. The forms created or destroyed in the clay can symbolize unresolved trauma, giving the client a physical way to address and transform these emotions.

The Clay Field functions as a solid therapeutic container, holding the complexities of the client's inner world. Unlike traditional therapeutic relationships, where the focus may primarily be on the therapist-client dynamic, the Clay Field allows for a more expansive exploration of the self. The clay becomes a physical manifestation of the client's psyche, enabling them to project their feelings and experiences into a tangible medium (Elbrecht, 2018).

Clay Field Therapy and Salugenesis

Through the physical engagement with clay, Clay Field Therapy helps the body release trauma and move into salugenesis—the body's natural process of healing and repair (see Chapter 7). By allowing the hands to explore and manipulate the clay, clients access the body's sensory system, which facilitates the release of stored trauma energy. This physical release supports the body's shift from the Cell Danger Response (CDR) to salugenesis.

The tactile nature of Clay Field Therapy also promotes neuroplasticity, as the brain responds to new sensory input, further supporting emotional and physical healing.

There are three main applications of Clay Field Therapy:

- **Developmental Trauma:** Clay Field Therapy is beneficial for individuals who experienced trauma in childhood and may struggle with verbal expression.

- **PTSD:** For clients with Post-Traumatic Stress Disorder, working with clay allows them to access and process trauma in a safe, controlled way.

- **Emotional regulation:** The sensory feedback from the clay helps individuals regulate their emotions by providing a physical outlet for tension and frustration.

Scientific Support

Research into sensorimotor therapies like Clay Field Therapy shows that engaging the senses—especially touch—can facilitate the release of trauma stored in the body. The sensory engagement with clay provides a powerful tool for processing trauma in a non-verbal, embodied way, allowing clients to move towards long-term emotional recovery.

Future Directions in Clay Field Therapy

As the practice of Clay Field therapy continues to evolve, it opens new avenues for research and application. Future studies could focus on quantifying the impact of this modality on various populations, including those with complex trauma, developmental disorders, or attachment issues. Research could explore how the Clay Field interacts with other therapeutic modalities, such as talk therapy or mindfulness practices, to create a more integrated approach to healing.

Training programs for therapists could also expand, incorporating findings from neuroscience and attachment theory to refine techniques within the Clay Field. By grounding the practice in current research, therapists can enhance their effectiveness and adaptability to meet diverse client needs. Elbrecht's work underscores the necessity of integrating artistic expression into therapeutic practices, highlighting the transformative potential of creative modalities (Elbrecht, 2018).

Final Reflections

Ultimately, the Clay Field is more than just another therapeutic tool; it is a profound opportunity to connect with one's inner self and reclaim the narrative of one's life. Through the creative process of working with clay, clients find not only a means of expression but also a pathway to healing and growth.

The legacy of the Clay Field resonates long after the clay has dried. It instils a sense of hope and possibility, encouraging clients to embrace their inherent capacity for transformation. As they leave the Clay Field behind, they move forward with the message that healing is not a destination but an ongoing journey—one that unfolds with each new creation.

Key Takeaways

- **Sensorimotor engagement:** Clay Field Therapy engages the sense of touch to help individuals process trauma stored in the body.

- **Non-verbal trauma processing:** By working with clay, clients can express and transform emotions without relying on words.

- **Facilitating salugenesis:** The tactile engagement helps release stored trauma energy, supporting the body's transition into salugenesis—the state of healing and cellular repair.

- **Versatile application:** Clay Field Therapy is effective for developmental trauma, PTSD, and emotional regulation.

Next Steps

If you are considering Clay Field Therapy for trauma recovery, here's how to proceed:

- **Find a certified sensorimotor therapist:** Ensure that the therapist is trained in sensorimotor therapies and experienced in working with clay as a medium.

- **Practice sensory mindfulness:** Engage in mindful activities that involve sensory engagement, such as gardening or crafting, to help prepare for Clay Field sessions.

- **Combine it with other therapies:** Clay Field Therapy can be used alongside therapies like Somatic Experiencing (see Chapter 21) or Brainspotting (see Chapter 22) to provide a comprehensive approach to trauma recovery.

- **Stay engaged with self-care:** Incorporate creative self-care activities like journaling or artmaking to support emotional healing outside of therapy.

Resources

Bowlby, J. (1982). *Attachment and Loss: Vol. 1. Attachment.* New York: Basic Books.

Elbrecht, C., & Antcliff, L. R. (2014). *Being touched through touch: Trauma treatment through haptic perception at the Clay Field: A sensorimotor art therapy. International Journal of Art Therapy*, 19(1), 19–30. https://doi.org/10.1080/17454832.2014.880932

Levine, P. A. (2010). *In an Unspoken Voice: How the Body Releases Trauma and Restores Goodness.* Berkeley, CA: North Atlantic Books.

Ogden, P., Minton, K., & Pain, C. (2006). *Sensorimotor Psychotherapy: Interventions for Trauma and Attachment.* New York: Norton & Company.

Porges, S. W. (2011). *The Polyvagal Theory: Neurophysiological Foundations of Emotions, Attachment, Communication, and Self-Regulation.* New York: Norton & Company.

Schore, A. N. (2003). *Affect Regulation and the Repair of the Self.* New York: W. W. Norton & Company.

Siegel, D. J. (2012). *The Developing Mind: How Relationships and the Brain Interact to Shape Who We Are.* New York: Guilford Press.

25.

SOMATIC ART THERAPY

Healing Through Creative Expression

Introduction

Somatic Art Therapy is a therapeutic approach that combines physical movement with art-making to help individuals process and release trauma. This therapy engages the body through creative expression, offering a non-verbal outlet for emotions that may be too difficult to express through words. By integrating movement and art, Somatic Art Therapy allows individuals to explore trauma in a safe and creative environment.

History of Somatic Art Therapy

Somatic Art Therapy has its roots in both Art Therapy and somatic psychology, which emerged in the mid-20th century. Art Therapy, initially developed in the 1940s, was founded on the belief that creative expression could facilitate psychological healing. Later, the rise of somatic psychology emphasized the importance of the body in processing trauma. Somatic Art Therapy evolved by combining these two fields, using both creative expression and body awareness to address trauma and its emotional challenges.

The Science Behind Somatic Art Therapy

Trauma often remains locked in the body, and traditional talk therapy may not always provide the tools needed to release these emotional blockages. Somatic Art Therapy taps into the body's wisdom by combining physical movement (which may include dance, stretching, or spontaneous gestures) with creative activities like painting, drawing, or sculpting. This approach helps individuals access deep-seated trauma and release it through the act of creation.

Engaging in artistic activities stimulates multiple brain areas, including the sensory-motor system, the limbic system (which processes emotions), and the prefrontal cortex (which supports self-regulation). By activating these systems simultaneously, Somatic Art Therapy allows clients to process trauma holistically.

How Somatic Art Therapy Works

In a typical session, the therapist guides the client through both physical movements and creative activities. Movement helps release physical tension, while art-making offers a way to externalize emotions. Clients are encouraged to explore their feelings through their body and their artwork.

Through physical engagement, the body's movements help discharge stored trauma energy, and through drawing, painting, or sculpting, clients give form to their inner experiences, helping them process difficult emotions in a non-verbal way.

Somatic Art Therapy and Salugenesis

By engaging both the body and mind, Somatic Art Therapy supports the body's transition into salugenesis—the process of healing and cellular repair (see Chapter 7). Physical movement helps to release trauma energy stored in the body, while the act of creation stimulates emotional release. This dual approach allows for deep healing, helping the nervous system move from the Cell Danger Response (CDR) to salugenesis, where restoration and emotional repair occur.

Applications of Somatic Art Therapy

- **Developmental Trauma:** Somatic Art Therapy is particularly effective for individuals who have experienced early trauma and struggle with verbal communication.

- **PTSD:** Clients with Post-Traumatic Stress Disorder (PTSD) can use the creative process to access and release stored trauma in a controlled and expressive manner.

- **Emotional regulation:** Engaging in art-making helps regulate emotions, offering a safe outlet for processing complicated feelings.

Scientific Support

Research on expressive arts therapies shows that combining movement with creative expression can lead to greater emotional release and trauma processing. By engaging the body, mind and soul in the creative process, Somatic Art Therapy provides a holistic approach to trauma recovery.

Key Takeaways

- **Body and creative engagement:** Somatic Art Therapy combines physical movement and art-making to help individuals process trauma.

- **Non-verbal emotional processing:** The therapy offers a non-verbal outlet for emotions, making it ideal for those who struggle with verbalizing trauma.

- **Facilitating salugenesis:** Somatic art therapy combines movement and creative expression to support the body's transition into salugenesis, promoting deep healing and repair.

- **Versatile application:** The therapy is effective for developmental trauma, PTSD, and emotional regulation.

Next Steps

If you are considering Somatic Art Therapy, here's how to get started:

- **Find an expressive arts therapist:** Ensure the therapist is trained in combining somatic movement with creative arts.

- **Practice creative self-expression:** Start experimenting with drawing or movement as a form of self-expression to help prepare for therapy.

- **Combine it with other therapies:** Somatic Art Therapy works well alongside other body-based trauma therapies, such as Somatic Experiencing or EMDR.

- **Engage in regular creative activities:** Continue practicing art-making or movement at home to support emotional release between therapy sessions.

Resources

Find a Somatic Art Therapist. (n.d.). Search for certified therapists who specialize in combining movement with art-making. Retrieved from https://www.arttherapy.org

Elbrecht, C. (n.d.). Sensorimotor art therapy. *Institute for Sensorimotor Art Therapy & School for Initiatic Art Therapy*. Retrieved December 4, 2024, from https://www.sensorimotorarttherapy.com/sensorimotor-art-therapy

Shafir, T., Orkibi, H., Baker, F. A., Gussak, D., & Kaimal, G. (2020). Editorial: The state of the art in creative arts therapies. *Frontiers in Psychology, 11*, 68. https://doi.org/10.3389/fpsyg.2020.00068

26

SANDPLAY THERAPY

Healing Through Symbolic Play

Introduction

Sandplay Therapy is a non-verbal, experiential therapy that allows clients to express and process trauma through symbolic interaction with sand and miniature figures. By creating scenes in a sandbox, clients externalize their inner world and work through unconscious emotions and trauma. Sandplay provides a safe, physical, and symbolic space for healing.

History of Sandplay Therapy

Dora Kalff developed Sandplay Therapy in the 1950s, drawing inspiration from the work of Carl Jung and Margaret Lowenfeld. Kalff integrated Jungian concepts into Lowenfeld's technique, using sand and miniature figures to access the unconscious mind through symbolic imagery. The therapy gained recognition for its ability to facilitate deep psychological healing, offering clients a way to express complex emotions nonverbally. Since its creation, Sandplay Therapy has been used worldwide to help individuals process trauma, grief, and unresolved feelings.

The Science Behind Sandplay Therapy

Sandplay Therapy is based on the idea that the unconscious mind can be accessed and expressed through symbolic play. Trauma often resides in the unconscious, making it difficult to access through traditional talk therapy. By using miniature figures and creating symbolic scenes in the sand, clients can project their inner experiences into a tangible form. This externalization allows for a deeper understanding and processing of trauma.

The tactile nature of sand, combined with the use of symbols, helps clients engage with both the body and mind, facilitating healing on multiple levels. Sandplay activates both the right hemisphere of the brain (responsible for creativity and emotion) and the limbic system, which holds emotional memories.

How Sandplay Therapy Works

In a typical session, the client is provided with a sandbox and a variety of miniature figures representing people, animals, and objects. The therapist encourages the client to use these figures to create scenes in the sand, allowing their unconscious mind to guide the process. The scenes often reflect unresolved emotions, conflicts, or trauma.

The figures and scenes created in the sand represent unconscious feelings and memories, helping clients externalize their inner world. By focusing on symbolic representation, clients can process trauma in a non-verbal way, which can be particularly beneficial for those who find verbal expression difficult.

Sandplay Therapy and Salugenesis

Sandplay Therapy helps the body and mind transition into salugenesis by providing a safe space for emotional expression and release. This emotional release supports the body's transition from the Cell Danger Response (CDR) to salugenesis, facilitating deep emotional and physical healing.

Applications of Sandplay Therapy:

- **Developmental trauma:** Sandplay Therapy is highly effective for individuals who experienced trauma in childhood and may struggle to verbalize their emotions.

- **PTSD:** Clients with Post-Traumatic Stress Disorder benefit from the non-verbal, symbolic processing that Sandplay offers, allowing them to access and release stored trauma.

- **Emotional exploration:** The use of symbols helps individuals explore and make sense of complex emotions in a safe and creative environment.

Scientific Support

Research into non-verbal therapies like Sandplay shows that symbolic interaction can facilitate the release of trauma stored in the body and unconscious mind. The physical and creative aspects of Sandplay allow for a holistic approach to trauma recovery, engaging both the body and the psyche.

Key Takeaways

- **Symbolic engagement:** Sandplay Therapy uses symbolic interaction with miniature figures and sand to help individuals process trauma.

- **Non-verbal emotional processing:** The therapy offers a non-verbal, creative outlet for expressing and resolving unconscious trauma.

- **Facilitating salugenesis:** Sandplay Therapy helps the body transition into salugenesis by engaging in symbolic play and supporting emotional and physical healing.

- **Versatile application:** Sandplay Therapy is effective for developmental trauma, PTSD, and emotional exploration.

Next Steps

If you are considering Sandplay Therapy for trauma recovery, here's how to get started:

- **Find a certified Sandplay therapist:** Ensure the therapist is trained in Sandplay Therapy and has experience working with trauma survivors.

- **Practice symbolic reflection:** Journaling or reflecting on symbols in dreams or everyday life can help prepare for Sandplay sessions.

- **Combine it with other therapies:** Sandplay Therapy can be integrated with other trauma-focused therapies, such as Somatic Experiencing or EMDR, to support comprehensive healing.

- **Explore creative self-care:** Between sessions, continue engaging in creative activities like drawing, painting, or writing to support emotional release.

Resources

Find a certified Sandplay therapist. (n.d.). You can search for certified Sandplay therapists near you using the Sandplay International directory. Retrieved from https://www.sandplay.org/find-therapist/

Sandplay Therapy overview. (n.d.). Learn more about how Sandplay Therapy works and its applications for trauma recovery. Retrieved from https://www.sandplay.org/what-is-sandplay-therapy

Tornero, M. D. L. A., & Capella, C. (2017). Change during psychotherapy through sand play tray in children that have been sexually abused. *Frontiers in Psychology, 8*, 617. https://doi.org/10.3389/fpsyg.2017.00617

27.

HAVENING TECHNIQUES

A Neurobiological Approach to Trauma Healing

Introduction

Havening, developed by Dr. Ronald Ruden, is a psychosensory therapy designed to create lasting change in the brain, particularly for
trauma survivors. It uses touch and pleasant imagery to modify how
the brain processes traumatic memories. This chapter will explore
the mechanisms behind Havening, its real-world applications, its
integration with other therapies, and Self-Havening as a tool for clients to manage trauma symptoms independently.

The Neurobiological Mechanisms of Havening

Havening works by stimulating delta brainwaves through touch,
which promotes neuroplasticity, enabling the brain to reprocess
traumatic memories and reduce their emotional impact. The process
specifically targets the amygdala, the part of the brain responsible
for emotional responses. This technique also engages the parasympathetic nervous system, calming the body's fight-or-flight response.

Havening decouples traumatic memories from their emotional
charge by rewiring the amygdala's response. This results in decreased
anxiety, intrusive thoughts, and hypervigilance in trauma survivors.

The rhythmic touch during Havening generates delta brainwaves, creating an environment where the brain can rewire emotional
responses.

The soothing touch and visualization reduce activation of the hypothalamic-pituitary-adrenal (HPA) axis, lowering cortisol levels and helping the body recover from chronic stress and trauma.

Applications of Havening in Trauma Therapy

Havening has shown efficacy in treating PTSD, phobias, anxiety, and stress-related disorders. Its immediate, body-centred approach enables clients to feel relief from their symptoms, often in just a few sessions.

Integration with Other Bottom-Up Therapies

Havening is a versatile tool that complements other body-based therapies, including Somatic Experiencing, Family Constellation Therapy, and Brainspotting. These therapies, like Havening, aim to address trauma stored in the body and help resolve emotional and physiological symptoms:

- **Somatic Experiencing:** Havening can accelerate the release of stored trauma by settling the nervous system and facilitating neuroplastic changes in how the brain processes emotional responses.

- **Family Constellation Therapy:** Havening's calming effect can help clients during emotionally intense moments in Family Constellation sessions, providing a safe space to process trauma.

- **Brainspotting:** The Havening touch can be used to calm clients during Brainspotting sessions, making it easier for them to access and process deep emotional material.

Self-Havening and Empowering Clients

Self-Havening is a practical tool that allows clients to manage their symptoms outside of therapy. By incorporating Self-Havening into daily life, clients can reduce stress, improve emotional regulation, and promote long-term recovery.

The Self-Havening Process

Self-Havening involves gentle touch applied to the arms, face, or palms, combined with visualization or affirmations. This simple process stimulates delta waves and fosters feelings of safety and calm.

Here's a step-by-step guide:

- **Find a quiet space:** Choose a calm environment without distractions.

- **Focus on a memory or feeling:** Concentrate on a distressing memory or sensation.

- **Apply Havening touch:** Gently stroke your arms, face, or palms in a rhythmic motion.

- **Visualization:** Imagine a safe place, such as a peaceful beach, while continuing the touch.

- **Repeat:** Perform as often as needed to reduce the emotional charge of distressing memories.

The Science of Self-Havening

Self-Havening works by engaging the parasympathetic nervous system, reducing the body's stress response, and promoting feelings of safety. The rhythmic touch also stimulates delta waves, facilitating neuroplastic changes that reduce the emotional intensity of traumatic memories over time (PTSD UK, 2022).

Benefits of Self-Havening for Trauma Recovery

Self-Havening offers several key **benefits:**

- **Empowerment:** It gives clients the tools to manage their trauma responses, fostering a sense of control over their healing process.

- **Immediate stress relief:** Clients can use Self-Havening to reduce anxiety and stress in real-time, whether during a stressful event or afterwards.

- **Long-term emotional regulation:** Regular practice of Self-Havening promotes emotional resilience, helping clients maintain progress between therapy sessions.

Integrating Self-Havening into Daily Life

Self-Havening is easy to incorporate into daily routines. Clients can practice it in the morning to start their day with a sense of calm, during breaks at work to manage stress, or at night to improve sleep quality. Many clients report a noticeable improvement in anxiety levels and overall emotional well-being with regular practice (Truitt, 2022).

Key Takeaways

- Havening uses a soothing touch to promote delta waves and neuroplasticity, reprocessing traumatic memories at a neurobiological level.

- Real-world case studies demonstrate its effectiveness in reducing PTSD, phobias, and anxiety.

- Self-Havening empowers clients by providing a simple, accessible tool for managing trauma responses between therapy sessions.

- Havening integrates well with other bottom-up therapies like Somatic Experiencing and Brainspotting, enhancing the overall trauma recovery process.

Next Steps

For both clients and practitioners, the next steps involve:

- **Training and certification:** Practitioners interested in Havening can pursue formal certification to integrate it into their practice ethically.

- **Client education:** Teaching clients how to practice Self-Havening between sessions empowers them to take control of their healing journey and reduces the likelihood of re-traumatization.

- **Further research:** Continued research on Havening is needed to explore its long-term efficacy across diverse trauma populations.

Resources

Nottingham Trent University. (2022). Nurturing touch technique shown to change brain activity and reduce distress. *Neuroscience News*. Retrieved from https://neurosciencenews.com/touch-therapy-trauma-20178/

PTSD UK. (2022). The Havening technique and PTSD. *PTSD UK*. Retrieved from https://www.ptsduk.org/the-havening-technique-and-ptsd/

Ruden, R. (2010). *When the Past is Always Present: Emotional traumatisation, causes, and cures*. Routledge.

Havening Techniques. (n.d.). *Havening Techniques official website*. Retrieved December 4, 2024, from https://www.havening.org/

Thandi, G., Tom, D., Gould, M., McKenna, P., & Greenberg, N. (2015). Impact of a single-session of Havening. *Health Science Journal, 9*(5), 1–5.

28

HEART RATE VARIABILITY (HRV)

The Window to Your Nervous System

Introduction

Heart Rate Variability (HRV) is a key indicator of the body's autonomic nervous system (ANS) balance. HRV measures the variation in time between each heartbeat and reflects how well the body can adapt to stress. High HRV indicates a flexible, adaptive nervous system, while low HRV suggests the body is stuck in a state of stress, anxiety or dysregulation. Monitoring and improving HRV will provide insight into one's ability to recover from trauma and chronic stress.

History of HRV

HRV was first studied in the 1960s when researchers explored the connection between heartbeat variations and the autonomic nervous system (see Chapter XX). Early studies found that HRV reflected how well the body could respond to, and recover from, stress. Since then, HRV has become widely used in various fields, including psychophysiology, sports science, and trauma recovery, as a method of monitoring emotional regulation, physical resilience, and the health of the nervous system.

The Science Behind HRV

HRV reflects the balance between the sympathetic nervous system (fight-or-flight) and the parasympathetic nervous system (rest-and-digest). The parasympathetic nervous system, controlled by the vagus nerve, plays a crucial role in calming the body and helping it recover from stress. High HRV indicates that the body can effectively switch between sympathetic arousal and parasympathetic relaxation, while low HRV may indicate chronic stress, trauma, or imbalance.

Multiple factors, including breathing patterns, sleep quality, exercise, and emotional states, can influence HRV. Trauma survivors often exhibit low HRV due to prolonged states of hyperarousal or emotional dysregulation.

How HRV Monitoring Works

HRV is typically measured using wearable devices or apps that track the time intervals between heartbeats. The more variability there is in the intervals between heartbeats, the higher the HRV score. Low HRV indicates that the body is in a state of chronic stress, whereas high HRV is a sign of resilience and recovery.

Deep, controlled breathing (such as diaphragmatic breathing) is known to increase HRV by activating the parasympathetic nervous system. HRV biofeedback training helps individuals learn to regulate their heart rate through breathing exercises and trauma-informed mindfulness practices.

HRV and Salugenesis

HRV plays a critical role in the transition to salugenesis (see Chapter 7). A higher HRV indicates that the body has the flexibility to move out of the Cell Danger Response (CDR) and into a state of healing. By improving HRV through practices like breathwork, meditation, and biofeedback, individuals can promote salugenesis and support trauma recovery. A balanced HRV signals that the body is moving away from chronic defence into repair and regeneration.

Applications of HRV

- **Trauma recovery:** Monitoring and improving HRV helps trauma survivors assess their nervous system balance and track their recovery progress.

- **Emotional regulation:** HRV is closely tied to emotional resilience, as higher HRV indicates better emotional regulation.

- **Stress management:** Increasing HRV through breathing exercises and biofeedback can reduce chronic stress and promote overall well-being.

Scientific Support

Research demonstrates that HRV is a reliable measure of the body's ability to manage stress and recover from trauma. Studies show that individuals with higher HRV tend to have better physical and emotional health, while low HRV is linked to chronic stress, depression, and anxiety. HRV biofeedback has been shown to improve emotional regulation and enhance recovery from trauma.

Key Takeaways

- **Measure of nervous system balance:** HRV reflects the balance between the sympathetic and parasympathetic nervous systems, offering insight into stress levels and recovery.

- **HRV and emotional regulation:** Higher HRV indicates better emotional regulation and resilience, while low HRV suggests chronic stress or trauma.

- **Facilitating salugenesis:** By improving HRV through practices like biofeedback and deep breathing, individuals can support the body's transition into salugenesis.

- **Versatile application:** HRV monitoring can be used to track trauma recovery, manage stress, and improve emotional regulation.

Next Steps

If you are interested in using HRV to support trauma recovery, here's how to proceed:

- Start monitoring HRV: Use a wearable device or smartphone app to track your HRV regularly.

- Practice deep breathing exercises: Engage in diaphragmatic breathing or coherence breathing techniques to naturally increase your HRV.

- Consider HRV biofeedback: Biofeedback training can help you regulate your HRV and promote emotional resilience.

- Combine HRV with other therapies: Use HRV monitoring alongside other trauma therapies, such as Somatic Experiencing or EMDR, to track your progress.

Resources

Arakaki, X., Arechavala, R. J., Choy, E. H., Bautista, J., Bliss, B., Molloy, C., Wu, D.-A., Shimojo, S., Jiang, Y., Kleinman, M. T., & Kloner, R. A. (2023). *The connection between heart rate variability (HRV), neurological health, and cognition: A literature review. Frontiers in Neuroscience,* 17, 1055445. https://doi.org/10.3389/fnins.2023.1055445

Goessl, V. C., Curtiss, J. E., & Hofmann, S. G. (2017). *The effect of heart rate variability biofeedback training on stress and anxiety: A meta-analysis. Psychological Medicine,* 47(15), 2578–2586. https://doi.org/10.1017/S0033291717001003

Heart rate variability explained. (n.d.). Learn more about HRV and how it reflects the body's autonomic nervous system balance. Retrieved from https://www.heartmath.org/science/research/heart-rate-variability

29.

FREQUENCY SPECIFIC MICROCURRENT (FSM)

Targeting Cellular Healing

Introduction

Frequency Specific Microcurrent (FSM) is a non-invasive therapy that uses low-level electrical currents to target specific tissues and cells in the body, promoting healing and reducing pain. By delivering microcurrents at specific frequencies, FSM stimulates the body's natural healing processes, helping to address inflammation, trauma, and chronic pain.

History of FSM

FSM was developed in the late 1990s by Dr. Carolyn McMakin, who discovered a list of frequencies that had been used in early 20th-century medicine for various conditions. McMakin refined these frequencies and combined them with modern microcurrent technology, creating FSM as we know it today. Since then, FSM has been widely used for pain management, inflammation reduction, and tissue repair, especially in cases of trauma and chronic pain.

The Science Behind FSM

FSM works by delivering extremely low-level electrical currents—measured in microamperes—through electrodes placed on the skin. These microcurrents mimic the body's own natural electrical signals, which are essential for cell function and communication. By applying specific frequencies to the body, FSM can target different tissues (muscles, nerves, fascia) and conditions (inflammation, trauma, scar tissue).

The frequencies used in FSM are believed to influence cellular activity, increasing **ATP (adenosine triphosphate) production**, improving protein synthesis, and reducing inflammation. This helps speed up tissue repair and relieve pain.

How FSM Works

During an FSM session, a therapist applies electrodes to the skin in areas related to the individual's pain or injury. The therapist then selects specific frequencies depending on the condition being treated. Different frequencies are thought to affect other tissues and conditions, such as nerve pain, muscle inflammation, or scar tissue.

FSM uses customized frequencies to target specific tissues, such as muscles, nerves, or ligaments. By boosting ATP production, FSM enhances cellular repair and energy, facilitating healing in damaged tissues.

FSM and Salugenesis

FSM can support salugenesis (see Chapter 7) by enhancing cellular energy and reducing inflammation. By increasing ATP production, FSM helps the body shift from a state of stress (such as chronic pain or trauma) to one of healing. This promotes salugenesis, enabling the body to recover and regenerate damaged tissues, reduce pain, and restore function.

FSM's ability to address specific tissues makes it a powerful tool for trauma survivors who may have pain, inflammation, or tissue damage resulting from long-term stress or injury.

Applications of FSM

- **Chronic pain:** FSM is widely used for managing chronic pain conditions, such as fibromyalgia, arthritis, and nerve pain.

- **Tissue repair:** FSM enhances tissue repair in injuries, including muscle strains, ligament tears, and post-surgical recovery.

- **Inflammation reduction:** By targeting inflammation at the cellular level, FSM can help reduce swelling and speed up recovery from trauma or injury.

Scientific Support

Research on FSM demonstrates its effectiveness in reducing pain, promoting tissue healing, and improving cellular function. Studies show that FSM can accelerate the healing process by boosting ATP production, reducing inflammation, and improving circulation. FSM is beneficial for conditions that involve chronic inflammation or tissue damage.

Key Takeaways

- **Non-invasive therapy:** FSM uses low-level electrical currents to target specific tissues and promote healing at the cellular level.

- **Customized frequencies:** Different frequencies are used to address specific tissues and conditions, such as pain, inflammation, or injury.

- **Facilitating salugenesis:** FSM enhances ATP production and cellular repair, supporting the body's transition into salugenesis.

- **Versatile application:** FSM is effective for chronic pain, inflammation, tissue repair, and trauma recovery.

Next Steps

If you are considering FSM for trauma recovery or pain management, here's how to proceed:

- **Find a certified FSM practitioner:** Look for a healthcare provider experienced in using FSM for chronic pain, inflammation, or trauma.

- **Consult on treatment areas:** Work with your practitioner to determine the most effective frequencies for your specific condition.

- **Combine FSM with other therapies:** FSM can be used alongside other trauma therapies, such as Somatic Experiencing or EMDR, to enhance recovery.

- **Monitor progress:** Track improvements in pain levels, tissue healing, and inflammation during and after FSM treatment.

Resources

Chaikin, L., Kashiwa, K., Bennet, M., Papastergiou, G., & Gregory, W. (2015). Microcurrent stimulation in the treatment of dry and wet macular degeneration. *Clinical Ophthalmology, 9*, 2345–2353. https://doi.org/10.2147/OPTH.S92296

Frequency-specific microcurrent overview. (n.d.). Learn more about FSM and its applications in pain management and trauma recovery. Retrieved December 4, 2024, from https://frequencyspecific.com

Kolimechkov, S., Seijo, M., Swaine, I., Thirkell, J., Colado, J. C., & Naclerio, F. (2023). Physiological effects of microcurrent and its application for maximising acute responses and chronic adaptations to exercise. *European Journal of Applied Physiology, 123*(2), 451–465. https://doi.org/10.1007/s00421-022-05097-w

30.

TRAUMA AND TEENAGERS

Introduction: The Unique Challenges of Trauma in Adolescence

Adolescence is a critical period of emotional, psychological, and physical development. Teenagers experience significant changes in their hormones, brain function, and identity as they navigate the transition from childhood to adulthood. When trauma occurs during this sensitive phase, its effects can be amplified, disrupting normal development and leading to long-lasting emotional and behavioural consequences.

In this chapter, we will explore how trauma impacts teenagers differently from adults and children, the specific challenges faced by teens in processing trauma, and the most effective therapeutic approaches tailored to support trauma recovery in adolescents.

The Developmental Impact of Trauma on Teenagers

Teenagers are in a state of rapid developmental change, particularly in terms of brain function and emotional regulation. Trauma can severely disrupt this process, leading to difficulties in managing emotions, forming healthy relationships, and navigating the challenges of adolescence.

The Teenage Brain and Trauma

Adolescent brains are still developing, particularly the prefrontal cortex, which is responsible for decision-making, impulse control, and emotional regulation. Trauma affects the prefrontal cortex's ability to function effectively, leaving teenagers more vulnerable to impulsive behaviour, emotional outbursts, and difficulty planning for the future.

The amygdala, the brain's fear centre, is more sensitive during adolescence, making teenagers more prone to heightened fear responses and emotional volatility after trauma. Since the prefrontal cortex is not fully developed until the mid-20s, teenagers may struggle with decision-making and impulse control when dealing with trauma, leading to risky behaviours such as substance use, self-harm, or recklessness.

Hormonal Changes and Emotional Dysregulation

Hormonal fluctuations during adolescence play a significant role in shaping teenagers' emotional experiences. Trauma can exacerbate these fluctuations, leading to increased emotional dysregulation, anxiety, and mood swings.

The Role of Hormones in Teenagers

- **Estrogen and progesterone in teenage girls:** Fluctuations in estrogen and progesterone can heighten emotional sensitivity and mood instability in teenage girls. Trauma during adolescence may amplify symptoms of anxiety, depression, and emotional dysregulation, especially during hormonal shifts in the menstrual cycle.

- **Testosterone in teenage boys:** Testosterone influences aggression, mood regulation, and risk-taking behaviours in boys. After trauma, teenage boys may exhibit increased irritability, anger, and a tendency toward externalizing behaviours like aggression or substance abuse as a way of coping with unresolved emotional pain.

Social and Identity Development

The development of identity and social connections marks the teenage years. Trauma can disrupt these processes, making it difficult for teens to form a stable sense of self and healthy relationships with peers.

Peer Relationships and Social Support

Trauma survivors may feel isolated from their peers or pressured to conform to certain behaviours that contradict their emotional needs. Peer pressure, bullying, or exclusion can worsen the effects of trauma, leading to low self-esteem and social withdrawal.

Adolescence is a critical period for developing a personal identity. Trauma can fragment a teenager's sense of self, making it difficult to establish a clear identity and increasing the risk of self-esteem issues and identity confusion.

Behavioural Challenges After Trauma

Teenagers often express trauma through behavioural changes, which can be misinterpreted as typical teenage rebellion or moodiness. However, trauma-related behaviours should be recognized and addressed as part of the healing process.

Common Behavioural Responses to Trauma in Teens

- **Risky behaviours:** Trauma can lead to an increase in risk-taking behaviours such as substance use, promiscuity, and reckless actions. These behaviours often serve as coping mechanisms for the emotional distress caused by trauma.

- **Self-harm and eating disorders:** Teenagers may engage in self-harming behaviours, such as cutting themselves or restrictive eating, as a way to regain control over their emotions or body after experiencing trauma. These behaviours often signal deeper emotional pain and the need for skilled intervention.

- **Academic decline:** Trauma can impact a teenager's ability to focus, concentrate, and retain information, leading to poor academic performance or a sudden drop in grades. This decline in school performance is often a sign that the teen is struggling to cope with unresolved trauma.

Trauma-Informed Approaches for Teenagers

Given the unique developmental and emotional challenges faced by teenagers, trauma treatment must be tailored to their specific needs. Therapeutic approaches for teens should incorporate emotional regulation, body-based therapies, and support for identity and relationship development.

Two bottom-up therapies are particularly effective for teenagers:

- **Somatic Experiencing (SE):** SE helps teenagers reconnect with their bodies, release stored trauma, and develop a sense of safety in the present moment. This is particularly important for teens who may feel disconnected from their emotions or overwhelmed by their physical reactions to trauma.

- **Trauma Releasing Exercises (TRE):** TRE can help teenagers discharge pent-up tension and energy caused by trauma, allowing them to process emotions in a controlled and safe way.

Creative and expressive therapies that work with teenagers include:

- **Art and music therapy:** Many teenagers find it difficult to express their emotions verbally, especially when it comes to trauma. Art and music therapy provides a non-verbal outlet for teens to explore and process their feelings through creative expression.

- **Clay Field Therapy:** Clay Field Therapy can help teenagers process trauma through sensory and motor engagement (see Chapter 25). This hands-on approach allows teens to express their trauma in a physical form, promoting emotional release and self-understanding.

For identity and relationship support, therapies include:

- **Family Constellation Therapy:** Family dynamics often play a significant role in how trauma is experienced and processed by teenagers (for more on Family Constellation Therapy, see Chapter 20). Family Constellation Therapy helps address generational trauma and relationship challenges, providing teens with a deeper understanding of their place within the family system.

- **Equine-Assisted Therapy:** Equine therapy helps teenagers develop emotional regulation skills and build trust through interactions with horses (for more on Equine-Assisted Therapy, see Chapter 24). This non-verbal form of treatment is particularly effective for teens who struggle with communication and trust in relationships.

For cognitive and emotional support, the following can be helpful for teenagers:

- **EMDR:** Eye Movement Desensitization and Reprocessing (EMDR) can help teenagers reprocess traumatic memories, reducing the emotional intensity of these memories and allowing them to move forward without being overwhelmed by the past. (For more on EMDR, see Chapter 13)

- **Emotional Freedom Techniques (EFT):** EFT taps into acupressure points, a helpful tool for teenagers to manage anxiety, reduce emotional distress, and create a sense of emotional control (see Chapter 13).

- **Mindfulness-Based Stress Reduction (MBSR):** Teaching teenagers trauma-informed mindfulness practices, such as breathing exercises and body scanning, will help them develop emotional awareness and regulate their stress responses.

Building Resilience in Teenagers After Trauma

Helping teenagers build resilience after trauma is critical for their long-term recovery and emotional well-being. Resilience-building strategies should focus on fostering emotional regulation, enhancing social support, and promoting a positive self-identity.

To help teenagers build resilience, help them build strong peer support networks and provide opportunities for positive social engagement. This can help teenagers feel connected and supported in their healing process.

Mentorship programs that focus on teenagers allow them to build trusting relationships with supportive adults, so developing a sense of safety and belonging.

Key Takeaways

- Trauma during adolescence can severely disrupt emotional regulation, identity development, and relationships, making this a critical period for intervention.

- Hormonal changes, peer pressure, and identity formation add layers of complexity to trauma recovery for teenagers.

- Bottom-up therapies, such as Somatic Experiencing (SE) and Trauma Releasing Exercises (TRE), and creative therapies like art and music therapy, are highly effective for teenagers.

- Building resilience through mindfulness, social support, and emotional regulation is essential for helping teens navigate trauma and recover fully.

Resources

Blakemore, S. J., & Mills, K. L. (2014). "Is adolescence a sensitive period for sociocultural processing?" *Annual Review of Psychology, 65,* 187-207. https://doi.org/10.1146/annurev-psych-010213-115202

Cicchetti, D., & Toth, S. L. (2005). "Child maltreatment." *Annual Review of Clinical Psychology, 1,* 409-438. https://doi.org/10.1146/annurev.clinpsy.1.102803.144029

Felitti, V. J., & Anda, R. F. (1998). "The Adverse Childhood Experiences (ACE) Study: Relationship of childhood abuse and household dysfunction to many of the leading causes of death in adults." *American Journal of Preventive Medicine, 14*(4), 245-258. https://doi.org/10.1016/S0749-3797(98)00017-8

Porges, S. W. (2011). *The Polyvagal Theory: Neurophysiological foundations of emotions, attachment, communication, and self-regulation.* W. W. Norton & Company.

Spear, L. P. (2000). "The adolescent brain and age-related behavioral manifestations." *Neuroscience & Biobehavioral Reviews, 24*(4), 417-463. https://doi.org/10.1016/S0149-7634(00)00014-2

Steinberg, L. (2005). "Cognitive and affective development in adolescence." *Trends in Cognitive Sciences, 9*(2), 69-74. https://doi.org/10.1016/j.tics.2004.12.005

31.

GENDER DIFFERENCES IN TRAUMA RESPONSE

Introduction: How Gender Influences Trauma Reactions

Gender plays a significant role in how individuals experience and respond to trauma. Men and women often have different emotional, psychological, and physiological reactions to traumatic events, and these differences influence the course of recovery. Biological factors, such as hormone levels, as well as cultural expectations, contribute to how trauma is processed and expressed by males and females.

This chapter explores the distinct ways trauma affects men and women, focusing on the hormonal, psychological, and societal factors that contribute to gender differences in trauma response. We will also discuss gender-specific treatment approaches that can help address these distinct needs, while emphasizing that bottom-up therapy remains effective across all genders.

Hormonal Differences and Trauma Responses

Hormones play a crucial role in regulating the body's stress response, and the differences in male and female hormone levels can lead to varying reactions to trauma. The interplay between estrogen, progesterone, and testosterone significantly impacts how men and women cope with and recover from traumatic experiences.

The Role of Estrogen and Progesterone in Women

Estrogen helps regulate mood and emotional stability by influencing neurotransmitters like serotonin and dopamine. After a traumatic event, estrogen can have a protective effect by reducing the intensity of the stress response. However, during times of hormonal fluctuations, such as menstruation, pregnancy, or menopause, women may become more vulnerable to emotional distress and PTSD symptoms due to lower levels of estrogen.

Progesterone has a calming effect on the brain and nervous system. Low levels of progesterone, which can occur during times of high stress, can lead to increased anxiety, irritability, and difficulty sleeping, further complicating trauma recovery in women.

The Role of Testosterone in Men

Testosterone is often associated with aggression and dominant behaviour, but it also plays a role in regulating mood and emotional resilience. In men, trauma can lead to a reduction in testosterone levels, which may result in symptoms such as depression, fatigue, and emotional withdrawal. Low testosterone levels are also linked to increased irritability and difficulties in emotional regulation following trauma.

Psychological and Emotional Differences in Trauma Processing

Men and women often process and express their emotions differently, which influences how they experience and recover from trauma. Cultural expectations around gender roles, emotional expression, and perceived vulnerability can impact how trauma is dealt with, and the likelihood of seeking help.

Emotional Expression in Women

Women are generally more encouraged to express emotions and seek social support, which can be beneficial for processing trauma. As a result, women may be more likely to experience **internalizing symptoms** of trauma, such as anxiety, depression, and self-blame.

Women tend to ruminate on traumatic experiences, repeatedly thinking about the event and its emotional impact. While this can help with emotional processing, excessive rumination can increase the risk of developing PTSD or depression.

Emotional Expression in Men

Cultural norms often discourage men from expressing vulnerability, which can make it harder for them to process emotions after trauma. Men may be more likely to engage in **externalizing behaviours**, such as aggression, substance use, or risky behaviours, as a way to cope with emotional pain.

Men are also more likely to suppress or avoid their emotions, which can lead to delayed processing of trauma and an increased risk of developing self-destructive behaviours, including addiction and anger-management issues.

Gender-Specific Trauma Reactions and PTSD Prevalence

While both men and women can develop PTSD after experiencing trauma, studies have shown that women are twice as likely to develop it than men. This gender difference is partly due to the types of trauma experienced, and the coping mechanisms employed.

Trauma Types and PTSD Risk

Women are more likely to experience sexual trauma, which has a higher risk of leading to PTSD than other forms of trauma. The emotional and psychological impacts of sexual violence are profound, often leading to feelings of shame, guilt, and fear, which can contribute to the development of PTSD.

Men, on the other hand, are more likely to experience physical violence and combat-related trauma. While these types of trauma can also lead to PTSD, men may be less likely to report their symptoms or seek help due to societal expectations of masculinity.

PTSD Symptom Presentation

Women with PTSD are more likely to experience symptoms such as hyperarousal, anxiety, and depression. They may also be more prone to developing co-occurring conditions like eating disorders or somatic complaints (physical symptoms without a medical cause).

Men with PTSD are more likely to exhibit symptoms of emotional numbing, aggression, and substance abuse. They may struggle with anger, irritability, and difficulty forming close relationships as a result of their trauma.

Gender Differences in Trauma Treatment and Recovery

While men and women may experience trauma differently, the core principles of trauma treatment are essentially the same for both genders. Brainspotting, Eye Movement Desensitization and Reprocessing (EMDR), Clay Field Therapy, Family Constellation Therapy, Emotional Freedom Techniques (EFT), Trauma Releasing Exercises (TRE), and Equine-Assisted Somatic Therapies are all very effective—regardless of gender.

The key to successful trauma treatment lies in adopting a bottom-up approach, which focuses on addressing trauma stored in the *body* rather than relying on *cognitive* (top-down) methods. Bottom-up therapies help regulate the nervous system and release stored trauma, making them the best choice for trauma recovery in both men and women.

Notably, group therapy is not part of the treatment model, as all therapy work is individualised and private.

Trauma Treatment for Both Genders

- **Brainspotting and EMDR:** Both therapies are highly effective for processing traumatic memories and reducing symptoms like anxiety, depression, and intrusive thoughts. They help access and resolve trauma stored deep within the brain, making them applicable to any gender.

- **Somatic Therapies:** Approaches like Somatic Experiencing (SE) and Trauma Releasing Exercises (TRE) are ideal for helping individuals release trauma stored in the body. These therapies help regulate the nervous system, reduce physical tension, and promote emotional regulation. Whether the client is male or female, somatic therapies provide a pathway to healing by reconnecting with the body and restoring balance.

- **Equine-Assisted Somatic Therapy:** Equine therapy offers a non-verbal approach to processing trauma through interactions with horses. The horses provide feedback based on the individual's emotional state. This therapy helps both men and women reconnect with their emotions in a safe and supportive environment.

- **Clay Field and Family Constellation Therapy:** These therapies address more profound relational and generational trauma, helping to process emotional wounds that may span multiple generations. They are equally effective for men and women, providing profound insights and healing at the family and systemic levels.

- **Emotional Freedom Techniques (EFT):** EFT, or "tapping", focuses on using specific acupressure points to release emotional blockages. This technique is effective for managing trauma-related anxiety, stress, and emotional dysregulation in both men and women.

Bottom-Up Therapy for Trauma Recovery

Bottom-up therapy is always the preferred approach for trauma recovery, regardless of gender. By focusing on how the body holds trauma, these therapies help survivors gradually release stored tension, process difficult emotions, and restore a sense of safety and comfort in the body. This method allows for deeper and more sustainable healing compared to traditional cognitive-based therapies (top-down approaches), which often bypass the somatic aspects of trauma.

No Group Work

Trauma treatment is individualised, and no group work is incorporated into these therapeutic approaches. Each session is private, ensuring that both men and women receive tailored, one-on-one support that addresses their unique trauma and emotional needs.

Hormonal Support for Trauma Recovery

Given the role of hormones in regulating emotional responses to trauma, incorporating hormonal support into trauma treatment can be beneficial for both men and women. Hormone imbalances caused by trauma can be addressed through lifestyle changes, supplementation, and integrative therapies.

Estrogen and progesterone in women can be supported with:

- **Adaptogenic herbs:** Adaptogens such as ashwagandha and rhodiola can help regulate cortisol and support hormonal balance in women, reducing the intensity of trauma symptoms during hormonal fluctuations.

- **Magnesium and vitamin B6:** These nutrients are essential for supporting progesterone levels and promoting relaxation, helping women manage anxiety and mood swings related to trauma.

Testosterone in men can be supported with:

- **Zinc:** Zinc plays a crucial role in testosterone production and can help improve mood, energy levels, and emotional resilience in men recovering from trauma.

- **Exercise:** Regular physical activity boosts testosterone levels, improves mood, and provides a healthy outlet for emotional tension.

Key Takeaways

- Hormonal differences between men and women significantly influence how they experience and recover from trauma.

- Women are more likely to experience internalizing symptoms, such as anxiety and depression, while men are more prone to externalizing behaviours like aggression and substance use.

- Gender-specific treatment approaches, including somatic therapies and emotional regulation techniques, can improve trauma recovery outcomes.

- Hormonal support through nutrition, lifestyle changes, and supplementation can help regulate the stress response and promote healing in both men and women.

Resources

Davis, E. P., & Pfaff, D. (2014). "Sexually dimorphic responses to early adversity: Implications for affective problems and autism spectrum disorder." *Psychoneuroendocrinology, 49*, 11–25. https://doi.org/10.1016/j.psyneuen.2014.06.014

Felitti, V. J., & Anda, R. F. (1998). The adverse childhood experiences (ACE) study: Relationship of childhood abuse and household dysfunction to many of the leading causes of death in adults. *American Journal of Preventive Medicine, 14*(4), 245-258. https://doi.org/10.1016/S0749-3797(98)00017-8

Porges, S. W. (2011). *The Polyvagal Theory: Neurophysiological foundations of emotions, attachment, communication, and self-regulation.* W. W. Norton & Company.

Schore, A. N. (2003). *Affect Regulation and the Repair of the Self.* W. W. Norton & Company.

Van der Kolk, B. A. (2015). *The Body Keeps the Score: Brain, mind, and body in the healing of trauma.* Penguin Books.

Wager, T. D., & Atlas, L. Y. (2015). The neuroscience of placebo effects: Connecting context, learning and health. *Nature Reviews Neuroscience, 16*(7), 403-418. https://doi.org/10.1038/nrn3976

Yehuda, R., Halligan, S. L., & Grossman, R. (2001). Childhood trauma and risk for PTSD: Relationship to intergenerational effects of trauma, parental PTSD, and cortisol excretion. *Development and Psychopathology, 13*(3), 733-753. https://doi.org/10.1017/S0954579401003170

32.

THE ROLE OF THE CENTRAL NERVOUS SYSTEM IN MUSCLE TIGHTENING

Musculoskeletal Health & Lactate Metabolism

Introduction: The Musculoskeletal System and Trauma

The musculoskeletal system plays a crucial role in trauma recovery. When trauma occurs, the body responds not only with emotional and psychological distress but also with physical tension, particularly in the muscles. For individuals with Post-Traumatic Stress Disorder (PTSD), chronic muscle tension can become a persistent issue, contributing to pain, stiffness, and even reduced mobility.

This chapter explores the relationship between trauma, the musculoskeletal system, and how the body metabolizes lactate. We will also examine how the central nervous system (CNS) contributes to muscle tightening, and how these processes impact trauma survivors.

The Role of the Musculoskeletal System in Trauma

When the body is exposed to stress or trauma, the musculoskeletal system responds with increased tension in order to protect itself. This response is driven by the "fight, flight, or freeze" mechanism, where the CNS signals muscles to contract in preparation for action.

However, for people with PTSD, this protective mechanism can remain activated long after the trauma has passed. Chronic tension, especially in areas like the neck, shoulders, and lower back, can be-

213

come a lasting symptom of trauma, leading to muscular pain, limited range of motion, and postural imbalances.

Central Nervous System and Muscle Tightening

The central nervous system (CNS), composed of the brain and spinal cord, plays a significant role in regulating muscle tone and tension. In response to perceived threats, the CNS activates the sympathetic nervous system, which causes muscles to contract, preparing the body for action.

In individuals with PTSD, the CNS can become overactive, leading to continuous muscle contraction, even in the absence of an immediate threat. This "muscle guarding" is a defence mechanism designed to protect the body. Still, when it becomes chronic, it leads to tight, painful muscles and contributes to conditions like **myofascial pain syndrome** and **chronic tension**.

The amygdala, the brain's "fear centre", is responsible for detecting danger and activating the body's stress response. In trauma survivors, an overactive amygdala constantly signals the CNS to keep muscles tense, contributing to chronic pain and stiffness.

The body has a "muscle memory", meaning that it can store the physical imprint of trauma. This is why people with PTSD often report feeling pain or tightness in their bodies *long* after the trauma has occurred.

Lactate Metabolism and Muscle Function

Lactate (or lactic acid) is a byproduct of anaerobic metabolism, which occurs when muscles work harder than the available oxygen can support. During intense exercise or periods of stress, the body produces lactate as a temporary energy source. In trauma survivors, prolonged muscle tension and stress can lead to an accumulation of lactate in the muscles, causing stiffness, soreness, and fatigue.

Lactate builds up in the muscles when the body switches from aerobic to anaerobic energy production, typically during periods of intense physical or emotional stress. This can result in muscle soreness and a feeling of heaviness or fatigue, especially in people with PTSD who experience chronic muscle tension.

Normally, the body clears lactate through the liver and converts it back into usable energy. However, in trauma survivors who may experience ongoing muscle tension and stress, the clearance process can be impaired, leading to higher levels of lactate and prolonged discomfort.

The Connection Between Lactate and the CNS

Lactate affects muscle function and has a direct impact on the CNS. Recent research shows that it can act as a signalling molecule in the brain, influencing mood, cognition, and the body's stress response.

Lactate has been found to promote neuroplasticity, the brain's ability to adapt and form new connections. This is crucial for trauma recovery, as neuroplasticity helps rewire the brain in response to therapy. However, excessive lactate buildup in the muscles can send distress signals to the CNS, exacerbating the stress response and further tightening muscles.

According to this hypothesis, lactate is shuttled between cells as an energy source, including brain cells. In trauma survivors, the high demand for energy during periods of stress can lead to imbalances in lactate metabolism, affecting both physical and emotional states.

The Impact of Trauma on Posture and Movement Patterns

Chronic muscle tension caused by CNS overactivity and impaired lactate metabolism can lead to postural imbalances. Trauma survivors often develop compensatory movement patterns, which involve tightening specific muscles while underusing others.

Individuals with PTSD may develop a hunched posture, tight shoulders, and forward head position as a result of chronic tension in the upper body. Over time, these postural imbalances can lead to musculoskeletal issues such as lower back pain, neck stiffness, and joint dysfunction.

Somatic therapies, trauma-informed yoga, and physical therapy can help restore balanced movement patterns, reduce muscle tension, and address such postural imbalances caused by trauma. These approaches encourage body awareness and help survivors release tension stored in the muscles.

Recovery Approaches for Musculoskeletal Health

Healing the musculoskeletal system after trauma involves a combination of physical therapies, nutritional support, and relaxation techniques that address both the body and CNS:

- **Somatic Therapy:** This therapeutic approach focuses on the connection between mind and body, helping trauma survivors release muscle tension by becoming more aware of their physical sensations.

- **Breathwork and Body Scanning:** These techniques help regulate the CNS and reduce muscle tension by promoting relaxation and mindfulness.

- **Nutritional support:** A diet rich in magnesium, potassium, and antioxidants can help reduce muscle tightness and support lactate clearance, aiding in recovery from chronic muscle tension.

- **Exercise and movement:** Gentle, restorative exercises like yoga or stretching help release muscle tension, improve posture, and reduce the buildup of lactate.

Trauma, Fascia, and Myofascial Release

In addition to muscles, trauma can also be stored in the body's fascia—a network of connective tissue that surrounds and supports muscles, organs, and other structures. Fascia is not merely a passive tissue; it is dynamic and plays an active role in the body's movement, posture, and response to stress. When trauma occurs—whether physical or emotional—the body often reacts by tightening or bracing, which can lead to restrictions and adhesions in the fascia.

Fascia holds tension and trauma in a similar way to muscles, and over time, this tension can become chronic, limiting mobility and contributing to pain. For trauma survivors, fascial restrictions may manifest as tightness, stiffness, and discomfort, particularly in areas like the neck, shoulders, and lower back. These patterns of fascial holding can also affect posture, leading to compensatory movement patterns that further perpetuate tension.

The Role of Myofascial Release in Trauma Recovery

Myofascial release and other body-based therapies, such as Somatic Experiencing, are key to addressing these fascial restrictions. By applying gentle, sustained pressure to areas of fascial tightness, these therapies can help release the stored tension and "unwind" the patterns of holding that are created by trauma. This process not only improves physical flexibility and reduces pain, but also allows for the emotional release of trauma that has been held in the body.

By freeing the fascia, the body can return to a more relaxed, balanced state, which in turn will help calm the nervous system. This release of physical tension often coincides with emotional and psychological relief, as the body and mind are deeply interconnected in the way they process and store traumatic experiences.

Key Takeaways

- Trauma affects the musculoskeletal system by increasing muscle tension through CNS overactivation, leading to chronic tightness and pain.

- Trauma can also be held in the fascia, the body's connective tissue, which stores physical and emotional tension. Releasing fascial restrictions through therapies like myofascial release can help relieve both physical and emotional trauma.

- Lactate metabolism plays a critical role in muscle function, and imbalances in lactate can contribute to physical and emotional stress in trauma survivors.

- Restoring balance in the musculoskeletal system requires a combination of somatic therapies, gentle movement, breathwork, and nutritional support to address both physical tension and CNS regulation.

References

Brooks, G. A. (2009). Cell-cell and intracellular lactate shuttles. *The Journal of Physiology, 587*(Pt 23), 5591-5600.

Clauw, D. J. (2014). Fibromyalgia: A clinical review. *JAMA, 311*(15), 1547-1555. https://doi.org/10.1001/jama.2014.3266

Holloszy, J. O., & Coyle, E. F. (1984). Adaptations of skeletal muscle to endurance exercise and their metabolic consequences. *Journal of Applied Physiology, 56*(4), 831-838. https://doi.org/10.1152/jappl.1984.56.4.831

Levine, P. (1997). *Waking the Tiger: Healing trauma.* North Atlantic Books.

Naviaux, R. K. (2014). Metabolic features of the cell danger response. *Mitochondrion, 16*, 7-17. This paper provides a foundational understanding of the Cell Danger Response (CDR), exploring how metabolic processes like lactate production are altered in response to trauma. https://doi.org/10.1016/j.mito.2013.08.006

Porges, S. W. (2011). *The Polyvagal Theory: Neurophysiological foundations of emotions, attachment, communication, and self-regulation.* W. W. Norton & Company.

Schleip, R. (2003). Fascial plasticity – A new neurobiological explanation: Part 1. *Journal of Bodywork and Movement Therapies, 7*(1), 11–19. https://doi.org/10.1016/S1360-8592(02)00067-0

33.

HARNESSING THE POWER OF HEAT AND COLD

Shock Proteins and the Cell Danger Response

Introduction

The body's response to trauma, stress, and cellular damage is intricately connected to the mechanisms of the Cell Danger Response (CDR), which halts normal cellular processes to focus on survival (see Chapter 3). One way that cells can recover from this danger state is through the activation of shock proteins, which are crucial in supporting cellular repair and recovery.

Heat shock proteins (HSPs) and cold shock proteins (CSPs) are molecular chaperones produced by the body in response to temperature changes. They play an important role in protecting cells under stress. Their impact on CDR resolution and overall healing offers new pathways for trauma recovery, leveraging natural temperature-based therapies to help shift the body from a defence state to one of repair and balance.

Heat Shock Proteins (HSPs)

Heat shock proteins (HSPs) are a group of proteins that protect cells from various forms of stress, including heat, toxins, and physical damage. First discovered in fruit flies subjected to high temperatures, HSPs are now known to play a critical role in stabilizing proteins and repairing damaged ones.

The most well-known types of HSPs are:

- **HSP70:** Involved in protein folding and protecting cells from apoptosis (cell death).

- **HSP90:** Stabilizes key proteins involved in cell cycle control and signalling.

- **HSP27:** Helps reduce oxidative stress and inflammation.

Mechanisms of Action

HSPs are vital in protecting cellular structures, particularly mitochondria, from stress-induced damage. By assisting in the folding of damaged proteins and preventing the aggregation of misfolded proteins, they help maintain cellular integrity. This is crucial for the resolution of the CDR, as a breakdown in protein function prolongs cellular stress signals and delays recovery.

Therapeutic Implications

HSPs can be stimulated through exposure to heat therapies, such as saunas, hyperthermia treatments, and hot baths. Studies suggest that repeated heat exposure can increase HSP production, leading to enhanced cellular resilience, improved protein repair, and the potential for faster recovery from stress and trauma-related conditions.

Cold Shock Proteins (CSPs)

Cold shock proteins are less studied but equally important in cellular protection. They are produced when the body is exposed to cold environments, and they help cells cope with temperature-induced stress by regulating metabolism, reducing inflammation, and promoting cellular repair.

The most well-known types of CSPs are:

- **RBM3 (RNA-binding motif protein 3):** Protects neurons during cold exposure, promoting synaptic plasticity and cognitive function.

- **CIRBP (Cold-inducible RNA-binding protein)**: Plays a role in reducing inflammation and protecting cells from damage during cold stress.

Mechanisms of Action

Cold shock proteins help prevent excessive apoptosis and improve mitochondrial function. By stabilizing RNA and proteins during cold exposure, CSPs protect neural and muscle tissue, which is particularly beneficial for trauma recovery. This ability to maintain cellular homeostasis supports CDR resolution by allowing cells to shift from a defensive state to one focused on repair and recovery.

Therapeutic Implications

Cold therapy has been used in various forms, such as cryotherapy, cold plunges, and ice baths. These therapies activate CSPs, which in turn reduce oxidative stress, lower inflammation, and promote synaptic resilience. Emerging evidence suggests that cold therapy may have profound effects on mental health, improving mood regulation and aiding trauma recovery.

The Connection Between Shock Proteins and the CDR

Heat and Cold Shock Proteins as Regulators of the Cell Danger Response

Both heat and cold shock proteins play pivotal roles in regulating the CDR by interacting with mitochondria, which are central to the cell's energy production and survival mechanisms. When the CDR is activated, cells enter a state of reduced function to survive. Shock proteins help these cells recover by reducing cellular stress, assisting with protein folding, and stabilizing mitochondrial function, allowing for a more rapid return to regular cellular activity.

Shock Proteins and the Immune System

HSPs and CSPs significantly impact immune modulation. They help reduce chronic inflammation by promoting cellular repair and protecting immune cells from damage. This is crucial for trauma survivors, as prolonged inflammation can perpetuate the CDR.

By enhancing immune tolerance and preventing unnecessary immune activation, shock proteins help bring the body back into balance.

Modulation of Shock Proteins for Trauma Recovery

When incorporated into trauma recovery protocols, therapies that promote HSP and CSP production—such as sauna sessions or cryotherapy—can help reset the CDR and accelerate the healing process. Shock protein activation enhances the body's ability to repair tissue, improve cognitive function, and regulate mood, making it a necessary adjunct therapy for those recovering from trauma.

Clinical Applications and Research

Evidence from Clinical Studies

Research indicates that heat and cold exposure therapies can significantly benefit trauma survivors by enhancing shock protein production, which helps regulate the CDR. Saunas and cryotherapy have shown promise in reducing PTSD symptoms, improving mood, and lowering inflammation, all of which are very important for trauma recovery.

Potential Therapeutic Protocols

Combining heat and cold therapies—such as alternating between saunas and cold plunges (contrast therapy)—may maximize the benefits of HSP and CSP activation. These protocols could work synergistically with other treatments like Frequency Specific Microcurrent (FSM) or Hyperbaric Oxygen Therapy (HBOT) to enhance cellular recovery and CDR resolution.

Key Takeaways

- Heat and cold shock proteins offer a powerful natural mechanism for enhancing cellular resilience and supporting the resolution of the Cell Danger Response.

- Integrating heat and cold therapies into trauma recovery programs provides a novel, non-invasive approach to improving mental and physical health, offering new hope for those impacted by trauma and chronic stress.

- Further research is warranted, but current evidence points to shock proteins as major players in unlocking the body's capacity for healing and recovery.

References

Esperland, D., de Weerd, L., & Mercer, J. B. (2022). Health effects of voluntary exposure to cold water: A continuing subject of debate. *Scandinavian Journal of Trauma, Resuscitation and Emergency Medicine*, 30(1), Article 2111789. https://pubmed.ncbi.nlm.nih.gov/36137565/

Lyman, M., Lloyd, D. G., Ji, X., & Vizcaychipi, M. P. (2018). Neuroinflammation: The role and consequences. *Neuroscience Research*, 133, 4–21. Available at: https://pmc.ncbi.nlm.nih.gov/articles/PMC6278532/

Singh, M. K., Shin, Y., Ju, S., Han, S., Choe, W., Yoon, K.-S., Kim, S. S., & Kang, I. (2023). Heat shock response and heat shock proteins: Current understanding and future opportunities in human diseases. *Frontiers in Cell and Developmental Biology*, 11, Article 11050489. https://pubmed.ncbi.nlm.nih.gov/38673794/

34

THE VAGUS NERVE AND THE CELL DANGER RESPONSE

Introduction

The vagus nerve, the longest cranial nerve in the body, plays a central role in the parasympathetic nervous system and is responsible for regulating the "rest-and-digest" functions. This nerve connects the brain to key organs such as the heart, lungs, and digestive system, making it an essential element in the body's ability to recover after a stressful or traumatic event. The vagus nerve also plays an integral role in deactivating the Cell Danger Response (CDR), a biological process triggered by trauma and stress to protect the body. When vagal function is compromised, the CDR remains activated, preventing the body from fully recovering from trauma.

Understanding and supporting vagal function is, therefore, critical in trauma recovery therapies.

The Vagus Nerve: Anatomy and Physiology

- **Structure:** The vagus nerve has two main branches: the ventral vagal complex, which promotes social engagement and calmness, and the dorsal vagal complex, which can trigger immobilization, or a "freeze" response, when the body perceives danger.

- **Functions:** This nerve influences heart rate, digestion, and inflammatory responses and regulates the immune system. Its role in maintaining homeostasis makes it critical in transitioning the body from a state of stress back to balance.

- **Vagal tone:** Vagal tone reflects the activity and health of the vagus nerve. A higher vagal tone indicates better stress resilience and faster recovery from trauma, whereas a lower vagal tone is often seen in individuals suffering from anxiety, depression, and PTSD.

Heart Rate Variability (HRV) as a Marker of Vagal Tone

HRV refers to the variation in time between heartbeats and is a key indicator of vagal tone. Higher HRV signifies better parasympathetic control and resilience, while lower HRV suggests chronic stress and vagal dysfunction. (For more on HRV, see Chapter 29.)

Trauma survivors often exhibit reduced HRV, reflecting diminished vagal tone and an impaired ability to regulate stress. HRV monitoring can, therefore, provide insights into the state of the nervous system and the body's ability to recover from trauma.

By monitoring HRV, therapists can track the effectiveness of interventions aimed at improving vagal tone, such as breathwork, neurofeedback, and vagus nerve stimulation techniques.

Polyvagal Theory

Developed by Dr. Stephen Porges, Polyvagal Theory explains how the vagus nerve governs three different physiological states: the social engagement state (ventral vagal), the fight/flight state (sympathetic nervous system), and the freeze state (dorsal vagal). Understanding how these states are activated can help explain the wide range of trauma responses.

Trauma dysregulates the autonomic nervous system, keeping individuals stuck in defensive states (fight, flight or freeze). Polyvagal Theory helps therapists understand how to move trauma survivors from defensive states back to safety, using the vagus nerve to restore balance.

The Vagus Nerve, Trauma, and the Cell Danger Response (CDR)

Trauma disrupts normal vagal function, preventing the body from shutting down the Cell Danger Response (CDR) and returning to a state of rest. This prolonged activation leads to chronic stress, inflammation, and various physical and emotional symptoms. The vagus nerve plays a key role in turning off the CDR, allowing the body to recover.

Trauma survivors often experience compromised immune function, leading to conditions such as chronic inflammation, autoimmune disorders, and gut dysfunction. This is due to the vagus nerve's role in regulating immune responses, which becomes impaired during trauma.

A healthy vagal tone is essential for deactivating the CDR. When the vagal tone is diminished, the body remains in a defensive state, preventing recovery from trauma and prolonging symptoms of anxiety, depression, and chronic illness.

Therapeutic Interventions Targeting the Vagus Nerve

- **Vagus Nerve Stimulation (VNS):** VNS is a technique that uses electrical impulses to stimulate the vagus nerve, promoting parasympathetic activity. VNS has been shown to improve symptoms of PTSD, anxiety, and depression by increasing vagal tone and helping the body transition out of the CDR.

- **Breathwork:** Controlled breathing exercises, such as diaphragmatic breathing or alternate nostril breathing, activate the vagus nerve, helping to reduce stress and improve vagal tone. Regular breathwork can help trauma survivors calm their nervous system and facilitate recovery.

- **Cold Exposure Therapy:** Cold exposure, such as cold showers or ice baths, stimulates the vagus nerve and increases vagal tone. By triggering the body's parasympathetic response, cold exposure can help deactivate the CDR and promote healing.

- **Neuroacoustic Sound Therapy:** Neuroacoustic Sound Therapy uses specific sound frequencies to influence brainwave activity and improve vagal regulation. Low-frequency sounds are known to stimulate the vagus nerve, promoting relaxation and reducing stress. Trauma survivors can benefit from neuroacoustic therapy as it helps regulate the nervous system and improve vagal tone, reducing symptoms of PTSD and anxiety.

- **Time in Nature/Forest Bathing:** Spending time in nature, also known as "forest bathing" or "shinrin-yoku", has been shown to reduce cortisol levels and improve parasympathetic activity, enhancing vagal tone. Nature immersion helps calm the nervous system, promoting recovery from trauma and supporting the body's ability to downregulate the CDR.

- **Frequency Specific Microcurrent (FSM):** FSM can directly improve vagal tone and help downregulate the CDR, reducing symptoms of anxiety, depression, and chronic pain. Clinical evidence and case studies show FSM's effectiveness in trauma recovery by supporting nervous system regulation and reducing inflammation. FSM uses low-level electrical currents tuned to specific frequencies to target and promote healing. Particular protocols include:

  - » **Vagus nerve (10 Hz):** Stimulates the vagus nerve, enhancing vagal tone and promoting calm.

  - » **Chronic inflammation (40 Hz):** Targets inflammation, reducing chronic stress responses in trauma survivors.

  - » **Central nervous system repair (81 Hz):** Supports nervous system regulation, helping trauma survivors calm overactive neural pathways.

  - » **Emotional trauma (89 Hz):** This treatment addresses the emotional and psychological components of trauma, helping the body release stored stress.

- **Somatic Therapies:** Somatic therapies, including body-based practices like Somatic Experiencing, yoga, and acupuncture, help trauma survivors re-establish safety and regulation in the body by activating the vagus nerve and promoting parasympathetic function.

Key Takeaways

- The vagus nerve is a powerful player in trauma recovery, helping the body move from defensive states to states of safety, relaxation, and healing.

- By understanding its connection to the Cell Danger Response (CDR) and using targeted interventions like vagus nerve stimulation (VNS), Frequency Specific Microcurrent (FSM), breathwork, and time in nature, trauma survivors can improve their vagal tone and begin the journey toward long-term recovery.

- Additionally, the vagus nerve is central to regulating the autonomic nervous system, and its activation promotes salugenesis signalling by shifting the body into a parasympathetic state. This relaxation response helps resolve the CDR, enabling the body to initiate cellular repair and restoration.

References

Frequency Specific Microcurrent (FSM). (2021). How FSM works in treating pain, inflammation, and trauma. *FSM Research Institute*. Available at: https://www.frequencyspecific.com/how-it-works/

HeartMath Institute. (2021). Heart rate variability, vagus nerve, and resilience. *HeartMath Research Library*. Available at: https://www.heartmath.org/research/research-library/

Porges, S. W. (2009). *The Polyvagal Theory: Neurophysiological foundations of emotions, attachment, communication, and self-regulation.* W.W. Norton & Company. Available at: https://wwnorton.com/books/9780393707007

Thayer, J. F., & Lane, R. D. (2000). A model of neurovisceral integration in emotion regulation and dysregulation. *Journal of Affective Disorders, 61*(3), 201-216. Available at: https://doi.org/10.1016/S0165-0327(00)00338-4

Thayer, J. F., & Sternberg, E. (2006). Beyond heart rate variability: Vagal regulation of allostatic systems. *Annals of the New York Academy of Sciences, 1088*(1), 361–372. https://doi.org/10.1196/annals.1366.014

35

ANAESTHESIA AND PTSD

Navigating Variant Responses in Trauma Survivors

Introduction

Post-Traumatic Stress Disorder (PTSD) affects millions worldwide, with impacts that go far beyond emotional and psychological distress. For individuals living with PTSD, medical procedures, including those involving anaesthesia, can present unique challenges. Research shows that people with PTSD may exhibit variant responses to anaesthesia due to neurobiological, physiological, and psychological alterations, many of which are rooted in the Cell Danger Response (CDR) (see Chapter 3 for more on CDR).

In addition, anaesthesia itself can be perceived as a threat by the central nervous system (CNS), further complicating the anaesthesia experience for trauma survivors.

This chapter explores how PTSD and the CDR influence the body's response to anaesthesia, delving into the mechanisms at play and offering practical considerations for healthcare providers, including the use of **pharmacogenomic (PGx) testing** to personalize anaesthesia plans.

The Neurobiology of PTSD, Anaesthesia, and the CDR

PTSD is a complex condition rooted in dysregulation of the nervous system, particularly the hypothalamic-pituitary-adrenal (HPA) axis and the autonomic nervous system (ANS). Both systems are heavily influenced by the CDR, which alters normal physiological functions in the presence of chronic stress and trauma.

Anaesthesia works by dampening neural activity, rendering a person unconscious or blocking pain signals during surgery. However, in individuals with PTSD, chronic activation of the CDR may make anaesthesia less predictable. When the body is stuck in a defence mode due to trauma, the typical response to anaesthesia can be altered. This may manifest in heightened sensitivity to anaesthetics, requiring adjusted doses, or in paradoxical responses where anaesthesia does not take effect as expected.

Anaesthesia as a Perceived Threat

For individuals with PTSD, anaesthesia can be perceived as a threat by the central nervous system. This is due to several factors, including:

- **Loss of control:** Anaesthesia involves a loss of consciousness, control, and awareness, which can be highly distressing for individuals whose trauma involved helplessness or lack of control. The experience of being sedated or unconscious can trigger the fight-flight-freeze response, even though the individual may not be fully aware of this during the procedure.

- **Dissociation:** Anaesthesia can mimic feelings of dissociation, where trauma survivors feel detached from their body or surroundings. This dissociative experience may act as a trigger for traumatic memories, increasing nervous system distress and causing the CNS to view anaesthesia as a danger.

- **Autonomic nervous system dysregulation:** In PTSD, the ANS—responsible for controlling involuntary bodily functions such as heart rate, breathing, and digestion—can become dysregulated. Anaesthesia disrupts these normal functions, which might be interpreted by the CNS as a signal of danger, leading to stress or threat responses.

- **Fear of vulnerability:** Being under anaesthesia can create feelings of extreme vulnerability, particularly challenging for trauma survivors. The sensation of being unable to protect oneself may be interpreted by the CNS as a danger signal, initiating the CDR and stress-related responses.

- **Sensory memory triggers:** The hospital environment, with its antiseptic smell, or even the sensation of anaesthesia may trigger trauma memories stored in the body. The brain may interpret these sensory experiences as a return to a dangerous situation, causing the CNS to activate defence mechanisms.

The Role of Mitochondrial Dysfunction

The CDR directly impacts mitochondria, the energy producers within cells. When the CDR is active, mitochondrial function becomes disrupted, leading to impaired energy production and metabolic regulation. Since anaesthesia relies on efficient cellular metabolism to process drugs and sustain sedation, mitochondrial dysfunction caused by the CDR may lead to unpredictable anaesthesia responses.

Patients with PTSD may therefore experience:

- Increased drug sensitivity, resulting in prolonged sedation or stronger side effects.

- Reduced efficacy of anaesthesia, where standard doses fail to sedate or manage pain fully.

- Prolonged recovery, due to the body's inability to process and recover from the anaesthetic efficiently.

Hyperarousal, CDR, and Pain Perception

One of the hallmark symptoms of PTSD is hyperarousal—an elevated state of alertness where the body remains on high alert. This is directly linked to the CDR, which keeps the nervous system in a defensive state. When the body is hyper-aroused, and the CDR is chronically engaged, anaesthesia might not be as effective in damp-ening the stress response. Patients may have difficulty achieving the deep sedation required for surgery, or they may experience height-ened distress upon waking from anaesthesia.

Additionally, pain perception is altered in PTSD due to the CDR's role in modulating inflammatory responses. Chronic activation of the CDR leads to increased inflammation, which can make post-op-erative pain more intense and difficult to manage.

Dissociation, Trauma-Triggered Responses, and the CDR

Dissociation is another core feature of PTSD, where trauma survi-vors feel disconnected from their surroundings or themselves. This dissociation, compounded by the CDR, may create heightened vulnerability during medical procedures involving anaesthesia. For some individuals, the experience of sedation, loss of control, or un-consciousness may serve as a trauma trigger, exacerbating PTSD symptoms or causing distressing flashbacks.

Trauma survivors may also have trouble reintegrating into their post-operative recovery due to the dissociative effects of anaesthesia, particularly in the presence of a dysregulated nervous system driven by the CDR.

PGx Testing: A Personalized Approach to Anaesthesia in PTSD Patients

Pharmacogenomic (PGx) testing has emerged as a powerful tool for predicting how individuals metabolize medications based on their genetic profile. This testing is particularly relevant for trauma sur-vivors with PTSD, as the chronic activation of the Cell Danger Re-sponse (CDR) and the genetic variability in drug metabolism can both influence how anaesthesia is processed.

PGx testing examines variations in genes responsible for drug me-tabolism, particularly those encoding cytochrome P450 enzymes (such as CYP2D6, CYP3A4, and CYP2C19). These enzymes play a crucial role in metabolizing anaesthetics and pain medications. By conducting PGx testing before surgery, clinicians can tailor anaesthesia and pain management plans to the individual's unique genetic profile, reducing the risk of adverse reactions or ineffective sedation.

How PGx Testing Can Improve Anaesthesia Outcomes for PTSD Patients

- **Personalised medication plans:** By identifying genetic variants that affect drug metabolism, PGx testing allows anaesthesiologists to adjust dosages and select anaesthetic agents more effectively. For example, individuals with specific CYP enzyme variants may metabolize anaesthesia too quickly, resulting in incomplete sedation, or too slowly, leading to prolonged sedation or side effects.

- **Predicting drug sensitivity:** PGx testing can identify patients who are more sensitive to certain anaesthetics or pain medications, such as opioids. This is particularly important for individuals with PTSD, who may already have heightened sensitivity due to chronic CDR activation. Knowing in advance which medications are likely to cause exaggerated responses can help prevent adverse reactions and improve patient safety.

- **Optimizing post-surgical pain management:** After surgery, PGx testing can guide the use of pain management medications. Trauma survivors with PTSD often require careful pain management due to altered pain perception and sensitivity. PGx testing can help select the most effective non-opioid alternatives and minimize the risk of complications associated with standard pain medications.

- **Minimizing risk of trauma triggers:** Since PGx testing helps reduce the trial-and-error approach to medication dosing, it can minimize the risk of anaesthesia-related complications, such as traumatic wake-ups or unexpected side effects. This approach enhances the overall safety and comfort of trauma survivors undergoing surgery.

Theoretical Case Study: Application of PGx Testing to Tailor Anaesthesia in PTSD

A 40-year-old veteran with PTSD underwent a laparoscopic chole-cystectomy (gallbladder removal). Pre-operative pharmacogenomic (PGx) testing revealed that the patient was a poor metaboliser for CYP2D6, a key enzyme involved in the metabolism of many anaesthetic and opioid pain medications. This information led the medical team to modify the anaesthetic regimen, avoiding drugs that rely heavily on CYP2D6 metabolism, such as codeine and certain benzodiazepines. Instead, they opted for alternatives like fentanyl for intraoperative management, and non-opioid alternatives for post-surgical pain.

The personalized anaesthesia plan, informed by the PGx results, resulted in effective sedation during surgery and a smoother recovery, with no PTSD-related symptoms triggered post-surgery. The patient experienced less post-operative sedation, and the pain was managed effectively without reliance on high doses of opioids, demonstrating how PGx testing can optimize care for trauma survivors with PTSD.

Key Takeaways

- Anaesthesia can be perceived as a threat by the central nervous system (CNS) in individuals with PTSD, leading to variant responses.

- The Cell Danger Response (CDR) can alter anaesthesia outcomes, resulting in unpredictable reactions such as heightened sensitivity or prolonged recovery.

- Pharmacogenomic (PGx) testing can provide valuable insights into how trauma survivors with PTSD metabolize anaesthetic drugs, helping clinicians tailor treatment plans.

- By using PGx testing, anaesthesia plans can be personalized to reduce risks, avoid trauma triggers, and optimize post-surgical pain management.

- A trauma-informed approach is essential when working with trauma survivors to minimize the stress associated with anaesthesia and medical procedures.

Next Steps

For healthcare professionals working with trauma survivors, especially those with PTSD, the delivery of anaesthesia requires more than a standard approach. The following are actionable steps for implementing trauma-informed anaesthesia care:

- **Training in trauma-informed care:** Medical teams, including anaesthesiologists, surgeons, and nursing staff, should undergo trauma-informed care training. This training focuses on recognizing trauma symptoms, minimizing re-traumatization, and adopting communication techniques that prioritize patient safety and comfort.

- **Pre-operative PTSD screening:** Incorporating routine PTSD screening into pre-operative assessments can help identify patients who may need special considerations. Tools such as the PTSD Checklist (PCL-5) can be administered to flag trauma histories.

- **Collaborative care plans:** An interdisciplinary team approach should be employed, involving collaboration between anaesthesiologists, psychologists, and trauma-informed therapists. This ensures that the patient's physical and emotional needs are considered at every stage of the surgical process.

- **Alternative pain management protocols:** Given the heightened sensitivity to pain and medication in PTSD patients, it's critical to explore alternative pain management strategies. This may include non-opioid medications, nerve blocks, Frequency Specific Microcurrent (FSM), acupuncture, and relaxation techniques such as guided meditation.

- **Post-operative support:** After surgery, individuals with PTSD may need extra support during recovery. Post-operative care should include psychological follow-up to monitor for PTSD flare-ups, dissociation, or other trauma-related symptoms.

- **Further research and innovation:** Encourage ongoing research into the impact of PTSD and the CDR on anaesthesia responses. This can help refine medical protocols and develop new, tailored approaches for trauma survivors, ensuring safer and more compassionate care.

Resources

Bremner, J. D. (2006). Traumatic stress: Effects on the brain. *Dialogues in Clinical Neuroscience, 8*(4), 445–461. https://www.ncbi.nlm.nih.gov/pmc/articles/PMC3181836/

Manley, E. L., Rametta, L., & Blau, A. (2022). PTSD: Anesthesia considerations for the patient with post-traumatic stress disorder. *AANA Journal, 90*(5), 359–365. PMID: 36173793.

McFadgen, K., Jensen, N., & Mahajan, P. B. (2019). Application of pharmacogenomics for trauma and critical care patients: A case report. *World Journal of Clinical Cases, 7*(23), 4045–4052. https://doi.org/10.12998/wjcc.v7.i23.4045

Raja, S., Hasnain, M., Hoersch, M., Gove-Yin, S., & Rajagopalan, C. (2015). Trauma-informed care in medicine: Current knowledge and future research directions. *Family & Community Health, 38*(3), 216–226. https://doi.org/10.1097/FCH.0000000000000071

Van der Kolk, B. A. (2014). *The Body Keeps the Score: Brain, mind, and body in the healing of trauma*. New York: Penguin Books.

36.

PSYCHEDELICS AND THE CELL DANGER RESPONSE (CDR)

Introduction: The Growing Interest in Psychedelics for Trauma Treatment

In recent years, there has been a surge of interest in using **psychedelics** such as **MDMA**, **psilocybin**, and **ketamine** to treat mental health conditions, particularly Post-Traumatic Stress Disorder (PTSD) and other trauma-related disorders. What makes psychedelics especially promising is their ability to induce profound emotional and cognitive shifts, allowing individuals to access and process traumatic memories in ways traditional therapies often struggle to achieve.

Psychedelics have been shown to reduce the emotional intensity of trauma and facilitate deep emotional healing. However, what is less known is how these substances might influence trauma's physiological effects, mainly through the lens of the Cell Danger Response (CDR). This chapter will explore the connection between psychedelics, the CDR, and their potential role in trauma recovery.

Considerations for Younger Adults: While psychedelics for adults show promise in trauma recovery, brain development in the young continues into the mid-20s, particularly in areas like the prefrontal cortex, which governs impulse control, decision-making, and future planning. Some researchers suggest that introducing psychedelics before this stage of development is complete could have unknown long-term effects. Early studies also indicate that psychedelics interact with mitochondrial function differently across individuals, including potential sex-based differences. While research is ongoing, careful consideration of risks and benefits is advised when exploring psychedelic-assisted therapy in individuals under 25 until more is known.

The Cell Danger Response (CDR) and Trauma

As discussed throughout this book, the Cell Danger Response (CDR) is a biological defence mechanism activated in response to trauma. When a person experiences trauma, the CDR shifts the body into a protective state, prioritizing survival over normal cellular functions such as growth, repair, and energy production.

For many trauma survivors, the CDR becomes chronically activated, keeping their bodies in a heightened state of alert long after the original trauma has passed. This prolonged activation leads to chronic stress, immune dysfunction, inflammation, and other physical health issues. Understanding how psychedelics may interact with the CDR offers new possibilities for resolving both the psychological and physical symptoms of trauma.

How Psychedelics Influence the Brain and Body

Psychedelics, including MDMA, psilocybin, and ketamine, induce altered states of consciousness by affecting neurotransmitter systems, particularly serotonin, dopamine, and glutamate. These substances temporarily reduce the activity of the **default mode network (DMN)**—the part of the brain responsible for self-reflection and rumination—which allows trauma survivors to process traumatic memories without being overwhelmed by fear or anxiety.

Beyond their psychological effects, psychedelics also appear to have profound effects on cellular and molecular processes, potentially influencing the CDR and the body's overall response to trauma.

MDMA and the CDR: Reducing Hypervigilance

MDMA (3,4-methylenedioxymethamphetamine) is one of the most studied psychedelics for treating PTSD. Known for its **empathogenic** effects, MDMA enhances emotional connection and reduces fear responses, making it easier for individuals to process traumatic memories during therapy.

MDMA's effect on the CDR

MDMA also appears to influence the CDR by:

- **Reducing the fight-or-flight response:** MDMA reduces the activity of the amygdala, the brain's fear centre, which is typically overactive in trauma survivors. By calming the fear response, MDMA may help shift the body out of the chronic CDR state, allowing the body to return to a state of safety and calm.

- **Facilitating cellular repair:** MDMA increases the release of oxytocin, which promotes feelings of trust and emotional connection. Oxytocin is also involved in tissue repair and anti-inflammatory processes, which can help resolve some of the physical effects of trauma, such as chronic inflammation and immune dysfunction.

In clinical trials, MDMA-assisted therapy has been shown to reduce PTSD symptoms significantly, and its potential to calm the CDR may explain why trauma survivors often experience both emotional and physical relief following treatment.

Psilocybin and the CDR: Neuroplasticity and Healing

Psilocybin, the active compound in "magic mushrooms", has also gained attention for its ability to treat depression, anxiety, and PTSD. Psilocybin's effects are primarily mediated through its action on serotonin receptors, particularly the **5-HT2A receptor**, which plays a role in mood regulation and cognition.

Psilocybin's influence on the CDR

Psilocybin's effects on the Cell Danger Response are potentially linked to its ability to promote neuroplasticity and the brain's ability to form new neural connections. By fostering neuroplasticity, psilocybin may help trauma survivors rewire their stress responses and shift out of the chronic CDR state. Some fundamental mechanisms include:

- **Reducing inflammation:** Psilocybin has been shown to have anti-inflammatory effects, which can help resolve chronic inflammation driven by the CDR. This reduction in inflammation may also support immune system regulation and improve gut health.

- **Promoting emotional processing:** Psilocybin enhances emotional processing by facilitating communication between the amygdala and the prefrontal cortex. This can help trauma survivors process their emotions more effectively and reduce the CDR's influence on emotional dysregulation.

Studies on psilocybin-assisted therapy have shown promising results in reducing symptoms of depression, anxiety, and PTSD. By promoting neuroplasticity and calming the CDR, psilocybin offers a unique approach to healing both the mind and body after trauma.

Ketamine and the CDR: Rapid Relief and Cellular Restoration

Ketamine, originally developed as an anaesthetic, has recently gained attention for its rapid-acting antidepressant and anti-anxiety effects. Unlike MDMA and psilocybin, which primarily affect serotonin, ketamine acts on the glutamate system, particularly through NMDA receptors.

Ketamine's effects on the CDR

Ketamine's ability to influence the Cell Danger Response lies in its rapid action on cellular processes that are dysregulated in trauma survivors:

- **Restoring cellular energy production:** Ketamine increases the production of brain-derived neurotrophic factor (BDNF), which plays a role in cellular repair and energy production. By enhancing BDNF levels, ketamine may help restore normal cellular functions that are disrupted by the chronic CDR state.

- **Reducing inflammatory markers:** Research has shown that ketamine reduces pro-inflammatory cytokines, which are typically elevated in trauma survivors due to the chronic activation of the CDR. This reduction in inflammation may help improve both mental and physical symptoms associated with trauma.

Ketamine is unique among psychedelics in that it provides rapid relief from symptoms of depression and anxiety, often within hours. By addressing the CDR at a cellular level, ketamine offers trauma survivors a way to alleviate the physical and emotional burden of trauma quickly.

Psychedelic-Assisted Therapy and Whole-Body Healing

Psychedelics offer more than just psychological relief for trauma survivors—they provide a pathway for whole-body healing. By influencing the Cell Danger Response, these substances help shift the body out of survival mode, allowing it to focus on repair, recovery, and growth. The combination of emotional processing and cellular restoration makes psychedelic-assisted therapy a powerful tool in the treatment of PTSD and trauma.

The Role of Integrative Approaches

While psychedelics can facilitate profound healing, their effects are enhanced when combined with integrative approaches that support whole-body health. For trauma survivors, this means combining psychedelic therapy with:

- **Nutrition and gut health:** Supporting the gut microbiome and reducing inflammation through diet can further calm the CDR and improve both mental and physical health.

- **Somatic therapies:** Techniques like Somatic Experiencing (SE) (Chapter 21) and Trauma Releasing Exercises (TRE) can help release trauma stored in the body, complementing the effects of psychedelics by promoting nervous system regulation.

- **Photobiomodulation (PBM) and Hyperbaric Oxygen Therapy (HBOT):** These therapies support cellular repair and help resolve the chronic activation of the CDR, making them valuable additions to psychedelic-assisted therapy.

Key Takeaways

- Psychedelics such as MDMA, psilocybin, and ketamine offer promising pathways for trauma recovery by influencing both the mind and body.

- These substances can help shift the body out of the chronic CDR state, reducing inflammation, promoting cellular repair, and enhancing neuroplasticity.

- MDMA calms the fear response and promotes emotional connection, which can help regulate the CDR and improve both the emotional and physical symptoms of trauma.

- Psilocybin promotes neuroplasticity, reduces inflammation, and facilitates emotional processing, offering a powerful approach to healing trauma's psychological and physical effects.

- Ketamine provides rapid relief by restoring cellular energy production and reducing inflammatory markers, making it especially effective for individuals experiencing severe trauma symptoms.

- Combining psychedelic therapy with integrative approaches, such as nutrition, somatic therapies, and cellular repair modalities, offers a comprehensive strategy for trauma recovery.

References

Bouso, J. C., Doblin, R., Farré, M., Alcázar, M. Á., & Gómez-Jarabo, G. (2008). MDMA-assisted psychotherapy using low doses in a small sample of women with chronic posttraumatic stress disorder. *Journal of Psychoactive Drugs, 40*(3), 225-236. https://doi.org/10.1080/02791072.2008.10400637

Carhart-Harris, R. L., & Goodwin, G. M. (2017). The therapeutic potential of psychedelic drugs: Past, present, and future. *Neuropsychopharmacology, 42*(11), 2105-2113. https://doi.org/10.1038/npp.2017.84

Mithoefer, M. C., Grob, C. S., & Brewerton, T. D. (2016). Novel psychopharmacological therapies for psychiatric disorders: Psilocybin and MDMA. *The Lancet Psychiatry, 3*(5), 481-488. https://doi.org/10.1016/S2215-0366(15)00576-3

Morris, H., & Wallach, J. (2014). From PCP to MXE: A comprehensive review of the non-medical use of dissociative drugs. *Drug Testing and Analysis, 6*(7-8), 614-632. https://doi.org/10.1002/dta.1620

Naviaux, R. K. (2014). Metabolic features of the cell danger response. *Mitochondrion, 16*, 7-17. https://doi.org/10.1016/j.mito.2013.08.006

Nichols, D. E. (2016). Psychedelics. *Pharmacological Reviews, 68*(2), 264-355. https://doi.org/10.1124/pr.115.011478

37

TRAUMA AND THE BRAIN

Understanding the Neurological
Impacts and Pathways to Recovery

Introduction

Trauma leaves an indelible mark not only on the body and mind, but also on the brain's structure and function. The effects of trauma—whether due to childhood adversity, acute traumatic events, or chronic stress—manifest in specific brain regions, altering neurobiological processes that regulate cognition, emotions, and behaviour. Understanding how trauma changes the brain is critical to identifying the appropriate interventions for healing and recovery.

This chapter explores how trauma affects critical brain regions, the role of neuroplasticity in recovery, and the long-term consequences of trauma on cognitive and emotional health.

The Impact of Trauma on Brain Regions

Trauma significantly affects the following brain structures:

- The amygdala

- The hippocampus

- The prefrontal cortex

We will look at each of these in turn.

The Amygdala: Hypervigilance and Emotional Reactivity

The amygdala is the brain's alarm system, responsible for detecting threats and triggering the fight-or-flight response. Trauma can lead to amygdala hyperactivation, resulting in increased emotional reactivity, hypervigilance, and heightened fear responses. Individuals exposed to trauma may find themselves in a constant state of arousal, easily triggered by reminders of the traumatic event or even unrelated stressors.

- **Hyperarousal:** The amygdala becomes hypersensitive to potential threats, even when none exist, leading to anxiety, irritability, and startle responses.

- **Emotional reactivity:** Emotional regulation becomes impaired as the amygdala overrides other brain regions responsible for processing emotions rationally.

The Hippocampus: Memory and Trauma

The hippocampus plays a crucial role in processing and storing memories. Trauma can cause atrophy of the hippocampus, particularly in cases of chronic stress or PTSD. This leads to fragmented, disorganized memories of the traumatic event, and difficulty distinguishing between past trauma and present experiences.

- **Impaired memory consolidation:** Trauma interferes with the hippocampus's ability to process and store memories, leading to flashbacks, intrusive thoughts, or memory gaps.

- **Contextualizing threats:** The hippocampus helps differentiate between past and present. Damage to this region makes it difficult to understand that a trauma response is no longer needed, exacerbating PTSD symptoms.

The Prefrontal Cortex: Executive Function and Regulation

The prefrontal cortex is responsible for higher-order functions such as decision-making, impulse control, and emotional regulation. Trauma can decrease the functionality of the prefrontal cortex, impairing an individual's ability to manage stress, regulate emotions, and engage in reflective thinking.

- **Reduced emotional regulation:** Trauma diminishes the prefrontal cortex's ability to regulate the emotional responses initiated by the amygdala.

- **Impaired decision-making:** Cognitive functions like planning, problem-solving, and impulse control are compromised, often resulting in poor decision-making or risk-taking behaviour.

Neuroplasticity: The Brain's Ability to Heal After Trauma

The brain is not a static organ; it has the remarkable ability to adapt and rewire itself through neuroplasticity. Neuroplasticity is the process by which the brain forms new neural connections, compensates for injury, and adapts to changes. In the context of trauma, neuroplasticity can either help the brain recover, or it can solidify maladaptive patterns that maintain trauma symptoms.

Negative Neuroplasticity

In cases of trauma, the brain may reinforce maladaptive neural pathways, perpetuating hypervigilance, anxiety, and emotional dysregulation. These maladaptive changes can contribute to the persistence of symptoms like flashbacks, dissociation, and mood instability.

Repeated trauma exposure strengthens fear circuits in the amygdala, leading to chronic anxiety and emotional dysregulation. Chronic trauma weakens connections in the prefrontal cortex, making it more challenging to engage in rational thought and emotional regulation.

Positive Neuroplasticity

Despite trauma's negative impacts, the brain's capacity for positive neuroplasticity provides hope for recovery. Through specific therapeutic interventions, it is possible to rewire the brain, forming new neural pathways that support emotional regulation, cognitive function, and resilience.

Somatic therapies, neurofeedback, and neurostimulation techniques (like TMS and tDCS) encourage the brain to form healthier neural connections and restore balance. Practices like mindfulness-based stress reduction (MBSR) and trauma-informed mindfulness strengthen the prefrontal cortex's ability to regulate emotions and reduce hyperactivity in the amygdala.

Long-Term Consequences of Trauma on Cognition and Emotion

The long-term effects of trauma on brain structure and function can manifest in both cognitive and emotional dysregulation, often contributing to conditions like PTSD, depression, anxiety, and dissociation. Understanding these long-term impacts is essential for recognizing how trauma continues to influence behaviour and thought patterns long after the traumatic event.

Cognitive consequences include:

- **Memory impairments:** Due to hippocampal atrophy, individuals with a history of trauma often experience difficulty forming coherent memories of the traumatic event and may struggle with memory retrieval in everyday life.

- **Concentration and attention impairments:** The chronic activation of the amygdala can hijack attention resources, making it difficult to concentrate or stay focused on tasks unrelated to the trauma.

Trauma's effects on emotional dysregulation include:

- **Persistent hypervigilance:** Even in the absence of immediate danger, the brain remains on high alert, leading to chronic anxiety, restlessness, and irritability.

- **Difficulty regulating emotions:** The decreased functionality of the prefrontal cortex, combined with an overactive amygdala, makes it difficult for trauma survivors to manage strong emotions or recover from emotional triggers.

Therapeutic Interventions for Brain Recovery After Trauma

Photobiomodulation (PBM) Therapy

Photobiomodulation (PBM), also known as low-level light therapy, involves using red or near-infrared light to stimulate cellular repair, reduce inflammation, and promote brain recovery. PBM has shown promise in improving cognitive function, enhancing mood, and supporting neuroplasticity in individuals recovering from trauma. By targeting the mitochondria, PBM helps the brain heal from trauma-induced oxidative stress and supports overall neural health.

PBM enhances neuroplasticity, reduces inflammation, and improves cognitive and emotional regulation.

Oxygen Therapy

Hyperbaric Oxygen Therapy (HBOT) involves breathing pure oxygen in a pressurized environment, which increases oxygen availability in the brain and promotes healing. Oxygen therapy enhances blood flow, supports tissue repair, and improves brain function by increasing oxygen delivery to areas affected by trauma. It has been shown to improve cognitive performance, memory, and emotional regulation in individuals with trauma-related brain injury.

HBOT increases oxygenation, enhances neurogenesis, and promotes cellular repair in brain regions affected by trauma.

Hydrogen Therapy

Hydrogen therapy, involving the inhalation or ingestion of molecular hydrogen, is emerging as a neuroprotective treatment. Hydrogen acts as a potent antioxidant, reducing oxidative stress and inflammation, which are commonly elevated in the brains of trauma survivors. This therapy supports brain recovery by protecting neurons from damage and enhancing cognitive function.

Hydrogen therapy reduces oxidative stress, protects neurons, and improves cognitive resilience.

Frequency Specific Microcurrent (FSM)

FSM is a non-invasive therapy that uses low-level electrical currents to target specific tissues and promote healing. In trauma recovery, FSM has been shown to reduce inflammation, alleviate pain, and improve brain function. By delivering microcurrents to dysregulated brain areas, FSM supports neuroplasticity and restores balance to the nervous system.

FSM reduces inflammation, improves neuroplasticity, and promotes brain recovery by targeting specific tissues with microcurrents.

Targeted Supplements

Targeted nutritional supplementation can play a significant role in supporting brain health after trauma. Certain supplements enhance neuroplasticity, reduce inflammation, and promote recovery in trauma-affected brain regions:

- **Magnesium:** Supports nervous system regulation, reduces anxiety, and improves sleep.

- **Omega-3 fatty acids:** Reduces inflammation and supports brain cell repair.

- **B-Vitamins:** Essential for cognitive function, energy production, and mood regulation.

Post-Traumatic Growth: Rewiring for Resilience

Post-traumatic growth (PTG) exemplifies the brain's capacity to heal from trauma and grow stronger. Through neuroplasticity, trauma survivors can create new neural pathways that foster emotional regulation, cognitive improvement, and personal resilience. PTG involves a process of rewiring in the brain, driven by neuroplasticity and neurogenesis, which allows for the formation of new neural connections and neurons, promoting both cognitive and emotional transformation.

Trauma survivors who experience PTG demonstrate improved resilience, emotional well-being, and a renewed sense of purpose after trauma. Therapeutic interventions like somatic therapy, neurostimulation, and mindfulness help stimulate the neuroplasticity necessary for PTG.

Conclusion: Healing the Brain After Trauma

Trauma dramatically alters the brain, leading to dysregulation in key regions responsible for memory, emotion, and decision-making. Understanding these changes is crucial for developing effective interventions. By leveraging the brain's natural neuroplasticity and employing therapies that target the disrupted brain circuits, we can guide the brain toward healing and recovery. Whether through Photobiomodulation, oxygen therapy, hydrogen therapy, FSM, or targeted supplements, restoring balance to the brain offers hope for trauma survivors seeking to regain cognitive and emotional well-being.

Post-traumatic growth provides further evidence of the brain's capacity to heal and thrive, offering trauma survivors the opportunity not only to recover but to emerge stronger, with new insights, resilience, and emotional depth.

References

McEwen, B. S. (2007). Physiology and neurobiology of stress and adaptation: Central role of the brain. *Physiological Reviews, 87*(3), 873–904. https://doi.org/10.1152/physrev.00041.2006

Porges, S. W. (2011). *The Polyvagal Theory: Neurophysiological foundations of emotions, attachment, communication, and self-regulation.* W. W. Norton & Company.

Sapolsky, R. M. (2004). *Why Zebras Don't Get Ulcers: The acclaimed guide to stress, stress-related diseases, and coping.* Holt Paperbacks.

Teicher, M. H., Samson, J. A., Anderson, C. M., & Ohashi, K. (2016). The effects of childhood maltreatment on brain structure, function, and connectivity. *Nature Reviews Neuroscience, 17*(10), 652–666. https://doi.org/10.1038/nrn.2016.111

Van der Kolk, B. A. (2014). *The Body Keeps the Score: Brain, mind, and body in the healing of trauma.* Penguin Books.

38.

CONCUSSION, TRAUMATIC BRAIN INJURY, AND THE CELL DANGER RESPONSE

The Cell Danger Response and Brain Injury

When a concussion or TBI occurs, the CDR (see Chapter 3) activates to protect the brain and initiate repair mechanisms. This involves:

- **Neuroinflammation:** The brain's immune cells (microglia) become hyperactive, leading to an inflammatory response intended to clear debris and repair damage. However, chronic neuroinflammation can cause further damage.

- **Mitochondrial dysfunction:** Mitochondria, the cell's powerhouses, shift their function toward managing the stress response, resulting in energy deficits and impaired cellular metabolism.

- **Disruption of cellular communication:** The CDR disrupts regular synaptic communication between neurons, which can cause cognitive and emotional symptoms to persist long after the injury has occurred.

While this protective mechanism is essential during the acute phase of injury, prolonged activation of the CDR can contribute to the development of chronic symptoms, including headaches, memory issues, mood disturbances, and sensory sensitivities, which complicate recovery from concussion and TBI.

Prolonged CDR Activation and Chronic Symptoms Post-TBI

When the CDR remains active long after the initial trauma has passed, individuals may experience a wide range of chronic symptoms, including:

- **Cognitive decline:** Memory impairments, poor attention, and executive function difficulties are common outcomes of long-term CDR activation.

- **Mood disorders:** Persistent inflammation and mitochondrial dysfunction may contribute to anxiety, depression, and irritability.

- **Sleep disruptions:** Chronic activation of the CDR can affect brain regions involved in regulating the sleep-wake cycle, leading to insomnia and disrupted sleep.

- **Headaches and sensory issues:** Ongoing neuroinflammation and energy deficits can cause headaches and heightened sensitivity to light, sound, and other stimuli.

Therapies Targeting the CDR for TBI Recovery

Various therapies have been explored to address the CDR in cases of concussion and TBI, helping to restore cellular function and reduce inflammation.

Hyperbaric Oxygen Therapy (HBOT)

HBOT is a powerful therapy that involves breathing pure oxygen in a pressurized environment, which significantly increases oxygen availability to tissues. For individuals recovering from TBI, HBOT can:

- **Support mitochondrial function:** By increasing oxygen availability, HBOT helps mitochondria resume energy production, facilitating cellular repair.

- **Reduce neuroinflammation:** HBOT has anti-inflammatory properties that reduce chronic inflammation in the brain, helping to deactivate the CDR.

- **Promote neurogenesis:** HBOT stimulates the growth of new neurons and blood vessels, both of which are vital for brain recovery.

Pulsed Electromagnetic Field (PEMF) Therapy

PEMF therapy uses electromagnetic fields to support cellular repair and reduce inflammation. In TBI recovery, PEMF:

- **Restores mitochondrial energy:** PEMF enhances ATP production, promoting energy restoration in neurons affected by the CDR.

- **Modulates inflammation:** PEMF therapy helps reduce inflammatory markers in the brain, resolving the prolonged neuroinflammation often seen in TBI.

- **Enhances neuroplasticity:** By encouraging synaptic regeneration, PEMF promotes brain adaptation and recovery.

Photobiomodulation (Red and Near-Infrared Light Therapy)

Photobiomodulation therapy uses light to penetrate the brain and stimulate mitochondrial activity, offering several **benefits:**

- **Restoring energy production:** By stimulating ATP production, Photobiomodulation supports energy restoration in brain cells.

- **Reduces neuroinflammation:** This therapy has anti-inflammatory effects that help resolve the prolonged immune activation associated with the CDR.

- **Promotes neuronal repair:** Photobiomodulation supports neurogenesis and synaptic repair, aiding in cognitive and emotional recovery.

Hydrogen Therapy

Molecular hydrogen (H_2), a relatively new therapeutic approach, has demonstrated potent antioxidant and anti-inflammatory properties, making it a promising therapy for addressing the CDR in concussion and TBI recovery. Hydrogen gas or hydrogen-enriched water can:

- **Neutralize oxidative stress:** Hydrogen has been shown to selectively reduce harmful free radicals, such as hydroxyl radicals, which accumulate during CDR activation and contribute to oxidative stress and mitochondrial dysfunction.

- **Reduce neuroinflammation:** Hydrogen therapy helps modulate inflammation in the brain, reducing the prolonged immune response triggered by the CDR. This anti-inflammatory effect has shown promise in lowering cognitive and emotional symptoms post-TBI.

- **Protect mitochondrial function:** Hydrogen gas supports mitochondrial health by reducing oxidative damage and improving the cells' ability to produce energy, helping to resolve the energy deficits caused by the CDR.

- **Enhance cognitive and motor recovery:** Preclinical studies suggest that hydrogen therapy can enhance the recovery of cognitive and motor functions by protecting neurons from further damage and promoting repair.

Hydrogen therapy is typically administered via inhalation of hydrogen gas or ingestion of hydrogen-enriched water. Both delivery methods effectively distribute molecular hydrogen throughout the body and brain, making it a safe, non-invasive intervention for individuals recovering from TBI.

Frequency Specific Microcurrent (FSM)

FSM delivers low-level electrical currents that help reduce inflammation and promote cellular healing. For TBI patients, FSM can:

- **Reduce neuroinflammation:** By targeting specific tissues and regions affected by TBI, FSM decreases inflammation and supports faster recovery.

- **Improve cellular communication:** FSM promotes better cellular signalling, helping neurons coordinate repair efforts and reduce the chronic CDR response.

- **Alleviate pain:** FSM is particularly effective in reducing chronic headaches and pain symptoms that accompany TBI.

Medicinal Mushrooms (Lion's Mane and Others)

Medicinal mushrooms, particularly Lion's Mane (*Hericium erinaceus*), offer neuroprotective benefits that make them a valuable addition to TBI recovery:

- **Neurogenesis support:** Lion's Mane stimulates nerve growth factor (NGF), which aids in the repair and growth of neurons and helps reverse CDR-related damage.

- **Anti-inflammatory effects:** Lion's Mane and other mushrooms like Reishi and Cordyceps have powerful anti-inflammatory properties, which help resolve chronic neuroinflammation and promote recovery.

- **Cognitive enhancement:** Lion's Mane has been shown to improve cognitive function, including memory and focus, which are often impaired following TBI.

Nutritional Approaches for TBI Recovery: Supporting the CDR

Ketogenic Diet

The ketogenic diet provides ketones as an alternative fuel source for the brain, bypassing the impaired glucose metabolism often seen in TBI. This helps:

- **Restore mitochondrial function:** The ketogenic diet provides ketones as an energy source, helping restore energy production and resolve the CDR.

- **Reduce inflammation:** The ketogenic diet has anti-inflammatory effects, which help deactivate the prolonged immune response seen in TBI recovery.

Anti-Inflammatory Nutrients

Nutrients such as omega-3 fatty acids, curcumin, and antioxidants play a critical role in modulating the CDR and reducing neuroinflammation. These compounds protect neurons and enhance cellular repair.

Neurostimulation Techniques for Modulating the CDR

Transcranial Magnetic Stimulation (TMS)

TMS stimulates specific brain regions using magnetic fields, helping to modulate neuronal activity and neuroplasticity. TMS can restore brain function by:

- **Promoting neuroplasticity:** TMS encourages the brain's ability to reorganize and adapt following injury, supporting recovery.

- **Modulating CDR activation:** By regulating brain activity, TMS helps reduce the prolonged CDR response seen in TBI patients.

Transcranial Direct Current Stimulation (tDCS)

A low electrical current to the brain in tDCS, acts by stimulating neurons and enhancing repair processes. This technique benefits in TBI recovery by:

- **Restoring synaptic communication:** tDCS improves the signalling between neurons, resolving the disruptions caused by the CDR.

- **Supporting cognitive recovery:** This non-invasive therapy has been shown to improve memory, attention, and mood in individuals recovering from TBI.

Key Takeaways

- The CDR plays a critical role in the brain's response to trauma but can become a barrier to recovery when it remains chronically activated.

- Therapies like HBOT, PEMF, Photobiomodulation, FSM, hydrogen therapy, and medicinal mushrooms such as Lion's Mane can help deactivate the CDR, reduce inflammation, restore mitochondrial function, and promote neuronal repair.

- Integrating these therapies into a comprehensive treatment plan offers hope for individuals recovering from the long-term effects of concussion and TBI.

References

Brandalise, F., Roda, E., Ratto, D., Goppa, L., Gargano, M. L., Cirlincione, F., Priori, E. C., Venuti, M. T., Pastorelli, E., Savino, E., & Rossi, P. (2023). *Hericium erinaceus* in neurodegenerative diseases: From bench to bedside and beyond, how far from the shoreline? *Frontiers in Pharmacology, 14*, Article 10218917. https://pmc.ncbi.nlm.nih.gov/articles/PMC10218917/

De Freitas, D. J., De Carvalho, D., Paglioni, V. M., Brunoni, A. R., Valiengo, L., Thome-Souza, M. S., Guirado, V. M. P., Zaninotto, A. L., & Paiva, W. S. (2021). Effects of transcranial direct current stimulation (tDCS) and concurrent cognitive training on episodic memory in patients with traumatic brain injury: A double-blind, randomised, placebo-controlled study. *BMJ Open, 11*(8), e045285. https://doi.org/10.1136/bmjopen-2020-045285

Harch, P. G., & McCullough, V. (2016). *The oxygen revolution: Hyperbaric oxygen therapy and the healing of the brain* (3rd ed.). Hatherleigh Press

Hu, H.-W., Chen, Z.-G., Liu, J.-G., & Chen, G. (2021). Role of hydrogen in traumatic brain injury: A narrative review. *Medical Gas Research, 11*(2), 54–63.

Stanford Medicine. (n.d.). *Metabolic Psychiatry Clinic*. Stanford Medicine. Retrieved December 4, 2024, from https://med.stanford.edu/psychiatry/patient_care/metabolic.html

39.

INTERGENERATIONAL TRAUMA AND EPIGENETICS

Introduction: The Legacy of Trauma Across Generations

Trauma is often viewed as an individual experience, but research into **intergenerational trauma** and **epigenetics** reveals that its effects can be passed down from one generation to the next. This means that the trauma experienced by parents, grandparents, or even great-grandparents can impact descendants at both biological *and* psychological levels.

The field of epigenetics—how external factors influence gene expression—provides insight into how trauma leaves a biological mark that future generations can inherit.

This chapter will explore the science of intergenerational trauma, the role of the Cell Danger Response (CDR) in trauma transmission, how epigenetic changes occur in response to trauma, and the ways in which healing one generation can positively affect future generations.

The Science of Intergenerational Trauma

Intergenerational trauma, also referred to as transgenerational trauma, occurs when the effects of trauma experienced by one generation are passed down to subsequent generations. This process can happen through social and psychological means—such as learned behaviours or familial patterns of emotional response—and through biological mechanisms, including the impact on cellular functions like the Cell Danger Response (CDR).

The Role of the Cell Danger Response in Intergenerational Trauma

The Cell Danger Response (CDR) is a critical mechanism that explains how trauma affects not just the mind, but also the body at a cellular level. The CDR is the body's protective reaction to stress or threat, which temporarily halts normal cellular functions to prioritize survival. However, as we have seen, when trauma is unresolved or chronic, the CDR can become stuck in an activated state, leading to long-term physical and psychological impacts. These cellular changes, caused by chronic trauma, may be passed down through generations, influencing how future descendants respond to stress and trauma at the cellular level.

Important implications of the CDR in intergenerational trauma include:

- **Chronic activation of the CDR:** When trauma is passed down through generations, it can leave descendants with a heightened stress response, where their bodies are primed for danger even in the absence of a direct threat. This can manifest as hypervigilance, anxiety, and chronic health issues.

- **Cellular memory of trauma:** Epigenetic changes influenced by the CDR can alter how genes related to stress, inflammation, and emotional regulation are expressed, making future generations more vulnerable to emotional dysregulation and physical health problems like autoimmune disorders and chronic pain.

Understanding Epigenetics: How Trauma Affects Gene Expression

Epigenetics refers to the study of how external environmental factors influence gene expression without changing the DNA sequence itself. Trauma can induce epigenetic changes through mechanisms like **DNA methylation** and **histone modification**, which alter gene activity. These trauma-induced epigenetic marks can be passed down through generations, influencing how descendants respond to stress and trauma.

The Mechanisms of Epigenetic Change and the CDR:

- **DNA methylation:** Trauma can lead to the addition of methyl groups to DNA, which silences or activates specific genes. For example, genes related to the body's stress response or immune function may become overactive or suppressed. This altered gene expression, maintained through epigenetic mechanisms, is often linked to the CDR, as the cellular environment is constantly on high alert due to the trauma signal.

- **Histone modification:** The structure of DNA around histone proteins can change in response to trauma, making specific genes more or less accessible. This can impact emotional regulation, stress response, and cellular repair, processes that are deeply connected to the CDR. Descendants of trauma survivors may inherit a heightened cellular defence mechanism, where the body remains in a state of chronic alert due to ancestral trauma.

The Psychological Impact of Inherited Trauma

In addition to biological changes, intergenerational trauma affects psychological development and emotional well-being. Families that have experienced trauma often develop specific behaviours, coping mechanisms, and emotional patterns that are unconsciously passed down through generations.

There are a number of emotional and behavioural patterns that can be seen in families:

- **Learned helplessness:** Trauma survivors may model a sense of powerlessness or helplessness that their descendants internalize, leading to similar emotional patterns in future generations. The chronic activation of the CDR reinforces this emotional state, as the body remains in a defensive mode.

- **Hypervigilance:** Families that have endured trauma may pass down a heightened state of alertness, where descendants are constantly scanning their environment for danger. The chronic activation of the CDR contributes to this hypervigilance, as the body perceives threats even in safe environments.

- **Attachment issues:** Trauma can disrupt attachment patterns, leading to difficulties in forming secure bonds. Descendants of trauma survivors may exhibit anxious or avoidant attachment styles, reflecting unresolved emotional wounds from prior generations. This, combined with the biological impact of the CDR, can lead to heightened emotional reactivity and stress in relationships.

The Epigenetic Legacy of Trauma: Research and Findings

Recent research on epigenetics and trauma has revealed how deeply trauma can influence gene expression across generations. The CDR plays a significant role in shaping how trauma is passed down biologically.

Epigenetic Studies on Trauma and the CDR

- **The Dutch famine study:** During World War II, a famine in the Netherlands led to pregnant women experiencing extreme stress. Decades later, researchers discovered that the children and grandchildren of these women had higher rates of metabolic disorders. This was traced back to epigenetic changes related to the body's response to stress and nutrient scarcity, a response influenced by the CDR.

- **Holocaust survivor studies:** Research on the descendants of Holocaust survivors has shown altered cortisol levels (the stress hormone) in both the survivors and their children, suggesting that trauma-induced changes to stress regulation were passed down epigenetically. The CDR's chronic activation likely played a role in these changes, as the body remained in a heightened state of alert for future generations.

Breaking the Cycle: Healing Generational Trauma

While the effects of intergenerational trauma can be profound, they are *not* irreversible. Healing in one generation can have a ripple effect, helping future generations break free from the patterns of trauma. Healing generational trauma requires addressing both the biological and psychological impacts, including resolving the chronic activation of the CDR.

Therapeutic Approaches for Intergenerational Trauma

- **Family Constellation Therapy:** This therapeutic approach is designed to explore family dynamics, uncover unresolved trauma, and bring awareness to how familial patterns are passed down. By addressing hidden dynamics, individuals can break free from inherited emotional burdens, potentially reversing the chronic activation of the CDR.

- **Somatic Therapies:** Trauma is stored in the body, and somatic therapies like Somatic Experiencing (SE) and Trauma Releasing Exercises (TRE) help release these stored patterns. Healing trauma in the body can shift epigenetic marks and reduce the CDR's influence on future generations.

- **EMDR for Inherited Trauma:** Eye Movement Desensitization and Reprocessing (EMDR) can be used to process both personal and inherited trauma. By resolving the emotional impact of past generations' experiences, individuals can disrupt the cycle of trauma transmission while calming the overactive CDR.

The Power of Conscious Healing

- **Awareness and acknowledgment:** Breaking the cycle of intergenerational trauma begins with awareness. Recognizing that certain emotional patterns, fears, or behaviours are inherited from past generations will provide a starting point for healing and regulating the CDR.

- **Healing future generations:** When one generation engages in trauma recovery, it can positively influence future generations by reducing the emotional and biological transmission of trauma. Healing the CDR's chronic activation can foster emotional resilience and well-being in descendants.

Practical Steps for Healing Generational Trauma

Healing intergenerational trauma is a long-term process, but there are practical steps individuals can take to begin breaking the cycle.

Emotional Healing

- **Trauma-informed mindfulness practices:** trauma-informed mindfulness practices help individuals become aware of inherited emotional patterns and interrupt them. By practicing emotional regulation techniques, survivors can begin to reshape their responses to stress and trauma and gradually shift the CDR into a more restful state.

- **Journaling:** Writing about family histories, inherited beliefs, and emotional experiences can help individuals process and release the weight of generational trauma.

- Biological Healing

- **Lifestyle changes:** A healthy lifestyle, including proper nutrition, exercise, and stress-reduction techniques, can mitigate some of the biological impacts of trauma on the body and help calm the CDR.

- **Epigenetic healing:** While epigenetic changes can be passed down, research suggests that positive lifestyle changes, such as reducing chronic stress and engaging in healthy social connections, can reverse some of the adverse effects of trauma-induced epigenetic marks. Calming the CDR through stress management can reduce inherited trauma's physical impact.

Key Takeaways

- Intergenerational trauma is passed down through both biological mechanisms, like epigenetic changes, and psychological patterns. The Cell Danger Response (CDR) plays a critical role in the transmission of trauma across generations.

- Epigenetic changes, such as DNA methylation and histone modification, influenced by the CDR, can alter gene expression, influencing how future generations respond to stress and trauma.

- Descendants of trauma survivors often experience emotional and behavioural patterns inherited from previous generations, including heightened anxiety.

References

Bengston, V. L., & Black, K. D. (1973). Intergenerational relations and continuities in socialisation. *Journal of Marriage and the Family, 35*(4), 871-883.

Bombay, A., Matheson, K., & Anisman, H. (2014). The intergenerational effects of Indian Residential Schools: Implications for the concept of historical trauma. *Transcultural Psychiatry, 51*(3), 320-338. https://doi.org/10.1177/1363461513503380

Kellermann, N. P. F. (2013). Epigenetic transmission of Holocaust trauma: Can nightmares be inherited? *Israel Journal of Psychiatry and Related Sciences, 50*(1), 33–39. PMID: 24029109

Klengel, T., & Binder, E. B. (2015). Epigenetics of stress-related psychiatric disorders and gene × environment interactions. *Neuron, 86*(6), 1343-1357. https://doi.org/10.1016/j.neuron.2015.05.032

Naviaux, R. K. (2014). Metabolic features of the cell danger response. *Mitochondrion, 16*, 7–17.

Szyf, M. (2011). The early life social environment and DNA methylation: DNA methylation mediating the long-term impact of social environments early in life. *Epigenetics, 6*(8), 971–978. https://doi.org/10.4161/epi.6.8.16793

Van der Kolk, B. A. (2014). *The Body Keeps the Score: Brain, mind, and body in the healing of trauma*. Penguin Books.

Yehuda, R., & Bierer, L. M. (2009). The relevance of epigenetics to PTSD: Implications for the DSM-V. *Journal of Traumatic Stress, 22*(5), 427–434. https://doi.org/10.1002/jts.20448

Yehuda, R., Flory, J. D., Pratchett, L. C., Buxbaum, J. D., Southwick, S., & Siever, L. J. (2010). Putative biological mechanisms for the association between early life adversity and the subsequent development of PTSD. *Psychopharmacology, 212*(3), 405–417. https://doi.org/10.1007/s00213-010-1969-6

40.

GENETIC INFLUENCES ON TRAUMA RECOVERY

MTHFR, MTR, COMT, VDR, and
the Cell Danger Response

Introduction

Genetic variations play a very important role in how the body responds to trauma and stress and how efficiently it recovers from these challenges. In the context of the Cell Danger Response (CDR), specific genetic mutations can perpetuate cellular stress, immune dysregulation, and metabolic imbalances, hindering trauma recovery.

This chapter explores genetic mutations—**MTHFR, MTR, COMT, VDR, MAO-A, SLC6A4, BDNF, GAD1, NR3C1,** and **ACE**—and their impact on the CDR and recovery from trauma. We also examine treatment approaches to mitigate the effects of these mutations and support the healing process.

MTHFR (Methylenetetrahydrofolate Reductase)

The MTHFR gene is responsible for converting folate into its active form (Methyl Folate), which is critical for DNA synthesis, detoxification, and neurotransmitter production. Mutations in MTHFR affect folate metabolism, leading to elevated homocysteine levels, impaired detoxification, and increased oxidative stress—all factors that prolong the CDR and impede trauma recovery.

Treatment includes:

- Methylfolate supplementation (L-5-MTHF) to bypass the impaired enzyme.

- B12 (Methylcobalamin) and B6 (Pyridoxal-5-Phosphate) support the methylation cycle.

- Betaine (TMG) to lower homocysteine levels.

- An anti-inflammatory diet rich in leafy greens and antioxidants to reduce oxidative stress and inflammation.

MTR (Methionine Synthase)

The MTR gene facilitates the conversion of homocysteine to methionine, a vital step in the methylation cycle necessary for DNA methylation and detoxification. Dysfunction in MTR can lead to elevated homocysteine levels, reducing methylation efficiency and sustaining the CDR.

Treatment includes:

- B12 (Hydroxycobalamin or Adenosylcobalamin) to improve the conversion of homocysteine.

- Support with methylfolate and trimethylglycine (TMG).

- Incorporate stress-reduction techniques like meditation and neurofeedback to reduce methylation strain.

COMT (Catechol-O-Methyltransferase)

The COMT gene is responsible for breaking down catecholamines such as dopamine, norepinephrine, and epinephrine. Mutations in COMT can result in altered emotional regulation, increased stress sensitivity, and difficulties in processing stress hormones, contributing to a prolonged CDR.

Treatment includes:

- Adaptogens like ashwagandha and rhodiola to improve stress resilience.

- Magnesium and B-vitamins to support neurotransmitter metabolism.

- DIM (Diindolylmethane) or calcium-d-glucarate helps with estrogen metabolism and hormonal balance, reducing the burden on the CDR.

- Engage in somatic therapies such as yoga and breathwork to calm the nervous system.

VDR (Vitamin D Receptor)

The VDR gene regulates vitamin D metabolism, which is essential for immune function, inflammation control, and cellular repair. Mutations in VDR can impair immune responses and exacerbate the CDR, delaying trauma recovery.

Treatment includes:

- Vitamin D supplementation, tailored to genetic needs and regularly monitored.

- Controlled sun exposure to boost natural vitamin D synthesis.

- Sulforaphane, found in cruciferous vegetables like broccoli, to support detoxification pathways and reduces inflammation, working synergistically with vitamin D.

- Probiotics and prebiotics support gut health, as 70% of immune function resides in the gut, and VDR mutations may impair immune regulation.

- An anti-inflammatory lifestyle with regular exercise and a diet rich in antioxidants to reduce chronic CDR activation.

MAO-A (Monoamine Oxidase A)

MAO-A is responsible for the breakdown of neurotransmitters such as serotonin, dopamine, and norepinephrine. Variants in MAO-A can lead to mood imbalances, heightened anxiety, and exaggerated stress responses, perpetuating the CDR.

Treatment includes:

- Supplementation with 5-HTP or tryptophan to support serotonin production.

- Magnesium, which regulates neurotransmitter breakdown.

- Mind-body therapies such as trauma-informed yoga and Somatic Experiencing to balance emotional regulation and stress responses.

SLC6A4 (Serotonin Transporter Gene)

The SLC6A4 gene regulates serotonin transport, a neurotransmitter crucial for mood and stress regulation. Mutations in SLC6A4 can affect serotonin levels, increasing vulnerability to depression, anxiety, and prolonged CDR activation.

Treatment includes:

- Omega-3 fatty acids, which support brain health and improve serotonin levels.

- Tryptophan or 5-HTP supplementation to naturally boost serotonin production.

- Mind-body therapies such as yoga, meditation, and trauma-informed mindfulness help regulate emotional and stress responses.

- Herbal support with St. John's Wort or Rhodiola Rosea (under medical supervision) to regulate serotonin levels naturally.

BDNF (Brain-Derived Neurotrophic Factor)

BDNF plays a crucial role in neuroplasticity, which is essential for brain healing and adaptation following trauma. Variants in BDNF can impair cognitive resilience and the brain's ability to recover from trauma, impacting the CDR.

Treatment includes:

- Exercise and cold therapy (such as cold showers) that stimulate BDNF production and neuroplasticity.

- Meditation and trauma-informed mindfulness to support cognitive flexibility and emotional balance.

- Lion's Mane Mushroom supplementation to enhance neuroplasticity and cognitive recovery.

GAD1 (Glutamate Decarboxylase)

GAD1 is responsible for converting the excitatory neurotransmitter glutamate into the inhibitory neurotransmitter GABA. Variants in GAD1 can disrupt this balance, leading to increased anxiety and prolonged CDR activation.

Treatment includes:

- Magnesium, Taurine, and GABA supplements to restore the balance between excitatory and inhibitory neurotransmission.

- Use of L-theanine and valerian root to promote GABA production and reduce anxiety.

NR3C1 (Glucocorticoid Receptor Gene)

The NR3C1 gene regulates how the body responds to cortisol (the stress hormone). Variants in this gene can influence the efficiency of the stress response system, contributing to a prolonged CDR.

Treatment includes:

- Phosphatidylserine supplementation to regulate cortisol levels and stress response.

- Adaptogenic herbs like ashwagandha and rhodiola modulate the body's stress response and support the hypothalamic-pituitary-adrenal (HPA) axis.

- Trauma-informed mindfulness practices to reduce the impact of chronic stress on cortisol production.

ACE (Angiotensin-Converting Enzyme)

The ACE gene plays a role in regulating blood pressure and stress responses. Variants in ACE have been linked to increased susceptibility to PTSD and other stress-related conditions, exacerbating the CDR. Treatment includes:

- CoQ10 and Magnesium support cardiovascular health and regulate stress responses.

- Heart rate variability (HRV) training and trauma-informed mindfulness practices to balance autonomic nervous system function.

- Hawthorn extract promotes heart health and reduces blood pressure, alleviating the stress burden on the body.

Integrating Genetic Understanding with Trauma Recovery

Understanding how these genetic mutations influence the Cell Danger Response provides an opportunity to tailor treatment approaches to the individual. By addressing genetic predispositions with personalized nutritional support, supplementation, mind-body therapies, and lifestyle changes, it is possible to bypass some of the limitations imposed by these genetic variations, promote healing, and accelerate trauma recovery.

References

Gilbody, S., Lewis, S., & Lightfoot, T. (2007). Methylenetetrahydrofolate reductase (MTHFR) genetic polymorphisms and psychiatric disorders: A HuGE review. *American Journal of Epidemiology, 165*(1), 1–13. https://doi.org/10.1093/aje/kwj347

Beyond MTHFR. (2013, October 1). A genetic cause of pain and anxiety – COMT, MAO and MTHFR. Retrieved from https://www.beyondmthfr.com/a-genetic-cause-of-pain-and-anxiety-comt-mao-and-mthfr/

Notaras, M., & van den Buuse, M. (2019). Brain-derived neurotrophic factor (BDNF): Novel insights into regulation and genetic variation. *The Neuroscientist, 25*(5), 434–454. https://doi.org/10.1177/1073858418810142

Wang, Z., Baker, D. G., Harrer, J., Hamner, M., Price, M., & Amstadter, A. B. (2011). The relationship between combat-related posttraumatic stress disorder and the 5-HTTLPR/rs25531 polymorphism. *Depression and Anxiety, 28*(12), 1067–1073. https://doi.org/10.1002/da.20872

Zannas, A. S., & Binder, E. B. (2014). Gene–environment interactions at the FKBP5 locus: Sensitive periods, mechanisms and pleiotropism. *Genes, Brain and Behavior, 13*(1), 25–37. https://doi.org/10.1111/gbb.12104

Zhang, Y., Tang, L., & Gonzalez, V. (2020). Anti-inflammatory effects of sulforaphane: A review of cellular mechanisms and applications. *Journal of Nutritional Biochemistry, 81*, 108295. https://doi.org/10.1016/j.jnutbio.2019.108295

41

TRAUMA AND CHILDHOOD ADVERSITY

(Adverse Childhood Experiences - ACEs)

Introduction: The Long-Term Impact of Childhood Trauma

Childhood is a formative period where emotional, psychological, and social development occurs at a rapid pace. Trauma during these critical years can leave a lasting imprint, affecting not only emotional well-being but also physical health, cognitive development, and social relationships. The term Adverse Childhood Experiences (ACEs) refers to a range of traumatic events that occur during childhood, including abuse, neglect, household dysfunction, and exposure to violence.

In this chapter, we will explore the profound impact of childhood trauma on long-term health, how ACEs influence behaviour and mental health, and the most effective strategies for healing the deep wounds caused by such childhood adversity.

What Are Adverse Childhood Experiences (ACEs)?

The term Adverse Childhood Experiences (ACEs) was coined following a groundbreaking study conducted by the Centers for Disease Control and Prevention (CDC) and Kaiser Permanente in the 1990s. This study revealed the significant impact of childhood trauma on lifelong health outcomes, showing a clear link between early adversity and long-term physical and mental health problems.

Common Types of ACEs

ACEs encompass a wide range of traumatic experiences that may occur before the age of 18. These include:

- **Physical, emotional, or sexual abuse:** Children who experience direct harm or emotional neglect from caregivers or others.

- **Parental substance abuse:** Living in a household where parents struggle with drug or alcohol addiction.

- **Parental mental illness:** Exposure to a caregiver with untreated mental health issues.

- **Divorce or separation:** Experiencing parental separation, especially if it is marked by conflict or hostility.

- **Domestic violence:** Witnessing violence between parents or caregivers.

- **Incarceration of a family member:** Having a close family member who is imprisoned.

These adverse experiences can disrupt the child's sense of safety, security, and trust, creating long-term emotional and psychological challenges.

The ACEs Study and Its Findings

The **ACE Study** found a clear link between the number of Adverse Childhood Experiences a person had and the likelihood of developing chronic physical and mental health issues later in life. As the number of ACEs increases, so does the risk for various health conditions, including:

- **Mental health issues:** Depression, anxiety, PTSD, and substance use disorders.

- **Chronic diseases:** Heart disease, diabetes, obesity, and cancer.

- **Behavioural challenges:** Risk-taking behaviours such as drug and alcohol abuse, unsafe sexual practices, and delinquency.

The ACEs Score

The ACE score is calculated by counting the number of different types of adverse experiences a person experienced during childhood. Higher scores are associated with increased health risks:

- **1–3 ACEs:** Moderate risk for health and emotional challenges.

- **Four or more ACEs:** Significantly higher risk of developing physical and mental health problems, including a higher likelihood of early death.

How Childhood Trauma Shapes Brain Development

The developing brain is especially vulnerable to the effects of trauma. During childhood, the brain undergoes rapid growth, particularly in areas that govern emotional regulation, learning, memory, and stress response. When children experience chronic or severe trauma, it alters the brain's architecture, making them more susceptible to emotional dysregulation, learning difficulties, and behavioural issues.

The Role of the Amygdala, Hippocampus, and Prefrontal Cortex

- **Amygdala:** The brain's emotional centre becomes hyperactive in children who experience trauma, leading to heightened fear responses and difficulties in managing emotions.

- **Hippocampus:** The hippocampus is responsible for memory and learning. The hippocampus can shrink in size due to chronic stress, making it difficult for children to process and store memories properly. This can lead to issues with learning and concentration.

- **Prefrontal cortex:** The part of the brain responsible for decision-making and impulse control develops more slowly in trauma-exposed children, making it harder for them to regulate their behaviour and emotions.

The Physical and Emotional Effects of ACEs

The long-term effects of childhood trauma are both physical and emotional, manifesting in different ways throughout an individual's life.

Emotional and mental health effects of ACEs include:

- **Anxiety and depression:** Children with high ACE scores are more likely to develop anxiety and depression in adolescence and adulthood. The chronic stress from early trauma can lead to dysregulation of the nervous system, making it difficult for individuals to manage their emotions.

- **Attachment disorders:** Early trauma can disrupt a child's ability to form healthy attachments with caregivers, leading to difficulties in trusting others, establishing relationships, and developing a stable sense of self.

- **Behavioural issues:** Children who experience ACEs are more likely to exhibit externalizing behaviours, such as aggression, defiance, and risk-taking, or internalizing behaviours, like withdrawal and isolation.

Physical health effects of ACEs include:

- **Chronic health conditions:** Chronic exposure to stress hormones, such as cortisol, can weaken the immune system and contribute to the development of chronic diseases, including heart disease, diabetes, and autoimmune disorders.

- **Inflammation and autoimmune disorders:** Chronic trauma leads to systemic inflammation, increasing the risk of developing conditions like rheumatoid arthritis, lupus, and chronic pain syndromes later in life.

Healing from Childhood Trauma: Therapeutic Approaches for ACEs

Healing from childhood adversity requires a holistic approach that addresses both the emotional and physical wounds caused by trauma. Trauma-informed care is essential for helping individuals process their early experiences, develop emotional resilience, and prevent further health complications.

Bottom-Up Therapies for ACEs Recovery

As with trauma in adulthood, bottom-up therapies that focus on healing the body and nervous system are essential for addressing the effects of ACEs.

Two therapies for facilitating recovery are:

- **Somatic Experiencing (SE):** This approach helps individuals release the stored energy of trauma in the body, allowing for emotional regulation and reducing physical symptoms related to stress.

- **Trauma Releasing Exercises (TRE):** TRE can help individuals process childhood trauma through physical release, reducing tension and restoring balance in the nervous system.

Family and Relational Therapies

Since many ACEs involve family dynamics, therapies that focus on repairing family relationships and addressing generational trauma can be incredibly effective.

Examples include:

- **Family Constellation Therapy:** This therapeutic approach helps individuals understand how family patterns and unresolved trauma from previous generations may be influencing their current emotional and relational challenges. By addressing these hidden dynamics, individuals can gain insights into their ACEs and find healing.

- **Clay Field Therapy:** Clay Field Therapy allows for sensory-based processing of trauma. It helps individuals, especially those who struggle with verbal expression, process childhood experiences in a hands-on, somatic way.

Cognitive and Emotional Support

Cognitive and emotional support can be offered using:

- **EMDR:** Eye Movement Desensitization and Reprocessing (EMDR) is a powerful tool for reprocessing traumatic childhood memories. It helps individuals reduce the emotional intensity of those memories and create new, healthier mental associations.

- **Mindfulness-Based Stress Reduction (MBSR):** Trauma-informed mindfulness practices help individuals develop greater awareness of their emotions and body, allowing them to regulate their stress response and break free from the patterns established by childhood trauma.

Building Resilience in Individuals with High ACEs

While the long-term effects of childhood trauma can be profound, building resilience is possible with the proper support and resources. Helping individuals develop emotional resilience, build healthy relationships, and engage in trauma-informed care can significantly reduce the long-term impacts of ACEs.

Developing Emotional Regulation Skills

Teaching individuals how to regulate their emotions through techniques like deep breathing, mindfulness, and grounding exercises can help them manage the intense emotions triggered by their childhood trauma.

Fostering Healthy Relationships

Since trauma often disrupts a child's ability to form healthy attachments, fostering supportive relationships is essential. Building trust, developing social skills, and engaging in safe, nurturing environments can help heal the relational wounds caused by childhood adversity.

Resilience-Based Approaches

- **Trauma-Informed Yoga:** Trauma-informed yoga helps individuals reconnect with their bodies, release tension, and promote nervous system regulation, which is critical for individuals recovering from childhood trauma.

- **Support networks:** Encouraging trauma survivors to build healthy support networks with family, friends, or support groups can provide the relational foundation necessary for emotional healing.

Key Takeaways

- Adverse Childhood Experiences (ACEs) have long-term effects on both mental and physical health, increasing the risk of chronic diseases, emotional dysregulation, and behavioural challenges.

- The ACE study highlights the significant impact of early trauma, showing that individuals with higher ACE scores are more likely to experience health problems later in life.

- Healing from childhood trauma requires bottom-up therapies, Family Constellation Work, and somatic approaches.

- Building resilience through emotional regulation skills, mindfulness, and supportive relationships is essential for individuals recovering from the effects of ACEs.

References

Anda, R. F., Felitti, V. J., Bremner, J. D., Walker, J. D., Whitfield, C., Perry, B. D., Dube, S. R., & Giles, W. H. (2006). The enduring effects of abuse and related adverse experiences in childhood: A convergence of evidence from neurobiology and epidemiology. *European Archives of Psychiatry and Clinical Neuroscience, 256*(3), 174–186. https://doi.org/10.1007/s00406-005-0624-4

Felitti, V. J., Anda, R. F., Nordenberg, D., Williamson, D. F., Spitz, A. M., Edwards, V., Koss, M. P., & Marks, J. S. (1998). Relationship of childhood abuse and household dysfunction to many of the leading causes of death in adults: The adverse childhood experiences (ACE) study. *American Journal of Preventive Medicine, 14*(4), 245–258. https://doi.org/10.1016/S0749-3797(98)00017-8

Levine, P. A. (2010). *In an unspoken voice: How the body releases trauma and restores goodness.* North Atlantic Books.

Porges, S. W. (2011). *The polyvagal theory: Neurophysiological foundations of emotions, attachment, communication, and self-regulation.* W. W. Norton & Company.

Sapolsky, R. M. (2004). *Why zebras don't get ulcers: The acclaimed guide to stress, stress-related diseases, and coping.* Holt Paperbacks.

Shonkoff, J. P., & Garner, A. S. (2012). The lifelong effects of early childhood adversity and toxic stress. *Pediatrics, 129*(1), e232–e246. https://doi.org/10.1542/peds.2011-2663

Teicher, M. H., Samson, J. A., Anderson, C. M., & Ohashi, K. (2016). The effects of childhood maltreatment on brain structure, function, and connectivity. *Nature Reviews Neuroscience, 17*(10), 652–666. https://doi.org/10.1038/nrn.2016.111

Van der Kolk, B. A. (2014). *The body keeps the score: Brain, mind, and body in the healing of trauma.* Penguin Books.

42.

TRAUMA AND SPIRITUALITY

Introduction: The Role of Spirituality in Trauma Recovery

Spirituality often plays a profound role in how individuals make sense of and recover from trauma. For many, trauma disrupts their sense of purpose, connection, and meaning in life. Exploring spirituality, whether through formal or informal religious practices, meditation, or a broader sense of connectedness, can help trauma survivors find hope, meaning, and healing in the aftermath of their experiences.

In this chapter, we will explore the connection between trauma and spirituality, how trauma can influence spiritual beliefs, and how integrating spiritual practices into trauma therapy can promote emotional, psychological, and physical healing.

The Spiritual Crisis of Trauma

Trauma often leads to a spiritual crisis—an existential questioning of life, purpose, and meaning. For many, trauma shakes the foundations of previously held beliefs about safety, justice, and the goodness of the world. This crisis can manifest as feelings of hopelessness, guilt, and disconnection from a higher power, or sense of purpose.

Loss of Meaning and Purpose

Trauma can make individuals question their beliefs and purpose, primarily if their faith or worldview cannot provide answers to why the traumatic event occurred. Survivors may experience a sense of abandonment, betrayal, or alienation from their spiritual or religious beliefs, leading to deep emotional and existential distress.

Many trauma survivors grapple with the question, "Why did this happen to me?" This can lead to a sense of isolation, as individuals feel that their suffering sets them apart from others, or the divine.

Survivors may also feel disconnected from their spiritual community, God, or a higher power, causing them to lose their sense of belonging or the support that their faith once provided.

How Trauma Can Affect Spiritual Beliefs

For some, trauma strengthens their spiritual beliefs, while for others, it causes doubt and disillusionment. The effects of trauma on spirituality are profoundly personal and vary depending on preexisting beliefs and the nature of the trauma experienced.

Strengthening Spiritual Beliefs

In some cases, trauma deepens an individual's spiritual beliefs as they seek comfort, guidance, and meaning through their faith. Religious or spiritual practices can provide solace, help individuals feel supported by a higher power, and offer a framework for making sense of suffering.

For trauma survivors who turn to their spiritual or religious beliefs, practices such as prayer, meditation, or rituals can become a source of strength and resilience during difficult times.

Spiritual communities often provide emotional and practical support for individuals recovering from trauma. The sense of belonging and shared beliefs can help survivors feel less isolated and more connected to others.

Spiritual Disillusionment

Conversely, trauma can lead to a spiritual crisis, where survivors feel abandoned or betrayed by their faith or higher power. This disillusionment can exacerbate feelings of despair, anxiety, and depression as the individual loses the sense of security or meaning that their faith once provided.

It can result in:

- **Questioning the divine:** Many trauma survivors question their faith or spiritual beliefs after experiencing trauma, especially if their worldview cannot explain or justify the suffering they endured.

- **Spiritual struggles:** Survivors may feel guilt or shame for doubting their faith, or experience fear that a higher power is punishing them for past actions. These spiritual struggles can lead to further emotional distress and hinder the recovery process.

The Healing Power of Spirituality

Despite the potential for spiritual disillusionment, spirituality can also be a powerful source of *healing* for trauma survivors. Spiritual practices can help individuals make sense of their experiences, reconnect with themselves and others, and find inner peace.

Trauma-informed Mindfulness and Meditation

Trauma-informed mindfulness and meditation practices, which often have spiritual or religious roots, help trauma survivors become more present, reduce anxiety, and cultivate a sense of inner calm. These practices allow individuals to focus on the present moment, release ruminative thoughts, and find peace in the here and now.

- **Trauma-informed mindfulness meditation:** Trauma-informed mindfulness teaches trauma survivors to observe their thoughts and emotions without judgement. This practice helps individuals regulate their emotions, reduce stress, and connect with a more profound sense of awareness.

- Loving-kindness meditation is a form of meditation that focuses on cultivating compassion toward oneself and others. This practice is beneficial for survivors who struggle with self-blame, guilt, or anger toward those involved in their trauma.

Connection to Nature

Nature-based spiritual practices, often referred to as **ecotherapy**, can provide a deep sense of grounding and connection to the world around us. Spending time in nature can help trauma survivors feel more connected to the Earth, experience a sense of renewal, and find meaning through the natural world's life cycles and growth.

An ancient Japanese practice called Shinrin-yoku (forest bathing) involves spending time in nature, engaging all the senses to connect with the environment. This practice promotes relaxation, reduces stress, and enhances emotional well-being, offering trauma survivors a spiritual and healing connection to the Earth.

Yoga and Breathwork

For many, yoga serves as both a physical and spiritual practice that helps integrate body, mind, and spirit. Trauma-informed yoga focuses on mindful movement and breath, helping trauma survivors reconnect with their bodies, release tension, and restore a sense of safety and control.

Conscious breathing exercises, often used in yoga and meditation, help regulate the nervous system and reduce trauma-related anxiety. Breathwork techniques such as box breathing or diaphragmatic breathing can calm the mind and bring a sense of inner peace and control.

Integrating Spirituality into Trauma Therapy

Incorporating spirituality into trauma therapy can enhance the healing process, particularly for individuals whose spiritual beliefs are central to their lives. Trauma-informed treatments that respect and support a client's spiritual framework can help them reconnect with their faith, find meaning in their experiences, and rebuild their sense of purpose.

Spiritual Counselling

Spiritual counselling, often provided by chaplains or faith-based counsellors, helps trauma survivors explore their spiritual questions and struggles in a supportive environment. By addressing spiritual concerns alongside psychological ones, spiritual counselling can foster a more holistic recovery process:

- **Addressing spiritual trauma:** Some individuals experience trauma specifically related to their religious or spiritual beliefs, such as abuse in a religious setting or feeling abandoned by a higher power. Spiritual counselling provides a space to address these issues with sensitivity and understanding.

- **Reconnecting with one's faith:** For survivors who have become disconnected from their faith, spiritual counselling can offer guidance on how to re-establish that connection, whether through religious practices, meditation, or personal reflection.

Meaning-Centred Therapy

Meaning-centred therapy, often associated with existential psychology, focuses on helping trauma survivors find meaning and purpose in their lives after trauma. This approach encourages individuals to explore their beliefs, values, and life purpose as part of the healing process.

Meaning-centred therapy helps individuals transform their trauma into a source of personal growth and wisdom, allowing them to reframe their experiences and find new purpose or direction in life.

Spiritual Practices for Trauma Survivors

In addition to formal spiritual counselling, trauma survivors can benefit from incorporating daily spiritual practices into their lives. These practices help individuals reconnect with their sense of self, explore their spirituality, and cultivate inner peace.

Daily Meditation or Prayer

Whether through traditional prayer, meditation, or quiet reflection, creating space for spiritual practices each day can help survivors process their trauma and find a sense of peace and meaning:

- Morning rituals: Starting the day with a moment of meditation or prayer sets a positive tone and helps survivors remain grounded in their spiritual beliefs.

- Gratitude practices: Engaging in a daily gratitude practice, where survivors reflect on the positive aspects of their lives, helps shift their focus from trauma to resilience, fostering a sense of hope and positivity.

Journaling for Spiritual Growth

Journaling is a powerful tool for exploring spiritual beliefs, processing emotions, and reflecting on one's experiences. Encouraging trauma survivors to journal about their spiritual journey can help them clarify their thoughts and feelings, work through spiritual struggles, and discover new insights.

Key Takeaways

- Trauma often leads to a spiritual crisis, where survivors question their sense of meaning, purpose, and connection to a higher power.

- Spirituality, whether through religious practices, meditation, or nature-based rituals, can help survivors find comfort, healing, and peace after trauma.

- Integrating spirituality into trauma therapy provides a holistic approach to recovery, helping survivors reconnect with their faith, find meaning in suffering, and rebuild a sense of purpose.

- Practices such as mindfulness, yoga, nature connection, and spiritual counselling can foster healing, growth, and inner peace for trauma survivors.

References

Bonanno, G. A., & Mancini, A. D. (2008). The human capacity to thrive in the face of potential trauma. *Pediatrics, 121*(2), 369–375. https://doi.org/10.1542/peds.2007-1648

Bryant-Davis, T., & Wong, E. C. (2013). Faith to move mountains: Religious coping, spirituality, and interpersonal trauma recovery. *American Psychologist, 68*(8), 675–684. https://doi.org/10.1037/a0034380

Kabat-Zinn, J. (1990). *Full catastrophe living: Using the wisdom of your body and mind to face stress, pain, and illness.* Delta.

Levine, P. A. (2010). *In an unspoken voice: How the body releases trauma and restores goodness.* North Atlantic Books.

Nash, W. P., & Litz, B. T. (2013). Moral injury: A mechanism for war-related psychological trauma in military family members. *Clinical Child and Family Psychology Review, 16*(4), 365–375. https://doi.org/10.1007/s10567-013-0146-y

Pargament, K. I., Smith, B. W., Koenig, H. G., & Perez, L. (1998). Patterns of positive and negative religious coping with major life stressors. *Journal for the Scientific Study of Religion, 37*(4), 710–724. https://doi.org/10.2307/1388152

Porges, S. W. (2011). *The polyvagal theory: Neurophysiological foundations of emotions, attachment, communication, and self-regulation.* W. W. Norton & Company.

Shapiro, S. L., Carlson, L. E., Astin, J. A., & Freedman, B. (2006). Mechanisms of mindfulness. *Journal of Clinical Psychology, 62*(3), 373–386. https://doi.org/10.1002/jclp.20237

Van der Kolk, B. A. (2014). *The body keeps the score: Brain, mind, and body in the healing of trauma.* Penguin Books.

Walsh, R., & Shapiro, S. L. (2006). The meeting of meditative disciplines and Western psychology: A mutually enriching dialogue. *American Psychologist, 61*(3), 227–239. https://doi.org/10.1037/0003-066X.61.3.227

43.

THE FUTURE OF PTSD TREATMENT

Advancing Trauma Recovery

Introduction: New Frontiers in Trauma Treatment

As our understanding of Post-Traumatic Stress Disorder (PTSD) evolves, so do the treatment options available to those who suffer from it. Traditional therapies, such as talk therapy and medication, have proven beneficial for many, but emerging therapies are paving the way for even more profound and long-lasting recovery.

In this chapter, we'll explore the cutting-edge approaches that are transforming PTSD treatment, including **Stellate Ganglion Blocks (SGB), Transcranial Direct Current Stimulation (TDCS), psychedelic-assisted therapy**, and **metabolic psychiatry**. These therapies offer hope for those who have not found relief through conventional methods.

Stellate Ganglion Blocks (SGB)

Stellate Ganglion Blocks (SGB) are an innovative treatment for PTSD: an injection of anaesthetic into the stellate ganglion—a collection of nerves in the neck that help regulate the body's stress response. By temporarily blocking these nerves, SGB can reset the sympathetic nervous system, reducing symptoms of hypervigilance, anxiety, and emotional dysregulation in individuals with PTSD.

How SGB Works

SGB interrupts the fight-or-flight response, calming the sympathetic nervous system and allowing the body to enter a state of relaxation. A medical professional typically performs this procedure under image guidance to ensure the precise placement of the injection.

Research on SGB

Studies have shown that SGB is effective in reducing PTSD symptoms, particularly in military veterans and first responders. Many individuals report immediate relief from anxiety, improved sleep, and a reduction in intrusive thoughts. The effects of SGB can last from several weeks to months, making it a promising option for those with treatment-resistant PTSD.

SGB for Military Veterans

In one study, a group of military veterans with PTSD underwent Stellate Ganglion Block treatment. After the procedure, 70% of participants reported significant reductions in anxiety and hypervigilance, with some experiencing sustained relief for up to six months.

Transcranial Direct Current Stimulation (TDCS)

Transcranial Direct Current Stimulation (TDCS) is a non-invasive therapy that uses low-level electrical currents to stimulate specific areas of the brain. This treatment has been shown to help individuals with PTSD by enhancing neuroplasticity, the brain's ability to reorganize and form new connections.

How TDCS Works

TDCS involves placing electrodes on the scalp to deliver a mild electrical current to targeted brain regions, such as the prefrontal cortex. By stimulating these areas, TDCS helps improve cognitive function, emotional regulation, and mood.

Research on TDCS

Several studies have demonstrated that TDCS can significantly reduce PTSD symptoms, particularly in individuals with cognitive impairments or emotional dysregulation. It has been shown to enhance the effects of traditional therapy, making it an ideal adjunct to Cognitive Behavioural Therapy (CBT) or EMDR.

Psychedelic-Assisted Therapy

Psychedelic-assisted therapy is a groundbreaking approach to treating PTSD that involves the use of psychedelic substances, such as MDMA, psilocybin, or ketamine, in a controlled therapeutic setting. These substances help individuals access deep emotional and psychological states, allowing for the processing and integration of traumatic memories.

How Psychedelics Work in Therapy

Psychedelics temporarily alter brain function, reducing activity in the default mode network (DMN)—the part of the brain responsible for self-reflection and rumination. This allows trauma survivors to access memories and emotions without being overwhelmed by fear or anxiety, facilitating deep emotional healing.

Research on Psychedelics for PTSD

Research on MDMA-assisted therapy for PTSD has shown remarkable results. In one phase 3 clinical trial, 67% of participants no longer met the criteria for PTSD after three MDMA therapy sessions, and 88% experienced significant reductions in symptoms. Similar results have been observed with psilocybin and ketamine, which have shown promise in treating depression, anxiety, and PTSD.

MDMA Therapy for PTSD

A man who had struggled with PTSD for over a decade participated in a clinical trial for MDMA-assisted therapy. After three sessions, he reported a complete cessation of nightmares, significant reductions in anxiety, and an ability to process traumatic memories without emotional overwhelm.

Metabolic Psychiatry: A New Frontier in Trauma Care

Metabolic psychiatry is an emerging field that focuses on the connection between metabolic health, brain function, and mental health. Trauma often disrupts the body's metabolic processes, leading to issues such as insulin resistance, inflammation, and **mitochondrial dysfunction**. Addressing these metabolic imbalances can help reduce PTSD symptoms and improve overall mental well-being.

How Metabolic Psychiatry Works

Metabolic psychiatry aims to treat PTSD by focusing on the gut-brain connection and optimizing metabolic pathways. Treatments may include anti-inflammatory diets, intermittent fasting, and the use of specific nutritional supplements to support brain health and reduce inflammation.

Research on Metabolic Psychiatry

Studies have shown that individuals with PTSD often have elevated levels of inflammation and oxidative stress, both of which can contribute to emotional dysregulation and cognitive dysfunction. By addressing these issues through diet and supplementation, metabolic psychiatry offers a holistic approach to healing trauma.

Virtual Reality Exposure Therapy (VRET)

Virtual Reality Exposure Therapy (VRET) is an innovative approach that uses virtual reality technology to simulate traumatic experiences in a controlled environment. This allows individuals to confront and process their trauma in a safe, therapeutic setting.

How VRET Works

Using VR headsets, individuals with PTSD are gradually exposed to virtual recreations of their traumatic experiences. The exposure is done in a controlled and supportive environment, allowing them to face their fears without becoming overwhelmed. Over time, this exposure helps reduce trauma-related distress and symptoms.

Research on VRET

Several studies have shown that VRET is effective in reducing PTSD symptoms, particularly in combat veterans and first responders. By allowing individuals to process trauma in a controlled way, VRET helps desensitize them to traumatic memories and reduce avoidance behaviours.

VRET for PTSD in First Responders

A group of first responders with PTSD participated in Virtual Reality Exposure Therapy. After several sessions, participants reported reduced flashbacks, improved emotional regulation, and an ability to confront trauma without experiencing overwhelming anxiety.

Key Takeaways

- Stellate Ganglion Blocks (SGB) offer a promising solution for reducing hypervigilance and anxiety in individuals with PTSD by resetting the sympathetic nervous system.

- Transcranial Direct Current Stimulation (TDCS) is a non-invasive technique that enhances neuroplasticity. It helps individuals regulate emotions and improve cognitive function.

- Psychedelic-assisted therapy, particularly with MDMA and psilocybin, has shown remarkable potential in helping trauma survivors to access and process traumatic memories deeply and therapeutically.

- Metabolic psychiatry connects trauma recovery with metabolic health, using anti-inflammatory diets, fasting, and supplements to reduce inflammation and improve mental well-being.

- Virtual Reality Exposure Therapy (VRET) allows individuals to confront and process trauma in a controlled, virtual environment, reducing avoidance behaviours and traumatic distress.

References

Rae Olmsted, K. L., Bartoszek, M., Mulvaney, S., McLean, B., Turabi, A., Young, R., Kim, E., Vandermaas-Peeler, R., Morgan, J. K., Constantinescu, O., Kane, S., Nguyen, C., Hirsch, S., Munoz, B., Wallace, D., Croxford, J., Lynch, J. H., White, R., & Walters, B. B. (2019). Effect of stellate ganglion block treatment on posttraumatic stress disorder symptoms: A randomized clinical trial. *JAMA Psychiatry, 76*(11), 130–138. https://doi.org/10.1001/jamapsychiatry.2019.3474

Cohen, H., Kaplan, Z., Kotler, M., Kouperman, I., Moisa, R., & Grisaru, N. (2004). Repetitive transcranial magnetic stimulation of the right dorsolateral prefrontal cortex in posttraumatic stress disorder: A double-blind, placebo-controlled study. *American Journal of Psychiatry, 161*(3), 515–524. https://doi.org/10.1176/appi.ajp.161.3.515

Mithoefer, M. C., Grob, C. S., & Brewerton, T. D. (2016). Novel psychopharmacological therapies for psychiatric disorders: Psilocybin and MDMA. *The Lancet Psychiatry, 3*(5), 481–488. [https://doi.org/10.1016/S2215-0366(15)00576-3]

Aucoin, M., LaChance, L., Naidoo, U., Remy, D., Shekdar, T., Sayar, N., Cardozo, V., Rawana, T., Chan, I., & Cooley, K. (2021). Diet and anxiety: A scoping review. *Nutrients, 13*(12), 4418. https://doi.org/10.3390/nu13124418

Maples-Keller, J. L., Bunnell, B. E., Kim, S. J., & Rothbaum, B. O. (2017). The use of virtual reality technology in the treatment of anxiety and other psychiatric disorders. *Harvard Review of Psychiatry, 25*(3), 103–113. https://doi.org/10.1097/HRP.0000000000000138

44.

HOLISTIC APPROACHES TO TRAUMA RECOVERY

Introduction: Healing the Whole Person: A Holistic Approach to Trauma Recovery

Recovering from trauma, especially from conditions like PTSD, requires a comprehensive approach that addresses the body, mind and spirit. Holistic approaches are essential for healing, as they focus on integrating various therapies and lifestyle changes that support the body's natural healing processes.

In this chapter, we explore how a combination of movement, nutrition, mindfulness, and spirituality can aid trauma survivors in their recovery journey and promote long-term resilience.

The Role of Nutrition in Trauma Recovery

Nutrition is a foundational aspect of trauma recovery, particularly in reducing inflammation and supporting brain function. Trauma may disrupt the body's metabolic processes and increase inflammation, but proper nutrition can counterbalance these effects and promote cellular repair.

Holistic therapies, such as nutrition, meditation, and vagus nerve activation, are integral to stimulating salugenesis signalling. These approaches help transition the body from a state of chronic stress and trauma (as triggered by the Cell Danger Response) into a state of cellular repair and healing, facilitating the body's innate ability to recover.

Anti-Inflammatory Diets

Chronic inflammation is a significant factor in many trauma-related physical symptoms. An anti-inflammatory diet rich in whole, unprocessed foods—such as vegetables, fruits, lean proteins, nuts, seeds, and healthy fats—helps reduce inflammation and support healing.

Essential anti-inflammatory foods include omega-3-rich fatty fish (salmon, mackerel), berries, dark leafy greens, nuts, and seeds. These foods contain antioxidants and essential fatty acids that reduce oxidative stress and promote cellular repair.

Nutritional Supplements for Brain and Body Health

In addition to a nutrient-rich diet, supplements can further support trauma recovery by promoting nervous system health and reducing inflammation. Some essential supplements include:

- **Magnesium:** Helps regulate the nervous system, supports restful sleep, and reduces anxiety.

- **B-Vitamins:** Essential for energy production, brain function, and mood regulation.

- **Probiotics:** Support gut health, which plays a significant role in regulating immune function and emotional health.

While nutrition plays a vital role, it should be seen as part of a more extensive, integrative approach to healing trauma.

Movement and Exercise for Trauma Recovery

Movement is one of the most potent tools for trauma recovery. It helps regulate the nervous system and release tension stored in the body. Regular physical activity also helps improve emotional well-being, cognitive function, and resilience to stress.

Trauma-Informed Yoga

Trauma-informed yoga is specifically designed to create a safe, supportive environment for trauma survivors. It focuses on gentle movements, breath awareness, and emotional regulation. This form of yoga encourages individuals to reconnect with their bodies in a non-judgmental way, releasing tension and promoting healing.

By focusing on body awareness and mindfulness, yoga can help trauma survivors gain control over their physical and emotional responses to stress.

Aerobic Exercise and Endorphin Release

Aerobic exercise, such as running, cycling, or swimming, is another powerful way to promote mental health. It triggers the release of endorphins, which are natural mood boosters. Regular aerobic exercise can improve mood, reduce anxiety, and help trauma survivors build emotional resilience.

Engaging in regular physical activity also helps regulate the autonomic nervous system, which can help balance the fight-or-flight response commonly seen in trauma survivors.

Trauma-informed Mindfulness and Trauma Recovery

Trauma-informed mindfulness practices play a central role in trauma recovery by helping individuals stay grounded in the present moment, regulate their emotions, and manage intrusive thoughts. Trauma-informed mindfulness can also reduce the likelihood of being overwhelmed by traumatic memories.

Trauma-Informed Mindfulness Meditation

Trauma-informed mindfulness meditation encourages individuals to focus on the present moment and observe thoughts and emotions without judgement. By practicing mindfulness, trauma survivors can reduce anxiety, increase self-awareness, and foster emotional stability.

Studies have shown that regular practice of trauma-informed mindfulness can help reduce the symptoms of PTSD, such as hypervigilance and emotional numbing, by calming the nervous system and promoting a sense of safety.

Body Scanning for Emotional Awareness

Body scanning is a simple yet effective trauma-informed mindfulness practice. In this practice, individuals focus on different parts of the body, noticing areas of tension or discomfort and releasing them through deep, slow breaths. This practice reduces physical tension and stress, and also helps individuals stay connected to their bodies and emotions.

Body scanning is beneficial for trauma survivors who may experience dissociation or disconnection from their physical sensations.

Spirituality and Trauma Recovery

For many individuals, spirituality is an essential part of their healing journey. Connecting with something greater than oneself, whether through meditation, prayer, or spiritual reflection, can provide comfort, meaning, and hope during the recovery process.

Meditation and Emotional Healing

Meditation is a powerful tool for reducing stress, promoting emotional balance, and fostering a sense of inner peace. Practices like trauma-informed mindfulness meditation, loving-kindness meditation, or transcendental meditation can help trauma survivors cultivate compassion for themselves and others.

By incorporating meditation into daily life, trauma survivors can shift their focus away from negative or traumatic thoughts, promoting healing and emotional resilience.

Nature Therapy (Ecotherapy)

Spending time in nature has been shown to reduce stress, lower cortisol levels, and promote overall well-being. Ecotherapy, or nature therapy, (forest bathing) involves reconnecting with the natural world through activities like walking in the woods, gardening, or simply sitting by a body of water.

Nature therapy can help trauma survivors feel more grounded, calm, and connected to the world around them. It offers a break from the demands of everyday life, giving the opportunity to reflect and heal in a peaceful environment.

Integrating Holistic Practices for Long-Term Recovery

Trauma recovery is not a linear process, and individuals often benefit from integrating *multiple* holistic practices into their daily routines. By combining nutrition, movement, mindfulness, and spirituality, trauma survivors will create a foundation for long-term emotional and physical healing.

Building a Daily Routine

Establishing a structured daily routine that includes time for self-care is critical for trauma recovery. Morning rituals such as meditation or stretching, regular meals that support brain health, and consistent movement practices will help stabilize emotions and reduce anxiety.

Self-Compassion and Healing

A central aspect of trauma recovery is learning to offer oneself kindness and understanding. Self-compassion practices, such as self-compassion meditation or journaling, help individuals develop a more positive relationship with themselves, reducing the shame and self-criticism that can accompany the experience of trauma.

Conclusion: A Holistic Path to Trauma Recovery

Healing from trauma requires addressing all aspects of the self—body, mind and spirit. Through a combination of nutrition, movement, mindfulness, and spirituality, trauma survivors can promote long-term healing and resilience. By integrating these holistic practices into daily life, individuals can rebuild emotional balance, restore physical health, and develop a deeper connection to themselves and the world around them.

Holistic therapies such as trauma-informed yoga, meditation, and nature therapy offer trauma survivors tools to reduce anxiety, increase self-awareness, and bring emotional stability. Likewise, nutrition plays a crucial role in reducing inflammation and supporting brain health, which are both essential in the trauma recovery process.

These integrative approaches create an environment for the body to transition from chronic stress and trauma into a state of healing, activating what is known as salugenesis.

Post-Traumatic Growth and Salugenesis

Post-traumatic growth (PTG) exemplifies the profound ability of the body and mind to not only heal from trauma but also to grow *stronger*. Research suggests that this growth involves a process of rewiring in the brain through neuroplasticity and neurogenesis. Neuroplasticity allows for the creation of new neural connections, while neurogenesis supports the formation of new neurons. These mechanisms are conducive to both cognitive and emotional transformation, enabling individuals to experience personal growth, enhanced mental resilience, and a renewed sense of purpose after trauma. PTG reflects not just recovery but a state of *thriving* following adversity.

Through salugenesis, trauma survivors not only heal but also develop resilience, strength, and a new understanding of their personal journey. The holistic methods explored in this chapter, from physical movement to spiritual practices, are instrumental in facilitating this growth, demonstrating that the path to recovery is as much about transformation as it is about healing.

Key Takeaways

- Nutrition and anti-inflammatory diets are crucial in reducing trauma-related inflammation and supporting brain health.

- Movement, such as trauma-informed yoga and aerobic exercise, helps regulate the nervous system and release stored tension.

- Trauma-informed mindfulness helps survivors stay grounded, manage emotions, and reduce the impact of traumatic memories.

- Spirituality, through practices like prayer, meditation and ecotherapy, can promote emotional healing and resilience.

- Post-Traumatic Growth (PTG) reflects how the brain can heal and grow stronger after trauma, facilitated by neuroplasticity and neurogenesis.

Next Steps

- Explore therapies that promote neuroplasticity and salugenesis in trauma recovery.

- Integrate holistic practices like nutrition, movement, mindfulness, and spirituality to support both emotional and physical healing.

- Encourage trauma survivors to establish daily routines that prioritize self-care and compassion.

References

Harch, P. G., & Fogarty, E. F. (2009). The Oxygen Revolution: Hyperbaric oxygen therapy. Hatherleigh Press.

Levine, P. A. (2010). In an Unspoken Voice: How the body releases trauma and restores goodness. North Atlantic Books.

McEwen, B. S. (2007). Physiology and neurobiology of stress and adaptation: Central role of the brain. *Physiological Reviews, 87*(3), 873–904. https://doi.org/10.1152/physrev.00041.2006

Naviaux, R. K. (2014). Metabolic features of the cell danger response. *Mitochondrion, 16*, 7–17. https://doi.org/10.1016/j.mito.2013.08.006

Neff, K. D. (2011). Self-compassion: The proven power of being kind to yourself. HarperCollins.

Porges, S. W. (2011). The Polyvagal Theory: Neurophysiological foundations of emotions, attachment, communication, and self-regulation. W. W. Norton & Company.

Van der Kolk, B. A. (2014). The Body Keeps the Score: Brain, mind, and body in the healing of trauma. Penguin Books.

45.

THE HOLISTIC PATH TO LASTING PTSD RECOVERY

Introduction: Sustaining Recovery Beyond Trauma

Recovering from Post-Traumatic Stress Disorder (PTSD) involves more than just addressing the immediate symptoms of trauma. To achieve long-term emotional and physical well-being, it's essential to integrate healing practices into daily life that support the body, mind, and spirit.

In this chapter, we build upon the previous chapter and further explore the holistic path to maintaining recovery, focusing on the integration of trauma-informed mindfulness practices, self-compassion, nutrition, exercise, and social connections that contribute to a lasting sense of balance and resilience.

Integrating Trauma-informed Mindfulness into Everyday Life

Trauma-informed mindfulness is a powerful tool for trauma recovery, helping individuals stay grounded in the present moment and reduce the likelihood of being overwhelmed by intrusive thoughts or emotional flashbacks. Once the initial stages of trauma therapy are complete, practicing trauma-informed mindfulness regularly can help trauma survivors maintain their sense of emotional regulation and clarity.

Trauma-informed Mindfulness Meditation for Long-Term Healing

Regular trauma-informed mindfulness meditation helps calm the nervous system, reduce stress, and improve emotional awareness. By training the mind to focus on the present moment, individuals can better manage anxiety and avoid getting caught in cycles of worry or rumination.

Body Scanning for Awareness

One simple but effective trauma-informed mindfulness practice is body scanning. This practice involves bringing full attention to different parts of the body, noticing areas of tension or discomfort, and releasing them through slow, deep breaths. It promotes a sense of calm and helps trauma survivors stay connected to their physical sensations, which is important for long-term healing.

Practicing Self-Compassion

Self-compassion is a critical element of sustaining recovery. Many individuals with PTSD struggle with feelings of shame, guilt, or self-criticism. Learning to practice self-compassion can help trauma survivors reframe their thoughts and treat themselves with kindness rather than judgement.

Loving-Kindness Meditation

One way to cultivate self-compassion is through loving-kindness meditation, which focuses on generating feelings of compassion and kindness toward oneself and others. By repeating phrases like "May I be happy, may I be healthy, may I be safe", trauma survivors can gradually shift their internal dialogue and thus promote emotional healing.

Challenging Negative Self-Talk

Another important aspect of self-compassion is learning to challenge negative self-talk. Many individuals with PTSD carry deep-rooted beliefs about their worthiness or ability to recover. By actively challenging these thoughts and replacing them with more compassionate and realistic affirmations, survivors can build a healthier relationship with themselves.

Nutrition and Gut-Brain Health

As discussed in previous chapters, nutrition plays a significant role in trauma recovery, particularly in supporting the gut-brain connection. Sustaining recovery requires adopting long-term dietary habits that reduce inflammation, support brain health, and promote emotional stability.

Anti-Inflammatory Diets for Ongoing Healing

An anti-inflammatory diet rich in whole foods, such as fruits, vegetables, lean proteins, and healthy fats, helps reduce the chronic inflammation that is often present in individuals with PTSD. Foods high in omega-3 fatty acids, antioxidants, and probiotics continue to support cognitive function, emotional regulation, and overall well-being long after the initial stages of recovery.

Probiotics and Gut Health

The gut is often referred to as the "second brain", and maintaining a healthy gut microbiome is essential for emotional stability. Regular consumption of probiotics and prebiotics (such as yoghurt, sauerkraut, and fibre-rich vegetables) helps regulate digestion and reduce inflammation, which can alleviate anxiety and depression symptoms over time.

Movement and Exercise for Trauma Recovery

Movement is an important component of trauma recovery, as it helps regulate the nervous system and release stored tension in the body. Integrating exercise into daily life is also essential for maintaining physical and emotional balance after recovery.

Trauma-Informed Yoga for Long-Term Stability

Practicing trauma-informed yoga on a regular basis provides ongoing benefits for both the body and mind. This gentle, mindful approach to movement helps trauma survivors stay connected to their physical sensations, release tension, and maintain emotional balance.

Aerobic Exercise and Endorphins

Aerobic exercise, such as running, swimming, or cycling, promotes the release of endorphins, the body's natural "feel-good" chemicals. Regular aerobic activity not only improves physical health but also enhances mood, reduces anxiety, and helps trauma survivors feel more resilient and emotionally stable.

Social Support and Connection

Social support is one of the most *important* factors in sustaining long-term recovery from trauma. Rebuilding and maintaining meaningful connections with others will reduce feelings of isolation, provides emotional validation, and offers practical support during challenging times.

The Importance of a Support Network

Having a solid support network of friends, family, or a peer group is critical to long-term recovery. Whether through formal support groups, community activities, or simply staying connected with loved ones, social interaction provides trauma survivors with a sense of belonging and safety.

Setting Boundaries and Maintaining Healthy Relationships

While social connections are important, it's equally crucial for trauma survivors to set boundaries and maintain relationships that are healthy and supportive. This may involve learning to say "no" to toxic or draining relationships and surrounding oneself with people who encourage growth and healing.

Building Emotional Resilience

Emotional resilience is the ability to bounce back from stress, adversity, or trauma. Building this resilience is essential for preventing relapse into PTSD symptoms and for navigating life's inevitable challenges with greater ease.

Resilience Practices

Resilience can be cultivated through practices such as gratitude journaling, where individuals reflect on positive aspects of their lives and focus on all the things they are thankful for. This practice helps shift attention away from negative thoughts and will support a more optimistic outlook on life.

Cognitive Restructuring

Cognitive restructuring is another tool for building resilience. This practice involves identifying and challenging irrational or unhelpful thoughts and replacing them with more balanced, realistic perspectives. Over time, this process helps trauma survivors feel more empowered to handle stress and adversity.

Key Takeaways

- Trauma-informed mindfulness practices, such as meditation and body scanning, help trauma survivors stay grounded in the present moment and maintain emotional regulation over time.

- Self-compassion is essential for long-term recovery. Learning to challenge negative self-talk and practice kindness toward oneself promotes emotional healing.

- Nutrition plays a crucial role in sustaining recovery. An anti-inflammatory diet and probiotics help maintain the gut-brain connection and support emotional well-being.

- Movement—trauma-informed yoga and/or aerobic exercise—helps regulate the nervous system, release tension, and promote emotional resilience.

- Social support provides important emotional validation, belonging, and emotional safety, but maintaining healthy boundaries with people is equally important for long-term recovery.

References

Neff, K. (2011). *Self-compassion: The proven power of being kind to yourself.* HarperCollins.

Schleip, R., & Jäger, H. (2015). *Fascia in sport and movement.* Handspring Publishing.

Siegel, D. (2010). *Mindsight: The new science of personal transformation.* Bantam Books.

Van der Kolk, B. (2015). *The Body Keeps the Score: Brain, mind, and body in the healing of trauma.* Penguin Books.

Walker, L. (2013). Nutritional psychiatry: Healing the brain through food. *Journal of Integrative Health, 12*(4), 187-194.

46.

INTEGRATING HEALING
INTO EVERYDAY LIFE

Practical Tools for PTSD Recovery

Introduction: Making Healing a Daily Practice

Healing from Post-Traumatic Stress Disorder (PTSD) is an ongoing process. While trauma therapy and holistic approaches provide powerful tools for recovery, the journey doesn't end when therapy is over. To maintain the progress made in recovery and continue healing, it's essential to incorporate daily practices that support emotional, mental, and physical well-being.

In this chapter, we provide practical tools for integrating healing into everyday life, helping trauma survivors develop resilience and continue their journey toward long-term recovery.

Establishing a Daily Routine

Creating a structured daily routine can help trauma survivors maintain stability and reduce anxiety. Routines provide a sense of control and predictability, which is especially important for individuals with PTSD who may feel overwhelmed by the uncertainty of day-to-day life.

Morning Rituals for Grounding

Start the day with a morning ritual that sets a positive tone. This could include a short meditation, breathing exercises, or setting an intention for the day. Beginning the day with trauma-informed mindfulness helps centre the mind and body, reducing stress and anxiety before challenges arise.

Consistency in Sleep and Nutrition

Consistency in sleep and nutrition is also crucial for sustaining recovery. Going to bed and waking up at around the same time each day promotes better sleep hygiene, while regular meals—especially those that support brain health—help maintain stable energy and mood levels throughout the day.

Practicing Trauma-informed Mindfulness in Daily Activities

Trauma-informed mindfulness doesn't need to be limited to formal meditation sessions. Trauma survivors can benefit from bringing trauma-informed mindfulness into everyday activities, helping them stay grounded and present.

Mindful Walking

One practical tool is mindful walking, where individuals focus on the sensation of their feet hitting the ground, the rhythm of their breath, and the environment around them. This practice helps reduce stress and keeps the mind focused on the present moment rather than dwelling on past trauma.

Mindful Eating

Mindful eating encourages individuals to slow down and fully experience their meals, paying attention to flavours, textures, and sensations. This practice not only improves digestion but also helps individuals to develop a deeper connection with the body, which can help trauma survivors rebuild trust in their physical sensations.

Journaling for Emotional Release

Journaling is a powerful tool for trauma recovery, providing a safe space for individuals to express their thoughts, emotions, and reflections. Regular journaling helps process unresolved feelings and can offer insight into emotional triggers and patterns.

Daily Gratitude Journaling

One very effective journaling practice is gratitude journaling, where individuals write down three things they are grateful for each day. This practice helps shift the focus away from negative or traumatic thoughts and encourages a more positive mindset.

Processing Emotions Through Writing

For those who find it difficult to talk about their trauma, free writing can be an excellent way to release pent-up emotions. Allowing thoughts and feelings to flow freely onto the page provides an outlet for emotional release and helps individuals gain clarity about their inner world.

Breathing Techniques for Stress Management

Breathing exercises are essential tools for managing stress and regulating the nervous system. By engaging in controlled breathing techniques, trauma survivors can activate the parasympathetic nervous system, promoting relaxation and reducing the intensity of trauma-related anxiety.

Box Breathing for Calm

One simple yet effective technique is box breathing, where individuals inhale for four counts, hold the breath for four counts, exhale for four counts, and hold again for four counts before repeating. This method helps slow the heart rate, reduce cortisol levels, and calm the body's fight-or-flight response.

Diaphragmatic Breathing for Nervous System Regulation

Diaphragmatic breathing, or deep belly breathing, is another tool that helps trauma survivors stay grounded in stressful situations. By focusing on breathing deeply into the diaphragm, individuals can lower their heart rate and blood pressure, promoting feelings of calm and safety.

Building a Supportive Social Environment

Social support is critical to maintaining recovery from PTSD. Reaching out to friends, family, or a more formal support network will help trauma survivors feel less isolated and more connected, offering emotional validation and encouragement along the way.

Identifying Supportive Relationships

It's important for trauma survivors to identify and nurture supportive relationships—those that provide understanding, encouragement, and kindness. This may involve seeking out *new* friendships or deepening connections with trusted individuals who offer positive reinforcement and a safe space for healing.

Communicating Boundaries

Maintaining healthy boundaries is essential for emotional well-being. Trauma survivors may need to set boundaries with individuals who trigger anxiety or bring negativity into their lives. Communicating these boundaries clearly and assertively will help maintain emotional safety and prevent relapse into PTSD symptoms.

Creating a Healing Space

The physical environment plays a significant role in emotional well-being. Creating a healing space at home can provide trauma survivors with a sense of peace, comfort, and security, helping them unwind and relax after stressful moments.

Decluttering for Mental Clarity

A clean, uncluttered space promotes mental clarity and reduces feelings of overwhelm. Regularly decluttering and organizing living spaces helps reduce stress and create a more harmonious environment that supports emotional well-being.

Incorporating Calming Elements

Incorporating calming elements—such as soft lighting, calming colours, essential oils, and soothing sounds—into the home environment can make it easier to relax and unwind. Creating a designated space for meditation, journaling, or quiet reflection will further support emotional balance.

Regular Movement and Exercise

Exercise continues to be one of the most effective tools for managing stress and maintaining mental health after trauma recovery. Whether through yoga, aerobic exercise, or gentle movement, staying active helps regulate the nervous system, release tension, and improve mood.

Morning Stretching for Energy

Starting the day with a few minutes of stretching helps release any tension that may have accumulated overnight and promotes better circulation. Incorporating gentle yoga poses or a simple stretching routine into the morning ritual can help individuals feel more energized and centred.

Regular Aerobic Exercise for Mental Health

Engaging in aerobic exercise for at least 30 minutes a day can significantly boost mood, reduce anxiety, and improve resilience. Whether it's jogging, biking, or swimming, regular movement helps trauma survivors maintain emotional stability and physical health.

Cultivating Emotional Resilience

Developing emotional resilience is key to handling life's inevitable stressors, without relapsing into PTSD symptoms. By strengthening resilience, trauma survivors can better navigate challenges, recover from setbacks, and continue *growing beyond* trauma.

Emotional Check-ins

One way to cultivate resilience is through emotional check-ins, where individuals take a moment to assess how they are feeling and identify any stressors or triggers that may need attention. This practice helps build self-awareness and prevents emotional overwhelm.

Affirmations and Positive Self-Talk

Using affirmations and positive self-talk can help trauma survivors challenge negative thinking patterns and replace them with empowering thoughts. Simple affirmations such as "I am strong", "I am capable", and "I am healing", reinforce positive beliefs and will build emotional resilience over time.

Key Takeaways

- Establishing a structured daily routine helps provide stability, reduce anxiety, and promote emotional well-being.

- Trauma-informed mindfulness can be integrated into daily activities, such as walking or eating, helping trauma survivors stay present and connected to their bodies.

- Journaling is a powerful tool for processing emotions and promoting self-awareness. Gratitude journaling, in particular, fosters a positive mindset.

- Breathing techniques, such as box breathing and diaphragmatic breathing, help regulate the nervous system and reduce stress.

- Social support is critical for maintaining recovery, and setting clear boundaries ensures that relationships remain healthy and supportive.

- Creating a healing space at home promotes relaxation and emotional balance, while regular movement supports both physical and emotional well-being.

- Emotional resilience can be cultivated through practices like emotional check-ins, positive affirmations, and maintaining self-awareness.

Next Steps

- Integrating these practical tools into everyday life provides trauma survivors with a roadmap for long-term healing and emotional well-being.

- By establishing routines, practicing mindfulness, nurturing supportive relationships, and cultivating resilience, individuals can continue to thrive beyond trauma and *reclaim their lives.*

References

Levine, P. (1997). *Waking the Tiger: Healing trauma.* North Atlantic Books.

Neff, K. (2011). *Self-compassion: The proven power of being kind to yourself.* HarperCollins.

Schleip, R., & Jäger, H. (2015). *Fascia in Sport and Movement.* Handspring Publishing.

Siegel, D. (2010). *Mindsight: The new science of personal transformation.* Bantam Books.

Walker, L. (2013). Nutritional psychiatry: Healing the brain through food. *Journal of Integrative Health, 12*(4), 187-194.

CONCLUSION

Understanding Trauma as Both a
Mental and Physical Illness

Trauma is often misconstrued as being purely a psychological event and issue, with a focus on emotional and mental health symptoms like anxiety, depression, and PTSD. However, as we've explored throughout this book, trauma is not just a mental illness—it is a profound psychological *and* physical condition that erodes the body over time. To truly heal trauma, we must consider its full impact on the body, mind and spirit, recognizing that trauma influences *every* system in the body, from the brain to the immune system; the nervous system; and down to the cellular level.

The Cell Danger Response (CDR) offers a groundbreaking perspective on how trauma affects the body at a cellular level. It explains why trauma survivors experience a wide range of physical symptoms, such as chronic inflammation, autoimmune disorders, digestive issues, and immune dysfunction. Trauma's effect on the body is not just an emotional imprint—it triggers a biological shift that changes how cells function, how the immune system responds, and how the body recovers from stress.

Reframing Trauma as a Whole-Body Experience

Traditional approaches to trauma have often been viewed mainly through a psychological lens, focusing on therapy, counselling, and emotional processing. While these treatments are essential, they only address *part* of the picture. Trauma is a whole-body experience that creates long-term changes in the brain, disrupts the body's immune and digestive systems, and activates the CDR, keeping the body in a constant state of defence. Understanding trauma as both a mental *and* physical illness is crucial for developing more effective treatment plans.

As we've seen in chapters focused on the immune system, sleep disturbances, and chronic pain, trauma's impact on the body is wide-reaching. The chronic activation of the CDR leads to long-term health consequences, including chronic fatigue, autoimmune diseases, and increased risk of cardiovascular issues. Addressing these physical symptoms is just as critical as resolving the emotional and psychological aspects of trauma.

The Role of the Cell Danger Response (CDR) in Trauma Recovery

The CDR is central to understanding trauma's long-term effects. When trauma strikes, the CDR activates to protect the body from immediate danger. In this state, normal cellular functions such as growth, repair, and metabolism are halted as the body prioritizes *survival.* While this response is vital for short-term survival, trauma survivors often experience prolonged or chronic activation of the CDR. This keeps the body in a state of heightened defence, even after the trauma has passed, leading to immune dysfunction, inflammation, and chronic disease.

By understanding the CDR, we can see why trauma is not merely a psychological issue but a condition that impacts every cell in the body. Trauma survivors often experience emotional pain alongside physical exhaustion, inflammation, and illness due to the body's inability to return to a state of calm and repair. Healing trauma, therefore, requires approaches that calm the CDR, restore normal cellular functions, and promote whole-body recovery.

Healing Trauma from the Inside Out

Incorporating the CDR into trauma treatment opens new avenues for healing. Therapies like Frequency Specific Microcurrent (FSM),

Hyperbaric Oxygen Therapy (HBOT), and Photobiomodulation (PBM) work at a cellular level to restore balance in the body. These therapies target the underlying biological disruptions caused by trauma, helping to shift the body out of its chronic defence state and into a place of healing and repair.

Supporting the immune system and gut health is equally important. As we've seen in our exploration of the gut-immune connection, trauma has a direct impact on the gut microbiome, which plays a critical role in regulating immune responses. Therapies that support gut health, such as probiotics, prebiotics, and anti-inflammatory diets, help the body recover from trauma's impact on the immune system and reduce chronic inflammation.

Mind-body therapies such as Somatic Experiencing (SE), Trauma Releasing Exercises (TRE), and Family Constellation Therapy also play a crucial role in trauma recovery. These therapies recognize that trauma is stored in the body, not just the mind, and that releasing physical tension and stress is essential for complete healing. By calming the nervous system and regulating the vagus nerve, these therapies help the body reset and recover from trauma's long-term effects.

Intergenerational Trauma: Healing Across Generations

Trauma's impact extends beyond the individual. As we've explored in the chapter on intergenerational trauma and epigenetics, trauma can be passed down through generations, both through learned behaviours and biological changes at the genetic level. The CDR plays a role in this transmission, as trauma-induced epigenetic changes can alter how future generations respond to stress, influencing their physical and emotional health.

Healing trauma, therefore, has the potential to create a ripple effect that benefits not only the individual—but also future generations. By addressing inherited trauma and breaking the cycle of chronic CDR activation, we can promote healing and emotional resilience across *entire* family systems.

The Path Forward: An Integrative Approach to Trauma Treatment

The key takeaway from this exploration of trauma and the Cell Danger Response is that healing trauma requires an *integrative* approach. Trauma affects both the mind and the body, and it demands treatment modalities that address *both*.

By combining cutting-edge therapies that target the CDR with traditional psychotherapy and holistic treatments, trauma survivors can experience profound healing. Approaches like EMDR, somatic therapies, and Neuroacoustic Sound Therapy provide the psychological and emotional support needed to reprocess trauma, while therapies like HBOT, PBM, and nutritional support help repair the body on a cellular level.

Why the CDR is Key to Healing Trauma

Understanding trauma from the perspective of the Cell Danger Response changes the way we approach trauma recovery. Instead of viewing trauma as solely an emotional issue, we now recognize it as a condition that affects every aspect of the body. The CDR explains why trauma survivors experience a wide range of physical symptoms and why traditional talk therapy alone may not be sufficient for recovery.

By addressing the CDR, we can help trauma survivors shift out of *survival mode* and into a state of *healing*. This requires a multi-pronged approach that includes psychological therapy, physical healing modalities, immune support, and lifestyle changes that promote overall well-being.

A Call to Action: Treating Trauma as a Whole-Body Illness

It's time to expand our understanding of trauma and recognize it for what it truly is—a whole-body illness. Trauma is not just about emotional wounds; it's about how those emotional wounds impact the brain, immune system, gut, and every cell in the body. By integrating the CDR into trauma treatment, we can develop more comprehensive and effective approaches to healing trauma.

The path to recovery involves treating both the mind and body, recognizing that trauma survivors need support at every level—emotional, physical, and cellular.

With this holistic approach, we can help trauma survivors not only heal from their past, but also *reclaim their lives, their health, and their sense of well-being.*

Evolving Trauma Treatment: The Path Ahead

As we continue to learn more about trauma, the treatment landscape will keep evolving. With advances in neuroscience, epigenetics, and integrative therapies, the future of trauma recovery holds great promise.

By remaining open to discoveries and approaches, we can continue to *refine* and *improve* the ways we support trauma survivors on their path to healing, ensuring they receive the most effective, comprehensive care possible.

Made in the USA
Monee, IL
26 May 2025

18216601R10199